**Preventing Sexual Violence as a Weapon of War**
**Verhinderung sexueller Gewalt als Kriegswaffe**
**Prévenir la violence sexuelle en tant qu'arme de guerre**

# International Studies on Military Ethics

THE SERIES IS EDITED UNDER THE AUSPICES OF THE INTERNATIONAL SOCIETY FOR MILITARY ETHICS IN EUROPE (EUROISME)



VOLUME 5

EURO ISME
International Society for Military Ethics in Europe

The titles published in this series are listed at *brill.com/isme*

# Preventing Sexual Violence as a Weapon of War
# Verhinderung sexueller Gewalt als Kriegswaffe
# Prévenir la violence sexuelle en tant qu'arme de guerre

*By*

Samantha J. Hope

BRILL
NIJHOFF

LEIDEN | BOSTON

The views expressed in this paper are those of the author and do not necessarily represent those of the UK Ministry of Defence or any other department of Her Britannic Majesty's Government of the United Kingdom. Furthermore such views should not be considered as constituting an official endorsement of factual accuracy, opinion, conclusion or recommendation of the UK Ministry of Defence or any other department of Her Britannic Majesty's Government of the United Kingdom.

German translation of the text by Gerta K. Valentine, French translation by Aurélia Boennec.

Library of Congress Cataloging-in-Publication Data

Names: Hope, Samantha J., author.
Title: Preventing sexual violence as a weapon of war = Verhinderung sexueller gewalt als kriegswaffe = Prevenir la violence sexuelle en tant qu'arme de guerre / by Samantha J. Hope.
Other titles: Verhinderung sexueller gewalt als kriegswaffe | Prevenir la violence sexuelle en tant qu'arme de guerre
Description: Leiden ; Boston : Brill Nijhoff, 2019. | Series: International studies on military ethics ; volume 5 | "Awarded the 2017 first prize in EuroISME's annual best thesis contest." | Includes bibliographical references.
Identifiers: LCCN 2019010102 (print) | LCCN 2019010683 (ebook) | ISBN 9789004396845 (Ebook) | ISBN 9789004396838 (hardback : alk. paper)
Subjects: LCSH: Rape as a weapon of war. | Rape as a weapon of war--Prevention. | IS (Organization).
Classification: LCC KZ7162 (ebook) | LCC KZ7162 .H67 2019 (print) | DDC 341.6/9--dc23
LC record available at https://lccn.loc.gov/2019010102

Typeface for the Latin, Greek, and Cyrillic scripts: "Brill". See and download: brill.com/brill-typeface.

ISSN 2214-7926
ISBN 978-90-04-39683-8 (hardback)
ISBN 978-90-04-39684-5 (e-book)



This book is printed on acid-free paper and produced in a sustainable manner.

Is it possible to prevent sexual violence as a weapon of war against women, men and children or only to manage the after-effects?

• • •

Ist es möglich, sexuelle Gewalt als Kriegswaffe gegen Frauen, Männer und Kinder zu verhüten oder nur die Nachwirkungen zu behandeln?

• • •

Est-il possible d'empêcher l'utilisation de la violence sexuelle en tant qu'arme de guerre contre les femmes, les hommes et les enfants, ou seulement d'en prévenir les conséquences ?

The jury of EuroISME's annual prize for the best student's thesis on military ethics consists of:

1. Colonel Rev. Prof.Dr. P.J. McCormack, MBE, (chairman, United Kingdom)
2. Lt.Col.(Ret) Daniel Beaudoin (France/Israel)
3. Dr. Veronika Bock (Germany)
4. MMag. Stefan Gugerel (Austria)
5. Col. (Ret) Prof.Dr. Boris Kashnikov (Russia)
6. Dr. Asta Maskaliūnaitė (Estonia)
7. Prof.Dr. Desiree Verweij (The Netherlands)
8. Mrs. Ivana Gošić (Serbia, Secretary)

Enquiries: secretariat.ethicsprize@euroisme.eu
www.euroisme.eu

The prize is financially supported by:

vfonds invests in PEACE

www.vfonds.nl

# Contents/Inhalt/Table des matières

## *Prévenir la violence sexuelle en tant qu'arme de guerre*

# Preventing Sexual Violence as a Weapon of War

> We can end sexual warfare conducted against innocent people.
> We can establish new norms that respect women, girls, men, and boys ...
> We can make clear to the world that we will no longer tolerate these horrific tactics ...
> We can say 'not now, not ever.'[1]

∴

## Introduction

Historically, sexual violence as a weapon of war against women, men and children was a hidden crime, with victims resigned to suffer in silence and without justice. It was perpetrated against both sexes for centuries: "from the rape of Sabine women in ancient Rome ... to ... castrations as a form of conquest carried out by Chinese, Persian, Amalekite, Egyptian and Norse armies."[2] Governments and humanitarian organisations, with limited resources, prioritised their assistance to support life-and-death cases. Survivors, ashamed of breaking social taboos, were uncertain where to go for help. Those seeking to negotiate peace agreements were wary of losing the trust of armed groups through broaching 'difficult' subjects interlaced with religious or traditional customs. Thus, at first sight, it seems that sexual violence is just one inevitable, grim feature of war that has always existed and always will.

However, this paper examines whether it is possible, in the twenty-first century, to prevent sexual violence as a weapon of war against women, men and children or only to manage the after-effects. It will begin by briefly explaining the background to the subject and discussing key terms, before reviewing the

---

* The views expressed in this paper are those of the author and do not necessarily represent those of the UK Ministry of Defence or any other department of Her Britannic Majesty's Government of the United Kingdom. Furthermore such views should not be considered as constituting an official endorsement of factual accuracy, opinion, conclusion or recommendation of the UK Ministry of Defence or any other department of Her Britannic Majesty's Government of the United Kingdom.

1 John Kerry, "Remarks at The Global Summit to End Sexual Violence in Conflict," US Department of State, June 2014, <http://www.state.gov/secretary/remarks/2014/06/227553.htm> (accessed November 27, 2015).

2 Sarah Solangon, and Preeti Patel, "Sexual violence against men in countries affected by armed conflict," *Conflict, Security and Development* 12(4) (2012), <doi:10.1080/14678802.2012.724794> (accessed November 27, 2015), 418-419.

current literature. It will then analyse existing prevention approaches, examine the specific case of Daesh[3] and, finally, consider possible additional preventive measures. The paper will aim to demonstrate that prevention can be achieved through improvements to existing measures, combined with an imaginative use of additional, multidisciplinary tools, which are tailored for each conflict, resourced and sustained. It will conclude that, despite immense challenges, it is possible to prevent sexual violence as a weapon of war.

By way of background, the 'Preventing Sexual Violence Initiative' (PSVI) was launched by the then UK Foreign Secretary, William Hague, in May 2012, who said: "Confronted by the greatest ills of our world it is all too easy to be overwhelmed and to turn away. But none of the strides we have made in human rights would ever have been possible without high ambition and resolute determination".[4] The following year, the UK promoted its PSVI agenda by using the G8 presidency to agree a G8 Declaration and sponsoring a United Nations' Security Council Resolution (UNSCR 2106). The UK also led on a UN General Assembly-endorsed 'Declaration of Commitment to End Sexual Violence in Conflict', which has since been signed by 155 countries.[5] In 2014, the UK hosted a global summit – the largest event of its kind. Hague's supporters in this endeavour were Zainab Bangura, the UN Secretary General's Special Representative on Sexual Violence in Conflict, and Angelina Jolie Pitt, a Special Envoy of the UN High Commissioner for Refugees. It seemed as if Hague – the biographer of William Wilberforce, who had successfully banned the slave trade in the nineteenth century – was determined to leave his own legacy before relinquishing power.

Before reviewing the current literature on sexual violence, it is important to clarify the key terms in the paper of 'prevent', 'sexual violence' and 'war'. The literature on sexual violence did not offer a theoretical or practical definition of 'prevent', including within the PSVI domain, so a dictionary definition will be followed: "to stop somebody from doing something; to stop something from happening".[6] By contrast, the UN Secretary General (UNSG) produces an an-

3 Spelling in accordance with Hansard: Parliament, "House of Commons Debates 29 June 2015: Tunisia, and European Council," Parliament June 2015), <http://www.publications.parliament.uk/pa/cm201516/cmhansrd/cm150629/debtext/150629-0001.htm#15062950000001> (accessed April 7, 2016), Column 1182.

4 Foreign & Commonwealth Office, "Foreign Secretary launches new Government initiative to prevent sexual violence in conflict," Foreign & Commonwealth Office May 2012), <https://www.gov.uk/government/speeches/foreign-secretary-launches-new-government-initiative-to-prevent-sexual-violence-in-conflict> (accessed March 21, 2016).

5 Paul Kirby, "Ending sexual violence in conflict: the Preventing Sexual Violence Initiative and its critics," *International Affairs*, 91(3) (2015), <doi:10.1111/1468-2346.12283> (accessed October 8, 2015), 457-458.

6 Oxford Learner's Dictionary, "Prevent," Oxford Learner's Dictionary, <http://www.oxfordlearnersdictionaries.com/definition/english/prevent?q=prevent> (accessed May 15, 2016).

nual report on 'Conflict-related sexual violence', where the term 'sexual violence' is formally defined as:

> rape, sexual slavery, forced prostitution, forced pregnancy, enforced sterilization and other forms of sexual violence of comparable gravity perpetrated against women, men, girls or boys that is linked, directly or indirectly (temporally, geographically or causally) to a conflict.[7]

The International Committee of the Red Cross (ICRC) recognises the types of activities in similar terms, and explains that: "Sexual violence can be broadly defined as acts of a sexual nature imposed by force, threat of force or coercion, or by taking advantage of a coercive environment or a person's incapacity to give genuine consent."[8] Legislation on sexual violence will be addressed as part of the literature review, however, it can be seen that, in non-legalistic language, the UNSG and ICRC's terminology slightly differs. For the purposes of this paper, the UNSG's definition will be adhered to – given the UN's leading role in this matter, its inclusion of 'women, men and children' in the definition, and its recognition that other activities could be included within the term. Regarding the use of the word 'war' in the title, a non-legal definition will also be adopted, taken from 'UK Defence Doctrine' as: "War is a state of armed conflict between different countries, or different groups within a country."[9] Therefore, 'weapon of war' in the title is a symbolic phrase and should be understood within the UK Defence Doctrine definition of 'war' just cited.

In terms of the paper's parameters and given the word limit, the paper will not attempt to evaluate specific UK policies, but will examine how the issues have been addressed by academics, international organisations, governments and Non-Governmental Organisations (NGOs). Furthermore, the paper will not conduct a comparative assessment of the merits of PSVI and the Women, Peace and Security (WPS) agenda or focus on the role of women in post-conflict reconstruction issues. However, it will seek to demonstrate the considerable demands in managing the after-effects, for those involved in sexual violence in conflict, to emphasise the challenges involved in both prevention and remedy.

---

7 United Nations Secretary General, "Conflict-related sexual violence: Report of the Secretary General," United Nations, S/2015/203 (March 23, 2015), <http://www.stoprapenow.org/uploads/advocacyresources/1428937312.pdf> (accessed January 6, 2016), 1/33.

8 International Committee of the Red Cross (ICRC), "Sexual Violence in Armed Conflict: E-Briefing," ICRC December 2015) <https://app.icrc.org/e-briefing/sexual-violence-armed-conflict/> (accessed January 7, 2016), Part 3.

9 United Kingdom, Development, Concepts and Doctrine Centre, *UK Defence Doctrine*, Joint Doctrine Publication 0-01. 5th ed. Shrivenham: DCDC, 2014), 18.

## Literature Review

The next section reviews the current literature on the subject by examining the key findings in five areas: first, the reasons for using sexual violence in conflict; second, the evidence that men and boys can be victims and that women can be perpetrators; third, the challenges of managing the after-effects; fourth, the risks from securitisation and deflecting attention from the WPS agenda; and, finally, evidence of the non-inevitability of sexual violence in conflict.

### *Why sexual violence is used as a weapon of war*

The first key finding from the literature review was an explanation of the reasons for sexual violence to be utilised as a weapon of war. Although Wood has conducted extensive research in this area, she wrote as recently as 2014 that: "there is much we still do not understand about conflict-related sexual violence."[10] Solangon and Patel agreed, recommending a deeper investigation of sexual violence against men.[11] Despite their caution, the literature proffered a number of explanations which went a considerable way in explaining the reasons for using sexual violence in conflict. Watson propounded that: "The most important predictor of sexual violence in all cases is that the victim is in an environment where the perpetrator can commit violence or abuse with a high degree of impunity."[12] Solangon and Patel concurred: "it is clear that a culture of impunity promotes propensity for violence",[13] and they highlighted that: "socio-economic breakdown and poor living conditions ... may lead to impunity due to the collapse of law and order to safeguard civilians."[14] The ICRC agreed that: "Impunity for sexual violence remains at the heart of the problem in many contexts."[15]

---

10 Elizabeth Jean Wood, "Conflict-related sexual violence and the policy implications of recent research," International Review of the Red Cross 96(894) (2014), <doi:10.1017/S1816383115000077> (accessed January 7, 2016), 477.

11 Solangon and Patel, "Sexual violence against men in countries affected by armed conflict," 435-436.

12 Callum Watson, "Preventing and Responding to Sexual and Domestic Violence against Men: A Guidance Note for Security Sector Institutions," Democratic Control of the Armed Forces 2014), <http://www.dcaf.ch/Publications/Preventing-and-Responding-to-Sexual-and-Domestic-Violence-against-Men-A-Guidance-Note-for-Security-Sector-Institutions> (accessed January 19, 2016), 14.

13 Solangon and Patel, "Sexual violence against men in countries affected by armed conflict," 426.

14 Ibid., 425-426.

15 ICRC, "Sexual Violence in Armed Conflict: E-Briefing," Part 3.

Additionally, Solangon and Patel emphasised sexual violence's role as a: "display of power, domination and humiliation".[16] This was typified in a 2016 UN report which said that Daesh was targeting Iraqi tribal and religious leaders, doctors, journalists, lawyers and police officers[17] as a means of demonstrating Daesh's power over authority and respected figures. In other conflicts, human rights defenders are also targeted for similar reasons of control by those who oppose them. Watson explained that sexual violence was used to: "destroy community ties",[18] to displace people forcibly from their homes and destroy future generations through a loss of societal cohesion.

Regarding the planned use of sexual violence by armed groups, Wood said it: "appears to have been a strategy in, for example, Bosnia, Guatemala and Rwanda".[19] Kirby said: "Most notoriously, Serbian psychological operations units concluded that acts of rape (including against children) would have a deleterious effect on enemy morale during the Bosnian war, and adopted a rape policy accordingly."[20] Wood also mentioned Michele Leiby's research on its use by state forces, including in Peru, as a counter-insurgency strategy, to control communities that were supporting insurgents. Peruvian state forces also used sexual violence against captured insurgents to gain information, punish insurgents and demonstrate the government's power.[21] Solangon and Patel described how it could be used: "as part of a military strategy to terrorise and demoralise civilians and combatants."[22] Last year's annual report on conflict-related sexual violence by the UNSG noted that groups were using sexual violence to support their: "strategic objectives, ideology and funding … [for] tactical imperatives as recruitment; terrorizing populations … displacing com-

16 Solangon and Patel, "Sexual violence against men in countries affected by armed conflict," 425.

17 United Nations, "Report on the Protection of Civilians in the Armed Conflict in Iraq: 1 May – 31 October 2015," (January 2016), <http://www.uniraq.org/images/humanrights/UNAMI-OHCHR_%20POC%20Report_FINAL_01%20May-31%20October%202015_FINAL_11Jan2016.pdf> (accessed January 21, 2016), i.

18 Watson, "Preventing and Responding to Sexual and Domestic Violence against Men: A Guidance Note for Security Sector Institutions," 13.

19 Wood, "Conflict-related sexual violence and the policy implications of recent research," 472.

20 Kirby, "Ending sexual violence in conflict: Preventing Sexual Violence Initiative and its critics," 462.

21 Wood, "Conflict-related sexual violence and the policy implications of recent research," 472.

22 Solangon and Patel, "Sexual violence against men in countries affected by armed conflict," 425.

munities from strategic areas ... generating revenue; ... torture to elicit intelligence ... [and] establish, alter or dissolve kinship ties that bind communities."[23]

By contrast, Alcorn summarised Baaz and Stern's primary research of the state forces' use of sexual violence in the Democratic Republic of the Congo (DRC) which led them to conclude that: "if anything, it is the dysfunction of the military hierarchy that has created a space for opportunistic sexual violence to occur."[24] Solangon and Patel recognised that sexual violence could be deployed as a military strategy, but also accepted that it could be: "a consequence of poor combatant selection mechanisms, poor discipline, poor living conditions, poor training and weak cohesion amongst members."[25] Wood referred to the results of Cohen's research, where: "she shows that nonstate armed groups that practice forced recruitment are more likely to engage in high levels of sexual violence."[26] Wood also assessed that sexual violence could be ordered within an armed group or tolerated as a practice.[27]

To conclude this first key finding, the literature provided a number of explanations as to why sexual violence is still used as a weapon of war. The rationale could appear contradictory at times: for example, that it could be part of a defined military strategy or, at other times, as a consequence of the break down in military procedures. However, this is likely to reflect the different nature and phases of each conflict. Although some academics emphasised the need for more research, the literature was consistent in identifying the principal reasons for its use: a sense of impunity, a determination to exert power, and, either as a planned military strategy or as poor military practice.

### *Men and boys can be victims and women can be perpetrators*

The second key finding from the literature review was that men and boys could be victims and women could be perpetrators. Solangon and Patel noted that: "The results of the literature review indicate that evidence and conceptual dis-

23 UN Secretary General, "Conflict-related sexual violence: Report of Secretary General," 24/33.

24 Ted Alcorn, "Responding to sexual violence in armed conflict," *The Lancet* 383(9934) (2014), <http://www.thelancet.com/journals/lancet/article/PIIS0140-6736(14)60970-3/fulltext> (accessed January 18, 2016), 2036.

25 Solangon and Patel, "Sexual violence against men in countries affected by armed conflict," 429-430.

26 Elizabeth Jean Wood, "Rape is not inevitable during war," in Kathleen Kuehnast, Chantal de Jonge Oudraat, and Helga Hernes, eds., *Women and War: Power and Protection in the Twenty-First Century* Washington, DC: US Institute of Peace Press, 2011), 58.

27 Wood, "Conflict-related sexual violence and the policy implications of recent research," 467 & 470.

course on sexual violence against men in conflict-settings is quite limited."[28] Watson, writing a couple of years later, highlighted that progress had been made in the academic arena, but that information for practitioners was still under-developed.[29] Gathering accurate data was potentially more demanding than for women, because for men it was frequently recorded as 'torture'.[30] Other obstacles in data collection resulted from the shame men experienced from the stigma, the breaking of social taboos and possibly domestic laws, as well as demoralisation from an inability to defend oneself. Historically, there had also been a lack of awareness or support from the health-care, legal and media sectors. Skjelsboek suggested that the emasculation which some men felt could make it difficult to report cases to a woman: "For better access to data, it might be necessary to involve more men in this research."[31] This was supported by Hague's summary at the Global Summit in 2014: "Data-collection should not be gender-blind to men and boys."[32]

Although the research was more limited, the reasons for sexual violence against men were evident in the literature, particularly in Solangon and Patel's work. They explained that it could take place as part of initiation to a group following conscription or abduction, or to break another group's cohesion or as a form of: "Genocidal sexual violence ... [through] genital mutilation and beatings committed against men of certain ethnic groups, in order to render them impotent."[33] They also identified that: "most sexual violence cases against men occur in detention settings ... for interrogation and punitive processes."[34] Dr Aburabi, an ICRC doctor, explained that it was possible to identify those at risk in detention camps: "young detainees, first-time detainees, those with a

28 Solangon and Patel, "Sexual violence against men in countries affected by armed conflict," 422.

29 Watson, "Preventing and Responding to Sexual and Domestic Violence against Men: A Guidance Note for Security Sector Institutions," 3.

30 Solangon and Patel, "Sexual violence against men in countries affected by armed conflict," 422-423.

31 Inger Skjelsboek, "Sexual violence in the post-Yugoslav wars," in Kuehnast et al., eds., *Women and War: Power and Protection in Twenty-First Century*, 82.

32 Foreign & Commonwealth Office, "Statement of Action - Global Summit to End Sexual Violence in Conflict," Foreign & Commonwealth Office June 2014), <https://www.gov.uk/government/publications/statement-of-action-global-summit-to-end-sexual-violence-in-conflict> (accessed November 26, 2015).

33 Solangon and Patel, "Sexual violence against men in countries affected by armed conflict," 419 & 428-429.

34 Ibid., 429-430.

certain appearance, those with learning or other disabilities, as well as lesbian, gay, bisexual, transgender and intersex persons".[35]

The complexities of the subject were also revealed in the literature regarding women as perpetrators. Wood stated that US female soldiers were responsible for acts of sexual violence in Iraq, Afghanistan and Guantanamo Bay.[36] In 2015, the International Criminal Tribunal for Rwanda (ICTR) upheld its conviction of Pauline Nyiramasuhuko, the former Minister of Family and Women's Development, for helping to organise, and ordering others to undertake, rape during the Rwandan conflict in 1994.[37] Other literature identified female perpetrators in Sierra Leone,[38] Haiti and the DRC.[39] The literature emphasised that the reasons why women carry out sexual violence needed further investigation, but Edström et al. suggested that: "some causes may include women's adaptation to norms of militarised masculinity, the desire to redirect sexual violence, or to humiliate an enemy."[40]

Regarding the extent of men and boys as victims and women as perpetrators, the difficulties in obtaining reliable figures and the lack of research into the latter were apparent in the literature. Solangon and Patel stated that in one Bosnian camp in the 1990s, 80% of the five thousand men imprisoned there had been raped and sexual violence against men had been recorded in 25 modern-day conflicts around the world.[41] It might be assumed that male survivors represent extremely small proportions of the overall number of victims. However, given the nature of this 'hidden crime', more research and evidence is

35 Vincent Bernard, and Elvina Pothelet, "Through the eyes of a detention doctor: Interview with Raed Aburabi," *International Review of the Red Cross*, 96(894) (2014), <doi:10.1017/S1816383115000284> (accessed January 11, 2016), 482.

36 Wood, "Rape is not inevitable during war," in Kuehnast et al., eds., *Women and War: Power & Protection in Twenty-First Century*, 45.

37 Human Rights Watch, "Rwanda: International Tribunal Closing Its Doors," HRW December 2015), <https://www.hrw.org/news/2015/12/23/rwanda-international-tribunal-closing-its-doors> (accessed January 6, 2016) & Marianne Mollmann, "Rape in war: No more excuses," Human Rights Watch July 2011), <https://www.hrw.org/news/2011/07/22/rape-war-no-more-excuses> (accessed January 6, 2016).

38 Wood, "Rape is not inevitable during war," in Kuehnast et al., eds., *Women and War: Power & Protection in Twenty-First Century*, 45.

39 Jerker Edström, Alexa Hassink, Thea Shahrokh, and Erin Stern, eds., "Engendering Men: A Collaborative Review of Evidence of Men and Boys in Social Change and Gender Equality," EMERGE Evidence Review, Promundo-US, Sonke Gender Justice and the Institute of Development Studies. (September 2015), <http://opendocs.ids.ac.uk/opendocs/bitstream/handle/123456789/7059/EMERGE.pdf?sequence=1> (accessed January 22, 2016), 142.

40 Ibid.

41 Solangon and Patel, "Sexual violence against men in countries affected by armed conflict," 419.

required, especially in the reporting of 'torture' used against men. For female perpetrators, Cohen's research had suggested that: "female combatants participated in 25 percent of the RUF's gang rapes [Revolutionary United Front in Sierra Leone]".[42] Nonetheless, the main outcome of the literature was that: "much more research is needed to determine the actual number of female perpetrators, as well as the causes and consequences of female perpetration of sexual violence".[43]

To conclude this second key finding, the literature addressed preconceptions that sexual violence is solely a gender issue, whereby men exert dominance over women with impunity, by demonstrating that men and boys can be victims and women can be perpetrators. The literature detailed the different causes and contexts for sexual violence to be employed against men and boys. By contrast, it appeared that significantly more research would be required to understand the reasons for women carrying out sexual violence. The extent of men and boys as victims and women as perpetrators – in comparison to the number of women as victims and the number of men as perpetrators – was extremely unclear from the literature. Nonetheless, the review demonstrated that this was an aspect of sexual violence in conflict which should not be ignored. Furthermore, it is suggested that this second key finding does not contradict a later key finding (that sexual violence is not inevitable), as it could be argued that greater understanding of the subject serves to highlight its complexities. As will be explained later, sexual violence is not always utilised, but when it is, it can be against men and boys, as well as against women and girls.

### *Managing the after-effects*

The third key finding from the literature review concerned the challenges of managing the after-effects, including: providing medical and psychological help; dealing with the spread of sexually-transmitted diseases (STDs); addressing the issue of abortion; and offering tailored support to children and men. Bouvier described the requirement for medical care to be administered within 72 hours: "for the purpose of preventing sexually transmitted diseases, including HIV, and for emergency contraception."[44] He provided an example of the difficulties from a study of the DRC, where over 95% of survivors were unable

42 Wood, "Rape is not inevitable during war," in Kuehnast et al., eds., *Women and War: Power & Protection in Twenty-First Century*, 47.

43 Edström et al., eds., "Engendering Men: Collaborative Review of Evidence of Men & Boys in Social Change and Gender Equality," 142.

44 Paul Bouvier, "Sexual violence, health and humanitarian ethics: Towards a holistic, person-centred approach," *International Review of the Red Cross* 96(894) (2014). <doi:10.1017/S1816383115000430> (accessed January 11, 2016), 573.

to gain access to emergency medical help within that timeframe.[45] Skjelsboek noted the implications for individuals' reproductive health, as well as an additional stigma of having a STD, and suggested: "We need to know more about the extent to which sexual violence in armed conflicts contributes to the spread of HIV/Aids".[46] Solangon and Patel said there was an: "urgent need of … psychiatric attention in the management of trauma",[47] and Bouvier highlighted the requirement for longer-term support: "Continuity of care and regular follow-up are essential over a period of time, including medical care, mental health and psychosocial support."[48] Other challenges in managing the aftermath included dealing with possible legal ramifications, where rape was illegal and where abortions were not permitted. Bouvier stressed the need to support women after an abortion, when: "They may face humiliation, exclusion or stigmatization … violence, even lethal violence … [or be] prosecuted and jailed."[49]

The literature review revealed that children had particular needs, depending on whether they had experienced sexual violence, perpetrated it or were a result of it. Duroch and Schulte-Hillen described Médecins Sans Frontières' work: "Caring for children presents additional challenges, such as … dealing at times with severe physical and psychological trauma", as well as the need for genuine patient consent before medical help could be provided.[50] Solangon and Patel described: "the complexities in reintegrating child soldiers, who may have been used as sexual slaves or forced to commit acts of sexual violence".[51] The MenEngage Alliance and UN Population Fund (UNFPA)[52] said there was a need to: "Identify specific strategies and techniques to work with children and adolescent boys who have experienced, witnessed or committed sexual violence".[53] Steinberg noted from his time as US Ambassador to Angola in the

45 Ibid., 574.

46 Skjelsboek, "Sexual violence in post-Yugoslav wars," in Kuehnast et al., eds., *Women and War: Power & Protection in Twenty-First Century*, 81.

47 Solangon and Patel, "Sexual violence against men in countries affected by armed conflict," 434.

48 Bouvier, "Sexual violence, health and humanitarian ethics: Towards a holistic, person-centred approach," 576.

49 Ibid., 582.

50 Françoise Duroch, and Catrin Schulte-Hillen, "Care for victims of sexual violence, an organization pushed to its limits: The case of Médecins Sans Frontières," *International Review of the Red Cross*, 96(894) (2014), <doi:10.1017/S1816383115000107> (accessed January 11, 2016), 616 and 618-619.

51 Solangon and Patel, "Sexual violence against men in countries affected by armed conflict," 434.

52 Abbreviation conventionally adopted in accordance with its former name.

53 MenEngage Alliance and United Nations Population Fund, "Sexual Violence in Conflict

1990s that there were: "young boys, who had never learned how to interact on an equal basis with girls their own age."[54] Bouvier identified the requirement for early and long-term care for children born from sexually-violent acts: "they should be considered as vulnerable children, at high risk of negative outcomes in their health and development."[55] A 2015 UN report which reviewed the outcomes in Bosnia and Herzegovina twenty years after the end of the war noted the lack of support to: "children born of wartime rape, who face particular risk of stigma, abandonment, rejection and low socioeconomic status."[56]

The literature also revealed that men's needs, in dealing with the after-effects, differed from those of women and children. Solangon and Patel set out the challenges for those who had experienced sexual violence, not least where homosexuality was illegal, but also that: "Men are often socially ostracised from their communities, referred to as 'bush wives', emasculated, humiliated and sometimes blamed for the assault."[57] They promoted the need for tailored education and communication campaigns, and specific psychological help.[58] They also recognised the different challenges for those who had committed sexual violence: "Reintegrating men and boys, who were forced to rape a family or community member, into society, remains hugely problematic in many societies."[59] The MenEngage and UNFPA highlighted the needs of other men: "Understanding that witnessing violence against loved ones is a direct experience of violence and can result in the same type of deep and lasting trauma as survivors of assault experience."[60] Another aspect was the potential increase in domestic violence, which was identified by a number of writers, including Skjelsboek.[61] Steinberg described men who returned from the conflict in Angola, had few skills and were then unemployed in communities where

and Post-Conflict: Engaging Men and Boys," (July 2012), <http://menengage.org/resources/sexual-violence-conflict-post-conflict-engaging-men-boys/> (accessed January 12, 2016), 12.

54 Donald Steinberg, "Women and War: an Agenda for action,' in Kuehnast et al., eds., *Women and War: Power and Protection in Twenty-First Century*, 121.

55 Bouvier, "Sexual violence, health and humanitarian ethics: Towards a holistic, person-centred approach," 582-583.

56 UN Secretary General, "Conflict-related sexual violence: Report of Secretary General," 20/33.

57 Solangon and Patel, "Sexual violence against men in countries affected by armed conflict," 421.

58 Ibid., 432-433 & 435.

59 Ibid., 421.

60 MenEngage Alliance and UNFPA, "Sexual Violence in Conflict and Post-Conflict: Engaging Men and Boys," 11.

61 Skjelsboek, "Sexual violence in post-Yugoslav wars," in Kuehnast et al., eds., *Women and War: Power & Protection in Twenty-First Century*, 81.

women had learned to live without them. This had led to an increase in drug-taking and alcoholism, often resulting in domestic violence: "In effect, the end of the civil war simply unleashed a new era of violence against women and girls."[62] Edström et al. pointed to research findings which showed the: "continuation and prevalence [of sexual violence] in post-conflict settings."[63] They referred to research undertaken in Rwanda where men were: "more likely to use both physical and sexual violence against partners at home" if they had been involved in genocidal violence in that conflict.[64]

To sum up the third key finding from the literature review, it was apparent that the challenges of managing the after-math were considerable in both the immediate and long-term, with requirements for medical and psychological care; dealing with the spread of STDs; helping women to have, and those who had undergone, abortions; and providing tailored support to children and men. Additionally, breaking the cycle of violence emerged from the literature review as an important element of dealing with the after-effects, as sexual violence continued post-conflict. This would be a daunting prospect for most nations to deal with, but even more demanding for countries severely damaged in conflict, and where such support may not have existed in the first place.

### *The risks of securitisation and detracting from the Women, Peace and Security agenda*

The fourth key finding from the literature review concerned the risks from securitising the issue, as well as deflecting attention from the 'Women, Peace and Security' (WPS) agenda. Kirby said that: "a political project to foreground sexual violence ... must, if successful, have the corresponding political effect of directing material resources" and he warned that there was the potential to distort attention from the pressing needs to address both other war crimes and domestic violence.[65] He noted, for example, that: "in the eastern DRC, household survey data reveal extremely high levels of *intimate partner* sexual violence, despite the general fixation on atrocities by armed groups."[66] Wood concurred: "In some conflict settings, the frequency of sexual violence by

62 Steinberg, "Women and War: an Agenda for action," in Kuehnast et al., eds., *Women and War: Power and Protection in Twenty-First Century*, 121.

63 Edström et al., eds., "Engendering Men: Collaborative Review of Evidence of Men & Boys in Social Change and Gender Equality," 141.

64 Ibid., 143.

65 Kirby, "Ending sexual violence in conflict: Preventing Sexual Violence Initiative and its critics," 463.

66 Ibid., 462.

armed actors is significantly less than that by intimate partners, acquaintances or strangers",[67] as did Alcorn:

> surveys have repeatedly shown that survivors are far more likely to report a rape if it is perpetrated by a stranger than by a husband or boyfriend. In conflict and post-conflict settings, this disproportionate under-reporting of sexual violence within households can greatly inflate the share of sexual violence attributed to armed groups.[68]

The results of the literature review also revealed a growing recognition that as men and boys were victims of sexual violence, as well as perpetrators, this could detract from the hard won gains of the WPS agenda. Kuehnast et al. said that UNSCR 1325, passed in 2000, "handed civil society organizations and women peace activists from around the world a major victory and an authoritative instrument for further mobilization"[69] and Alison questioned in 2007: "if feminists stop talking about rape, who will?"[70] Kirby's critique of the PSVI, and its overt support for men and boys as survivors, included the possible implication that: "the UN and contributing states will now be less forceful in diagnosing and responding to patriarchal power relations and hierarchical gender orders ... [and] the expectation that existing programmes halve (or significantly decrease) the resources devoted to women and girls".[71] However, the ICRC seemed to welcome the new construct: "the focus has shifted from the particular plight of women in conflicts to a broader approach, based on the vulnerabilities experienced by both men and women on the basis of their gender and their sex."[72] This was supported by Solangon and Patel: "sexual violence against men must be brought to the fore, not as a challenge to female rights but as a partner in the fight against the war on gender-based sexual violence."[73] Although some academics, policy-makers and practitioners might not be entirely comfortable with this development, Kirby noted that it was possible to track the changes in language from women-focussed UNSCRs 1888 and 1960 in 2008 and 2009, to

67 Wood, "Conflict-related sexual violence and the policy implications of recent research," 460.

68 Alcorn, "Responding to sexual violence in armed conflict," 2035.

69 Kuehnast et al., eds., *Women and War: Power & Protection in Twenty-First Century*, 2.

70 Solangon and Patel, "Sexual violence against men in countries affected by armed conflict," 424.

71 Kirby, "Ending sexual violence in conflict: Preventing Sexual Violence Initiative and its critics," 471.

72 ICRC, "Sexual Violence in Armed Conflict: E-Briefing," Introduction.

73 Solangon and Patel, "Sexual violence against men in countries affected by armed conflict," 436.

'women and gender advisers' in UNSCR 2106 in June 2013 to 'gender advisers' in UNSCR 2122 in October 2013.[74] This suggests an increasing recognition of, and acceptance from, the international community that the issue of sexual violence in conflict should be approached for its impact on men and boys, as well as women and girls.

To conclude the fourth key finding, the results of the literature review showed that it was important to keep sexual violence as a weapon of war in perspective with the potentially higher rates of *domestic* violence in conflict, post-conflict and non-conflict situations. Additionally, although this paper aims to undertake a more even-handed analysis of the subject, the importance of addressing the role of women in peace and security matters should not be underestimated – both in terms of effectively managing the after-effects and preventing future occurrences of sexual violence in conflict.

### *Sexual violence in conflict is not inevitable*

The fifth key finding from the literature review demonstrated that sexual violence in conflict is not inevitable. From Wood's own research and a synthesis of other academics' findings, she identified that the extent of sexual violence, the forms it took, the timing within a conflict, its place within a repertoire of violent methods, and whether it was symmetrical or asymmetrical were different in each conflict. Furthermore, she discovered that such differences could not be accounted for by the type of conflict, nor by prevailing traditional norms, the religions practiced or the opportunities available to undertake sexual violence. Additionally, the differences could not be explained by difficulties in obtaining reliable figures.[75] Wood concluded therefore that: "The neglected fact of variation, including the relative absence of wartime sexual violence by one or more armed groups, has important policy implications: rape is not inevitable in war as is sometimes claimed."[76] Wood provided examples of some armed groups which had not employed sexual violence in El Salvador, Israel/Palestine, Vietnam and Sri Lanka.[77] However, she also cautioned that: "By the absence of sexual violence, I mean the (relative) absence of sexual violence: sexual violence by a group is very rare (but not completely absent)."[78]

74 Kirby, "Ending sexual violence in conflict: Preventing Sexual Violence Initiative and its critics," 470.

75 Wood, "Rape is not inevitable during war," in Kuehnast et al., eds., *Women and War: Power & Protection in Twenty-First Century*, 37-39 and 43-45.

76 Ibid., 39.

77 Ibid., 40 & 43.

78 Ibid., 39.

In a later work, Wood identified another element of variation: whether sexual violence was used against women only or against both genders.[79] She also provided figures from other academic research. For example, she cited from Nordås who claimed that: "59% of 177 armed actors in the civil wars between 2000 and 2009 in twenty African countries were not reported to have engaged in rape or other forms of sexual violence."[80] She also referred to Cohen's findings: "where one party to the war promotes sexual violence while the other does not, a pattern true of almost 40% of civil wars."[81] Additionally, she drew from Cohen and Nordås' combined work:

> The best cross-national dataset available confirms that sexual violence (including rape) varies across State militaries, insurgent organizations and pro-government militias; indeed, for all three types of armed actors, a strong majority is not reported to have perpetrated sexual violence between 1989 and 2009.[82]

Solangon and Patel in their research on sexual violence against men recognised that: "Sexual violence is no longer primarily viewed as a biological sexual desire but increasingly seen as a display of power, dominance and humiliation".[83] The ICRC concurred: "It is no longer tenable to claim that sexual violence is simply an ugly facet of our worst human inclinations and an unfortunate companion of war; today it is widely acknowledged that sexual violence is not an inevitable consequence of armed conflict."[84] This was a key finding in the literature review, because it suggested that if sexual violence was not always used as a weapon of war, then preventive measures should be identified from these conflicts and applied to prevent future outbreaks of sexual violence in war.

### *Summary of the Literature Review's key findings*

To conclude this review of the literature, analysis by academics and practitioners provided a number of reasons for using sexual violence in conflict, and evidence that men and boys could be victims and women could be perpetrators. It revealed the non-inevitability of sexual violence in conflict – given that

79 Wood, "Conflict-related sexual violence and the policy implications of recent research," 461.
80 Ibid., 458.
81 Ibid., 462.
82 Ibid., 459.
83 Solangon and Patel, "Sexual violence against men in countries affected by armed conflict," 425.
84 ICRC, "Sexual Violence in Armed Conflict: E-Briefing," Part 4.

it was not employed by all armed groups in all conflicts at all times. It also highlighted the challenges of managing the after-effects; the risk from securitisation so that other war crimes and domestic violence are insufficiently resourced; and the risk of deflecting attention from the WPS agenda.

## Current Prevention Approaches

### *Understanding*

Turning now to an analysis of existing prevention approaches, which will cover four areas: understanding; high-level support; training; and legislation. First, in order to prevent something happening, it is necessary to understand the issues. The previous section on the results of the literature review sought to demonstrate that comprehension of the issues concerning sexual violence as a weapon of war has increased. Although, the literature promoted the need for further research, there now appears to be a solid foundation of work, which has improved understanding of the subject. The ICRC noted that: "its prevalence and horrific toll on individuals and societies, as well as the dynamics behind it, have been progressively better understood over the last two decades."[85] For example, although Médecins Sans Frontières was established in 1971, it was not until 1999 that it devised its first treatment package for survivors of sexual violence.[86]

The literature also demonstrated an understanding of the known vulnerable locations and times when sexual violence could be perpetrated. For example, Solangon and Patel described some of the vulnerable locations, such as in displacement camps, at border crossings, in isolated areas such as in fields and, by contrast, in markets and some trade routes where a concentration of people gathered. They also suggested vulnerable times, such as when collecting water or firewood, going to school, at night time and around elections.[87] For men in particular, Dr Aburabi, an ICRC detention doctor, described known vulnerable times, such as: "during initial detention, when the detainee is most disoriented and isolated from the usual support systems. … There is also a high prevalence in interrogation centres".[88] Skjelsboek suggested an indicator that people could

85 ICRC, "Sexual Violence in Armed Conflict: E-Briefing," Introduction.

86 Duroch and Schulte-Hillen, "Care for victims of sexual violence, an organization pushed to its limits: case of Médecins Sans Frontières," 603.

87 Solangon and Patel, "Sexual violence against men in countries affected by armed conflict," 432.

88 Bernard and Pothelet, "Through eyes of a detention doctor: Interview with Raed Aburabi," 481.

be vulnerable to sexual violence was when: "political discourses become sexualized".[89] Watson noted that one element of prevention of sexual violence against men (although it could equally apply to women and children), was: "by reducing the number of wrong places and wrong times that exist."[90] Therefore, despite more research being required, it is suggested that the current level of understanding of the issues provides a good basis for effective prevention strategies to be designed, implemented and evaluated.

### *High-level support*

The second area to be examined for its contribution to current prevention approaches is the degree of high-level international support. In 2009, under UNSCR 1888, the post of 'Special Representative of the Secretary General on Sexual Violence in Conflict' was established. A year later, UNSCR 1960 mandated the UNSG to produce an annual report listing all the armed groups carrying out sexual violence in conflict as part of 'naming and shaming'. The 2015 report provided details of 45 state and non-state groups, thirteen of which were listed for the first time.[91] Additionally, 'UN Action against Sexual Violence in Conflict' undertakes: "a number of strategic initiatives to improve system-wide coordination, knowledge-building, advocacy and technical country-level support."[92] Since 2013, 155 countries have endorsed a UN General Assembly Declaration to end sexual violence in conflict.[93] Through its presidency of the G8 in 2013, the UK secured a Declaration, whereby G8 members agreed to support a range of measures. These included: financial help, training, advice on documenting evidence, recognition that sexual violence could amount to grave breaches under the Geneva Convention (and thereby be prosecuted internationally under universal jurisdiction), the need to address sexual violence in the first phase of any response, and that no amnesty should be offered, in

89 Skjelsboek, "Sexual violence in post-Yugoslav wars," in Kuehnast et al., eds., *Women and War: Power & Protection in Twenty-First Century*, 81.

90 Callum Watson, "Bad apples or bad apple trees? An examination of the contexts in which sexual violence against men takes place," paper presented at a workshop entitled, 'Sexual Violence Against Men during Conflicts: Bridging the Gap between Theory and Practice', *The Graduate Institute of International and Development Studies*, Geneva February 26-27, 2015), 9.

91 UN Secretary General, "Conflict-related sexual violence: Report of Secretary General," 1/33.

92 Ibid., 25/33.

93 G7, "G7 Report on the Implementation of the G8 Declaration on Preventing Sexual Violence in Conflict," G7 November 2015), <https://www.g7germany.de/Content/EN/_Anlagen/G7/2015-11-24-g7-erklaerung_svc_en.pdf?__blob=publicationFile&v=3> (accessed January 7, 2016), 2.

subsequent peace agreements, for those who perpetrate sexual violence.[94] They also agreed to produce a follow-up report under Germany's G8 presidency in 2015 to report on progress, which they duly undertook (by then, acting as the G7).[95]

In June 2014, the UK hosted a Global Summit, with 120 nations[96] and representation from all G7 members, including four G7 foreign ministers and the EU High Representative for Foreign Affairs and Security Policy.[97] The US' Secretary of State, John Kerry, who closed the event, outlined the US' support, which included an initiative 'Safe from the Start' announced in 2013, which by November 2015, the US had funded to the tune of $22M. The UK Prime Minister appointed a 'Special Representative on Preventing Sexual Violence in Conflict', Baroness Anelay, and last year's National Security Strategy made a commitment to: "expand its [the PSVI's] reach and implementation".[98] From the time the UK launched the PSVI in 2012 until the end of 2015, the UK government had allocated £29M to support it.[99] The North Atlantic Treaty Organisation (NATO) established a permanent post of Special Representative for WPS in 2014. For their current mission in Afghanistan, Operation Resolute Support, NATO incorporated WPS in the planning process from the outset, demonstrating that it was: "no longer an afterthought: a gender perspective was integrated from the political decision-making level down to the drafting of the operational plan for the mission and the troop generation process."[100] The ICRC has revised its way of working to assume that sexual violence has taken place in a conflict, until there is evidence to suggest otherwise.[101]

---

94 Foreign & Commonwealth Office, "The Foreign Secretary William Hague, Angelina Jolie and Zainab Hawa Bangura launch G8 Declaration on Preventing Sexual Violence in Conflict," Foreign & Commonwealth Office April 2013), <https://www.gov.uk/government/news/g8-declaration-on-preventing-sexual-violence-in-conflict> (accessed November 27, 2015).

95 G7, "G7 Report on the Implementation of the G8 Declaration on Preventing Sexual Violence in Conflict."

96 Kirby, "Ending sexual violence in conflict: Preventing Sexual Violence Initiative and its critics," 457.

97 G7, "G7 Report on the Implementation of the G8 Declaration on Preventing Sexual Violence in Conflict," 2.

98 United Kingdom Government, *National Security Strategy and Strategic Defence and Security Review 2015: A Secure and Prosperous United Kingdom*, Cm 9161 November 2015), 63.

99 G7, "G7 Report on the Implementation of the G8 Declaration on Preventing Sexual Violence in Conflict," 5.

100 Marriët Schuurman, "NATO and the Women, Peace and Security Agenda: Time to Bring It Home." *Connections: The Quarterly Journal*, XIV(3) (2015), <http://www.nato.int/cps/en/natohq/opinions_124032.htm?selectedLocale=en> (accessed January 12, 2016).

101 ICRC, "Sexual Violence in Armed Conflict: E-Briefing," Part 2.

It would seem, therefore, that there is a degree of high-level international support, from the UN, G7, NATO, ICRC and individual countries, for dealing with sexual violence as a weapon of war. This is an important enabler for leading on prevention and helping others to implement preventive measures. However, given the challenges involved, more resources will be required and sustained engagement from the international community to strengthen current preventive measures and cement improvements. Also, international support needs to be seen to be coming from non-western organisations. For example, searches of the English-version websites of the African Union (AU), Commonwealth, Arab League, Gulf Cooperation Council, Association of South East Asian Nations and the Organization of American States revealed little, if any, information on their policies to prevent sexual violence as a weapon of war. Such organisations need to be proactive in voicing their condemnation of sexual violence in conflict, reinforced by concrete action. Their commitment of financial and other support would assist the rest of the international community, itself under resource pressures, as well as demonstrating non-western organisations' genuine opposition to sexual violence in conflict.

### *Training*

The third issue to be assessed for its contribution to preventing conflict-related sexual violence concerns the current provision for training armed and civil forces. In 2010, UN Action developed: "scenario-based predeployment training … to improve the operational readiness of military and police peacekeepers to react swiftly and appropriately",[102] which continues to be rolled out in UN training centres. In 2014, NATO members agreed a new Education and Training Plan for Gender in Military Operations: "which unifies and synchronizes gender education and training at all levels."[103] The following year, NATO's most senior, politico-military crisis management exercise: "was the first at that level … [which] included indicators that conflict related sexual violence takes place as a tactic of war, and tested how these indicators might influence strategic decision-making."[104] The same year, the UK announced new funding worth £700,000 to train AU peacekeepers to prevent and respond to sexual violence in conflict.[105] The UK also said that all UK forces deployed overseas would be

102 UN Secretary General, "Conflict-related sexual violence: Report of Secretary General," 26/33.

103 Schuurman, "NATO and Women, Peace and Security Agenda: Time to Bring It Home."

104 Ibid.

105 Foreign & Commonwealth Office, "Angelina Jolie Pitt joins Baroness Anelay to chart next steps on tackling sexual violence," Foreign & Commonwealth Office June 2015),

trained in WPS and the PSVI by November 2016.[106] Furthermore, by November 2015, the UK had trained more than 8,000 African peacekeeping and police personnel, 2,500 Malian armed forces and 800 Iraqi Peshmerga troops.[107] Whilst there are still cases of UN and AU peacekeepers committing sexual violence themselves, rather than preventing or halting it, the current training provisions go some way to ensuring improved behaviour. Therefore, training can be seen as an important measure in giving armed forces and police officials the skills and understanding to deal with outbreaks of sexual violence and prevent future occurrences. It also establishes them as role models to: "help shape universal notions of how armed actors should behave and what their roles and responsibilities in conflict are … even rebel groups may emulate them in the hope that one day they will be recognised as legitimate national actors."[108] This view was echoed by the then Foreign Secretary, William Hague, in 2013: "members of armed forces are often the first to come into contact with survivors, and could also have an important role to play in helping to change male attitudes."[109]

Thus, there is evidence to suggest that training packages have been developed by the UN, NATO and individual countries, like the UK, which are being implemented for UN and AU peacekeepers, as well as for state armed forces and police officials. It will be important that such training is regularly assessed for its effectiveness (and refined), and continued to be rolled-out to multinational and national forces, as well as providing refresher training, and taking prompt and punitive action against those who commit sexual violence when they should be protecting others from such violence.

### *Legislation*

The fourth, and final, element to be examined for its contribution to current prevention approaches concerns legislation, which will cover: the body of law, implementation and deterrence. First, on the law itself, Gaggioli, a lawyer and

<https://www.gov.uk/government/news/angelina-jolie-pitt-joins-baroness-anelay-to-chart-next-steps-on-tackling-sexual-violence> (accessed January 12, 2016).

106 Baroness Sandip Verma, "The UK firmly believes that the 15th anniversary must represent the start of a new era on Women, Peace and Security," UK Government October 13, 2015), <https://www.gov.uk/government/speeches/the-uk-firmly-believes-that-the-15th-anniversary-must-represent-the-start-of-a-new-era-on-women-peace-and-security> (accessed November 26, 2015).

107 G7, "G7 Report on the Implementation of the G8 Declaration on Preventing Sexual Violence in Conflict," 7.

108 Watson, "Bad apples or bad apple trees? Examination of contexts in which sexual violence against men takes place," 10.

109 FCO, "Foreign Secretary William Hague, Angelina Jolie and Zainab Hawa Bangura launch G8 Declaration on Preventing Sexual Violence in Conflict."

academic, reviewed the current legislative provisions within International Humanitarian Law (IHL) and international human rights law. She found that: "The IHL prohibition of rape and other forms of sexual violence applies to both international and non-international armed conflicts and is also part of customary law. Human rights law prohibits sexual violence at all times."[110] She also identified that: "Rape and other forms of sexual violence can amount to international crimes – war crimes, crimes against humanity and acts of genocide – when the conditions for such crimes ... are fulfilled. As such, they entail individual criminal responsibility."[111] Gaggioli concluded that: "The international legal framework ... is thus extremely strong, even if imperfect ... the different international law branches (IHL, human rights law, international criminal law) echo and reinforce each other, providing for an essential complementarity."[112] A G8 Declaration in 2013 noted that: "international humanitarian law maintains a long-standing prohibition ... and that ... when it is part of a widespread or systematic attack against a civilian population can constitute a crime against humanity and can be a constitutive act with respect to genocide."[113] A recent House of Lords' Select Committee review: "examined the case for further international law ... [but] concluded that existing provisions are adequate".[114] Therefore, it would seem as if the legislative provisions – on paper at least – are sufficiently robust.

Whilst there were no calls for additional legislation from the literature review, there was an emphasis on implementation. For instance, Gaggioli called for: "better implementation of existing rules at the domestic level and effective prosecutions of perpetrators of sexual crimes at the domestic and international levels."[115] In 2013 the G8 supported: "the deployment of international experts

---

110 Gloria Gaggioli, "Sexual violence in armed conflicts: A violation of international humanitarian law and human rights law," *International Review of the Red Cross* 96(894) (2014), <doi:10.1017/S1816383115000211> (accessed January 11, 2016), 537.

111 Ibid.

112 Ibid.

113 Foreign & Commonwealth Office, "Declaration on Preventing Sexual Violence in Conflict," Foreign & Commonwealth Office April 2013), <https://www.gov.uk/government/uploads/system/uploads/attachment_data/file/185008/G8_PSVI_Declaration_-_FINAL.pdf> (accessed November 27, 2015).

114 House of Lords, "Select Committee on Sexual Violence in Conflict: Report of Session 2015-16: Sexual Violence in Conflict: A War Crime," House of Lords, HL Paper 123 April 12, 2016), <http://www.publications.parliament.uk/pa/ld201516/ldselect/ldsvc/123/123.pdf> (accessed April 15, 2016), 8.

115 Gaggioli, "Sexual violence in armed conflicts: violation of international humanitarian law and human rights law," 533.

to help build up the judicial, investigative and legal capacity of other countries".[116] The ICRC recommended: "Authorities must ensure that adequate mechanisms are in place allowing victims to report the violence in a safe and confidential manner."[117] They also called for: "appropriate sensitization of legal personnel, specific technical arrangements regarding time and place of the hearings, and adequate legal assistance to all alleged perpetrators."[118]

Although this would appear to be a significant undertaking, there are organisations which are helping countries to improve their legal processes. For example, a G7 report in 2015 highlighted the work of 'Justice Rapid Response' (JRR), an inter-governmental body that works with the UN. It explained that JRR maintains rosters of rapidly-deployable criminal justice experts (over 500 individuals) and investigative experts (nearly 150 people), the latter undertaking more detailed enquiries.[119] JRR's own website highlighted that the rapidly-deployable experts represent 60 professions and: "come from over 95 countries and speak over 80 languages. JRR's roster is more than 40% from the global South and over 50% [are] women".[120] In less than six years, JRR had undertaken nearly 70 investigations, including in Syria and Iraq.[121] The UK has also established its own team of more than 70 experts, spanning a range of fields, including police and forensic scientists,[122] which has worked on 17 projects in 13 countries, including on the border with Syria, to, inter alia: "improve investigations, and increase prosecutions of sexual violence in conflict."[123] Furthermore, G8 Foreign Ministers agreed in 2013 to produce an *International Protocol on the Documentation and Investigation of Sexual Violence in Conflict*. It was devised by UK officials, with expert input, and launched at the Global Summit in 2014 to: "help strengthen the evidence base for bringing perpetrators to

116 FCO, "Foreign Secretary William Hague, Angelina Jolie and Zainab Hawa Bangura launch G8 Declaration on Preventing Sexual Violence in Conflict."

117 ICRC, "Sexual Violence in Armed Conflict: E-Briefing," Part 3.

118 Ibid.

119 G7, "G7 Report on the Implementation of the G8 Declaration on Preventing Sexual Violence in Conflict," 7.

120 Justice Rapid Response, "Justice Rapid Response welcomes UN Women and Draper Richards Kaplan Foundation to its Executive Board," JRR November 2015), <http://www.justicerapidresponse.org/justice-rapid-response-welcomes-un-women-and-draper-richards-kaplan-foundation-to-its-executive-board/> (accessed January 7, 2016).

121 Ibid. & G7, "G7 Report on the Implementation of the G8 Declaration on Preventing Sexual Violence in Conflict," 7.

122 FCO, "Foreign Secretary William Hague, Angelina Jolie and Zainab Hawa Bangura launch G8 Declaration on Preventing Sexual Violence in Conflict."

123 G7, "G7 Report on the Implementation of the G8 Declaration on Preventing Sexual Violence in Conflict," 7.

justice".[124] Since then, the UK has developed a training package and translated the Protocol into other languages, including Arabic. The UK has also helped several countries to use the Protocol, including Bosnia, Colombia and Uganda.[125] The medical profession has also recognised that it has a role to play in gathering evidence. This is not necessarily a straightforward development, as their primary role is to treat patients, not act in a policing role. However, since 2011, 'Physicians for Human Rights' has brought together health-care workers and legal professionals to improve their combined efforts: "[Clinicians] are the first people to come across what constitutes evidence, so they have to start labelling it and preserving it in a way that will make it court admissible down the road."[126] Thus, it would seem as if the international community has recognised the need to help countries improve their legal practices and taken a number of steps to support change. Nonetheless, this will require sustained international and national engagement, training, mentoring and resources to embed good practices and ensure better application of the relevant legislation if it is to have any real effect as a preventive measure. This would seem to be an area which needs addressing further. Once states have been persuaded to adopt the relevant legislation, the international community needs to assist and ensure it is applied.

The final aspect of legislation which should be examined is its effectiveness as a deterrent. One of Kirby's major criticisms of the PSVI was its focus on ending impunity: "the principal impunity hypothesis – that increasing prosecution will deter future atrocity – faces considerable challenge on grounds of efficacy, cost and clarity of purpose."[127] Kirby recalled that the average cost of convicting one person in the International Criminal Tribunals for the Former Yugoslavia and Rwanda was a staggering $35M and £39M respectively.[128] He also highlighted that the: "victors and the vanquished are not equal before the law."[129] Human Rights Watch noted that the criticisms of the International Criminal Tribunal for Rwanda (ICTR) included cost, cumbersome processes,

124 Foreign & Commonwealth Office, "Chair's Summary: Global Summit to End Sexual Violence in Conflict," Foreign & Commonwealth Office June 2014), <https://www.gov.uk/government/publications/chairs-summary-global-summit-to-end-sexual-violence-in-conflict/chairs-summary-global-summit-to-end-sexual-violence-in-conflict> (accessed November 27, 2015).

125 G7, "G7 Report on the Implementation of the G8 Declaration on Preventing Sexual Violence in Conflict," 5-6.

126 Alcorn, "Responding to sexual violence in armed conflict," 2037.

127 Kirby, "Ending sexual violence in conflict: Preventing Sexual Violence Initiative and its critics," 464.

128 Ibid., 465.

129 Ibid.

few cases tried, the time taken, allowing those convicted to speak to the media, lack of reparations for survivors, and not prosecuting the 'winners' from the Rwandan Patriotic Front.[130] It would seem that the prospect of longer-term punishment can be negated by the short-term opportunities of winning a war.

However, the ICTR did convict the former Prime Minister, Army Chief of Staff and Defence Ministry Chief of Staff,[131] as well as the first woman of committing genocide, war crimes and crimes against humanity, Pauline Nyiramasuhuko.[132] Other landmark cases included Duško Tadić, who was the first to be convicted of sexually violent war crimes against men in 1997.[133] In 2014, General Kakwavu and 'Colonel 106' were found guilty of sexual violence crimes in the DRC, which the UN noted as: "These convictions mark a milestone in efforts to hold high-ranking officers to account."[134] In March 2016, the ICC secured its first conviction for sexual violence in conflict (including against men) against Jean-Pierre Bemba. It was also the first time the ICC had successfully prosecuted an individual for their 'command responsibilities', in Bemba's role as the President and Commander-in-Chief of the 'Mouvement de libération du Congo'.[135] The ICRC noted the symbolic importance of prosecuting individuals for the message it sent to others and providing some form of recognition to survivors.[136] The results of the literature review, described earlier, indicated that a sense of impunity was a key factor in accounting for sexual violence as a weapon of war. Therefore, the successful prosecution of politicians, senior and middle-ranking military and police officers, and members of state and non-state groups is a necessary condition to prevent sexual violence being employed as a weapon of war in future conflicts. However, it would seem that considerably more needs to be achieved in this area for it to be an effective preventive measure.

### *Summary of current prevention approaches*

From this assessment of current preventive measures, it is suggested that there are effective measures in operation, but there is a requirement to make improvements. On the positive side, there is a high-degree of understanding of

130 Human Rights Watch, "Rwanda: International Tribunal Closing Its Doors."

131 Ibid.

132 Mollmann, "Rape in war: No more excuses."

133 Watson, "Bad apples or bad apple trees? Examination of contexts in which sexual violence against men takes place," 3.

134 UN Secretary General, "Conflict-related sexual violence: Report of Secretary General," 8/33.

135 House of Lords, "Select Committee on Sexual Violence in Conflict: Report of Session 2015-16: Sexual Violence in Conflict: A War Crime," 22.

136 ICRC, "Sexual Violence in Armed Conflict: E-Briefing," Part 3.

the subject, which has enabled prevention strategies to be designed and implemented, including training packages. There is also strong support from key elements of the international community, which has devoted resources to the issue and galvanised action. Training is being delivered to thousands of armed and civil forces, and action is being taken when peacekeepers disobey orders. The legislative provisions are substantial, evidence is being gathered and prosecutions are being made. On the improvements side, more research is required to deepen understanding and devise additional prevention approaches (for example, to prevent women from carrying out sexual violence). Additional resources are required and sustained engagement from the international community. International support and funding needs to be visibly coming from non-western organisations, such as the AU, Arab League and Gulf Cooperation Council. Given ongoing cases of peacekeepers and law enforcers committing sexual violence, more training needs to be delivered and refresher training provided (as well as legal action). The impact of training should be evaluated and adjustments made, as required. Training and exercises need to be based on complex scenarios, to test students' understanding and responses. Further long-term assistance should be given to those countries that have weak legal systems and poor procedures for prosecuting cases effectively. More individuals should be brought to trial more quickly, including UN/AU peacekeepers and those on the winning side, to reduce the sense of impunity (and the cost). Thus, it is suggested that there is a solid foundation on which to build, but the current prevention approaches require further development if they are to prevent sexual violence in conflict more systematically and comprehensively.

## Case Study: Daesh[137]

### *Daesh's modus operandi*

This paper will now examine the case of Daesh and its current use of sexual violence as a weapon of war in Iraq and Syria. It will consider Daesh's approach in light of the literature findings and assess the effectiveness of existing prevention methods, as just described, as a means of preventing Daesh using sexual violence in the future. The UNSG described the: "Egregious forms of conflict-related sexual violence"[138] undertaken by Daesh since 2014, and a G7

137 See Footnote 3 for spelling rationale.

138 UN Secretary General, "Conflict-related sexual violence: Report of Secretary General," 24/33.

report concurred.[139] The UNSG's annual report, listing armed groups perpetrating sexual violence in conflict, described Daesh's modus operandi in Iraq: "Sexual violence has been used as part of the ISIL strategy of spreading terror, persecuting ethnic and religious minorities and suppressing communities that oppose its ideology."[140] In a subsequent report, the UN stated that Daesh employed sexual violence as: "a tactic of war."[141] This was supported by Wood's view of Daesh as a group that: "has purposefully adopted ... sexual violence in pursuit of organization objectives, and it is therefore a strategy."[142] Daesh's use of sexual violence has also been identified in detention and displacement camps, and at border controls.[143] Such features are consistent with the literature review's findings that sexual violence can be used to exert power, neutralise community resistance, support political-military goals and elicit information. It also appears to have occurred in known vulnerable locations.

However, there are elements of Daesh's use of sexual violence that seem to differ from the literature findings or be more exaggerated in their form. For instance, it could be argued that Daesh carries out sexual violence to destroy women's rights and their value in society. Thus, the UNSG's Special Representative on Sexual Violence in Conflict noted that: "the notorious Mount Sinjar offensive of August 2014 has been considered as much a sexual conquest ... as it was a territorial advance."[144] In towns like Raqqa, markets have been established to sell naked women, with a Daesh 'regulation' specifying the market-rate for women and girls based on their age.[145] Another element of Daesh's approach is the capture of women and girls as hostages, which the G7 described as a: "disturbing new dimension".[146] They noted this was not unique to

139 G7, "G7 Report on the Implementation of the G8 Declaration on Preventing Sexual Violence in Conflict," 1.

140 UN Secretary General, "Conflict-related sexual violence: Report of Secretary General," 9/33.

141 United Nations, "Report on Protection of Civilians in Armed Conflict in Iraq: 1 May – 31 October 2015," 32.

142 Wood, "Conflict-related sexual violence and the policy implications of recent research," 472.

143 UN Secretary General, "Conflict-related sexual violence: Report of Secretary General," 18/33.

144 Zainab Bangura, "Faith in Islam & Faith in Women: Why Gender Justice is Key to an Islam Without Extremes," International Crisis Group October 2015), <https://medium.com/the-future-of-conflict/faith-in-islam-faith-in-women-why-gender-justice-is-key-to-an-islam-without-extremes-8920277ef674#.dkjeo08jg> (accessed January 6, 2016).

145 UN Secretary General, "Conflict-related sexual violence: Report of Secretary General," 10/33.

146 G7, "G7 Report on the Implementation of the G8 Declaration on Preventing Sexual Violence in Conflict," 1.

Daesh and referred to the example of 270 school girls taken from Chibok in Nigeria in April 2014.[147] The UN also identified the connection: "the same ideology and objectives that motivate Boko Haram to abduct women and girls in Nigeria also spur ISIL to enslave women and girls in the Syrian Arab Republic and Iraq."[148] An Amnesty International report in December 2014 stated that thousands of women and girls were being held by Daesh[149] and a UN report in January 2016 said the phenomenon continued with around 3,500 enslaved Yezidis and other minority groups.[150] Additionally, sexual violence against women was: "part of the political economy ... used to generate revenue through the trafficking, trading and ransoming of women and girls ... women have become part of the currency ISIL uses to consolidate its power. They have been monetised as the 'spoils of war'".[151] The UNSG also suggested it was a form of nation-building with the creation of 'marriage bureaux' to sell women to Daesh members to produce the next generation.[152] Thus, it appears Daesh uses sexual violence to achieve its strategic political and military objectives.

Most of the reports reviewed on Daesh's methods focused on sexual violence against women and girls. However, a 2016 UN report identified that 800-900 boys had been abducted from around Mosul in June 2015 and those: "who refused to obey ISIL orders were flogged, tortured or raped."[153] Additionally, the same report stated that: "UNAMI/OHCHR also verified a number of reports of individuals murdered (by throwing them from buildings) by ISIL for being homosexual."[154] The UNSG also recorded sexual violence against: "lesbian, gay, bisexual, transgender and intersex individuals ... as a form of 'moral cleansing'"[155] and as: "a form of social control" by Daesh in both Iraq and Syria.[156]

---

147 Ibid.

148 UN Secretary General, "Conflict-related sexual violence: Report of Secretary General," 25/33.

149 Amnesty International, "Escape from Hell: Torture and Sexual Slavery in Islamic State Captivity in Iraq," Amnesty International, MDE 14/021/2014 December 2014), <http://www.amnesty.org.uk/sites/default/files/escape_from_hell_-_torture_and_sexual_slavery_in_islamic_state_captivity_in_iraq_-_english_2.pdf> (accessed January 7, 2016), 5-6.

150 United Nations, "Report on Protection of Civilians in Armed Conflict in Iraq: 1 May – 31 October 2015," 18.

151 Bangura, "Faith in Islam & Faith in Women: Why Gender Justice is Key to Islam without Extremes".

152 UN Secretary General, "Conflict-related sexual violence: Report of Secretary General," 25/33.

153 United Nations, "Report on Protection of Civilians in Armed Conflict in Iraq: 1 May – 31 October 2015," 14.

154 Ibid., 17.

155 UN Secretary General, "Conflict-related sexual violence: Report of Secretary General," 10/33.

156 Ibid., 2/33.

Finally, a further key feature of Daesh's form of sexual violence described by the UNSG's Special Representative is that: "ISIL flagrantly publicises its [sexual] abuses".[157] Amnesty International noted that: "more than any other group, it has gone to great efforts to publicize gruesome details of the atrocities ... giving them ample resonance through videos and statements widely distributed on social media, often in multiple languages."[158] Amnesty International believed this technique had been deployed to: "instil fear in its enemies and anyone else in its path."[159] It is possible that this is all the more intimidating because Daesh is challenging traditional religious and cultural taboos. The UNSG suggested that: "social media has converted brutality into a form of propaganda to incite, radicalize and attract recruits."[160] The use of sexual violence through: "forced marriage to foreign fighters" was recorded in the same report.[161] It appears that another reason for Daesh's policy of sexual violence is to encourage individuals from outside Iraq and Syria to join the group. Thus, Daesh has deliberately communicated its perpetration of sexual violence against women, men, children, homosexuals and others by exploiting social media to reach a global audience, with the threefold aim of terrifying, attracting and garnering media headlines to promote its core message.

Therefore, whilst Daesh's use of sexual violence is consistent with most of the literature findings, Daesh's strategy also involves: degrading women (partly as an attack on western values), seeking to eliminate non-heterosexuals, sexual violence for fund-raising and external recruitment, and a targeted sexual violence information campaign. Daesh is not unique in its modus operandi, but the case study revealed particular aspects to its approach.

### *Preventive measures against Daesh's sexual violence*

The paper will now assess the effectiveness of existing prevention methods, as described earlier (understanding; high-level support; training; and legislation), as a means of preventing Daesh using sexual violence in the future. First, an understanding of how and why sexual violence is used by Daesh seems to be in place with comprehensive reports by, for example, the UN, G7 and Amnesty International. This is despite the UN's reported difficulties in obtaining

157 Bangura, "Faith in Islam & Faith in Women: Why Gender Justice is Key to Islam without Extremes".

158 Amnesty International, "Escape from Hell: Torture and Sexual Slavery in Islamic State Captivity in Iraq," 11.

159 Ibid.

160 UN Secretary General, "Conflict-related sexual violence: Report of Secretary General," 25/33.

161 Ibid.

accurate statistics,[162] but seemingly counteracted by Daesh's clear intent to publicise its use of sexual violence, rather than hide or deny it, as some other groups do. Second, high-level support exists for tackling Daesh's prevalent use of sexual violence. For instance, last year's National Security Strategy said the PSVI would be extended particularly to Syria and Iraq.[163] A G7 report in 2015 on implementation of a 2013 'G8 Declaration' on the PSVI included details of assistance to Iraq and Syria. For example, the UK had provided Peshmerga troops with training on prevention. The UK had also trained Iraqi and Syrian human rights' defenders on gathering evidence through the 'International Protocol on the Documentation and Investigation of Sexual Violence in Conflict' and the US had funded Syrian doctors in forensic documentation. The Canadians had funded investigations and help for survivors. The French were funding 'Gynaecologists without Borders' to help Syrian refugees in Jordan. The Germans had financed the 'Berlin Center for Torture Victims', to give assistance in six Iraqi provinces, and also an Iraqi radio station that addresses sexual violence in conflict.[164] Similarly, the UK had funded: "training Syrian media activists in the use of radio to empower women and engage men in overturning social norms around the reporting of sexual violence".[165] The UNSG said: "I condemn the use of sexual violence by ISIL" and recommended: "Programmes to support the social reintegration of women and girls released from captivity".[166] Thus, it would seem that high-level international support exists, as demonstrated by the range of actions taken, including training for Peshmerga forces, human rights' defenders, doctors and media activists.

This just leaves the fourth prevention method examined in the literature review, namely the legislation, especially the aspects of deterrence and implementation. The literature review had confirmed that: "sexual violence is absolutely and adequately prohibited under international law".[167] However, this has seemingly had no effect on Daesh's strategy for using it, which supports Kirby's criticism of the PSVI, covered earlier. Daesh's sense of impunity appears undiminished despite the international glare of publicity and condemnation from

162 Ibid., 18/33.

163 United Kingdom Government, *National Security Strategy and Strategic Defence and Security Review 2015: Secure and Prosperous United Kingdom*, 63.

164 G7, "G7 Report on the Implementation of the G8 Declaration on Preventing Sexual Violence in Conflict," 3-4, 6-7.

165 Foreign & Commonwealth Office, "Angelina Jolie Pitt joins Baroness Anelay to chart next steps on tackling sexual violence".

166 UN Secretary General, "Conflict-related sexual violence: Report of Secretary General," 19/33 & 10/33.

167 Gaggioli, "Sexual violence in armed conflicts: violation of international humanitarian law and human rights law," 505.

the highest levels. Amnesty International has claimed that Daesh is responsible for war crimes and crimes against humanity, partly as a result of committing sexual violence in Iraq.[168] It stated that International Humanitarian Law applied to Daesh and that its civilian and military leaders: "can be held criminally responsible for war crimes" including the actions of their subordinates through a commission to act or an omission to prevent such action.[169] A UN report published this year agreed that Daesh had committed war crimes, crimes against humanity and: "possibly genocide".[170] The UN High Commissioner for Human Rights, Zeid Ra'ad Al Hussein, said: "The international community … should continue to closely follow the situation in Iraq with a view to ensuring that perpetrators of gross violations and abuses of human rights and serious violations of international humanitarian law are held accountable."[171] In the same report, the UN urged the Iraqi government to amend its own legislation so that Iraqi courts could have jurisdiction for international crimes. It also urged Iraq to refer such sexual violence matters to the International Criminal Court (ICC) or become a party to the ICC[172] (however, this seems unlikely as the same report also claimed the Iraqi State Force had violated international humanitarian and human rights laws).[173] Daesh also seems undeterred by G7 members' efforts to collect and document evidence, as described above, or by the work of the International Commission of Inquiry in Syria and the Fact-Finding Commission in Iraq, which the Justice Rapid Response team of experts had supported.[174] Thus, despite efforts to gather evidence and credible accusations that Daesh's sexual violence amounts to war crimes, crimes against humanity and possibly genocide, Daesh appears undeterred.

### *Daesh conclusions*

To conclude this review of Daesh as a case study, it has revealed itself to be both typical and distinctive. Many of Daesh's reasons for employing sexual violence as a weapon of war reflect the literature findings: a considerable sense of impunity, an objective to exert power and neutralise community resistance, and part of a planned military strategy to acquire territory. Most sexual

168 Amnesty International, "Escape from Hell: Torture and Sexual Slavery in Islamic State Captivity in Iraq," 4.

169 Ibid., 15.

170 United Nations, "Report on Protection of Civilians in Armed Conflict in Iraq: 1 May – 31 October 2015," i.

171 Ibid., start of report (no page number).

172 Ibid., ii.

173 Ibid.

174 G7, "G7 Report on the Implementation of the G8 Declaration on Preventing Sexual Violence in Conflict," 7.

violence appears to have been directed against women and girls, especially religious and ethnic minorities. However, sexual violence against men and boys has also been used to elicit information and suppress opposition. It has been committed in known vulnerable locations, such as displacement and detention camps, and at border checkpoints. Other elements, which reflect the literature findings, include the extent of the shame experienced by survivors, which has exacerbated challenges of accessing help and gathering reliable data. Amnesty International highlighted the number of Yezidi families who denied that their own relatives had been subjected to sexual violence, but insisted that it had been perpetrated systematically against members of their community.[175] Amnesty International also described the difficulties for survivors to obtain medical and psychological help, due to lack of awareness, the geographical distances involved, costs and the logistics of accessing support-services[176] – again the literature review had identified such problems as part of the numerous challenges in dealing with the after-effects.

The literature review emphasised that each conflict is different, which is why prevention approaches demand a deep appreciation of the context and bespoke responses. Daesh's policy to publicise its use of sexual violence through the latest communication channels serves three objectives: to terrorise people in Iraq and Syria into submitting to Daesh; to attract new recruits; and to ensure their broader message of establishing an Islamic Caliphate is transmitted around the world. Daesh seems to have an information operation at the heart of its military campaign and sexual violence as one of the main narratives to amplify their message. Other features which differed from the main findings of the literature review included an ideological and financial policy of using sexual violence to reduce women's status and transform women into a commodity to raise funds for their war efforts. They also used sexual violence to try to eliminate non-heterosexuals, which was mentioned in the literature but only to a limited extent.

Regarding current prevention methods identified in the literature, the Daesh case study reflected most of the literature findings. There appears to be a good comprehension, of why and how Daesh employs sexual violence, by the UN, G7 and Amnesty International, with academics such as Wood already researching their methods. There is also international support at the highest levels, including from the UNSG, his Special Representative on Sexual Violence in Conflict and the UN High Commissioner for Human Rights, as well as the G7.

175 Amnesty International, "Escape from Hell: Torture and Sexual Slavery in Islamic State Captivity in Iraq," 13-14.

176 Ibid., 13.

As with the literature findings, such international support reflects a western bias, and it would be useful to see other bodies engaging in the issue, such as the Arab League and Gulf Cooperation Council. Nonetheless, the high level support has been matched with resources to support a range of measures, including training Peshmerga forces, human rights' defenders, doctors and media activists. Yet the fourth strand of existing prevention strategies – deterrence through legislation – seems woefully inadequate. This is despite attempts to gather evidence and credible accusations from the UN and Amnesty International that Daesh's sexual violence amounts to war crimes, crimes against humanity and possibly genocide. Daesh remains undeterred.

There are few other prevention measures in place against Daesh's use of sexual violence as a weapon of war. Journalists have made strenuous efforts to report Daesh's actions – often encouraged by community activists and sometimes by family members. Perhaps as an unintended consequence, this has introduced unwelcome pressure on survivors to speak to the press. As a result, Amnesty International has called for more responsible journalism and for local leaders and activists to be more sensitive.[177] Yet, it will be important for the international media to remain engaged so that Daesh's sexually violent activities do not become hidden from world leaders who will need to drive through any future prevention strategies. Another aspect is the role of the Yezidi spiritual leader, Baba Sheikh, who spoke publicly in February 2015 to urge his community to support Yezidi women who had escaped from Daesh.[178] Although this was primarily aimed at helping survivors to reintegrate, it also served the function of challenging Daesh's strategy of degrading women. However, such messages will need to be reiterated on a regular basis by a range of religious and community leaders if they are to counterbalance Daesh's dedicated communication efforts. Although it is too early to know whether these additional preventive measures will have any impact, it is suggested that other prevention strategies need to be introduced if Daesh is ever to desist from its sexual violence strategy. This seems all the more pressing, given the lack of impact from existing prevention methods outlined in the literature and which are in place against Daesh, but with apparently no effect to-date.

177 Ibid., 17.

178 Bangura, "Faith in Islam & Faith in Women: Why Gender Justice is Key to Islam without Extremes".

## Additional Preventive Measures

The academic and practitioner literature offered few practical preventive measures, beyond those covered previously in this paper, with the limitations of these existing approaches identified in the Daesh case study just examined. This final section will, therefore, briefly consider possible additional preventive tools. It is not an exhaustive list, but focuses on: learning from groups which have desisted from using sexual violence; the role of civil society actors and soft power; the application of research in other fields to armed groups; and exploiting the capabilities of social media.

First, the ICRC advocated that it was important to learn from those groups which had not used sexual violence in conflict.[179] In examining individual cases, Wood noted that: "An armed group's leadership may prohibit sexual violence for strategic, normative, or practical reasons."[180] Wood identified the principal reasons for the prohibition of sexual violence as: avoiding losing control of subordinates; setting the moral high-ground; obtaining funding and resources from others; and winning the peace, as well as the war, to assume future power.[181] It is possible that such arguments could persuade armed groups to avoid, or stop using, sexual violence by highlighting the military-strategic and operational-level benefits which other armed groups have realised. A bespoke combination of incentives and sanctions, which reflects a deep understanding of an armed group's hierarchy, actors, culture and methods of violence, could help to prevent sexual violence being used by that group, especially if the benefits could be articulated by those who had foregone the use of sexual violence in their own armed struggles.

As well as using credible military leaders to achieve positive outcomes, the role of civil society actors could be better utilised. Focusing on positive male role models (although it could equally apply to female role models), the MenEngage Alliance and UNFPA highlighted that service-providers could: "play an important role in ... recasting social norms" – not just through their professional roles, but due to their status within that society.[182] In Hague's summing up of the Global Summit in 2014, he endorsed the role of faith groups: "Through their networks, they often have access and influence with local communities that no other actor has. As such, they are uniquely placed to change

179 ICRC, "Sexual Violence in Armed Conflict: E-Briefing," Part 4.

180 Wood, "Rape is not inevitable during war," in Kuehnast et al., eds., *Women and War: Power & Protection in Twenty-First Century*, 54.

181 Ibid., 54-55.

182 MenEngage Alliance and UNFPA, "Sexual Violence in Conflict and Post-Conflict: Engaging Men and Boys," 7.

hearts and minds".[183] Women's and men's organisations could be given more resources to support their endeavours within their own societies. The use of 'soft power' by organisations such as the British Council, UN and NGOs, as well as by individual campaigners, has long been established. However, few examples were cited within the literature regarding practical measures to prevent sexual violence in conflict. Wood suggested that lessons should be identified from other campaigns, such as those to stop 'blood diamonds', child soldiers and land mines, and then applied to preventing sexual violence in conflict.[184] A recent review by the House of Lords' on this subject concluded that: "There is a compelling case that programmes to effect behavioural and attitudinal change can assist in the prevention of sexual violence in conflict."[185]

Turning to other specialisms, Steffens et al. conducted research to understand how followers identify with particular leaders and the importance of shared social identities to enable group behaviour.[186] Other academics have investigated the factors behind military group cohesion.[187] By contrast, other research has examined why groups commit mass murder, such as during the Holocaust. For example, Haslam and Reicher suggested that: "groups *transform* the individuals who join them by changing the dispositions of their members".[188] Additionally, Wood contemplated whether research results into rape in university campuses, youth gangs, sports clubs and prisons could be applied to sexual violence in conflict.[189] She also considered that: "The small-group dynamics that lead to unit norms promoting or constraining the occurrence of sexual violence appears a promising avenue of research."[190] Thus, further research

183 FCO, "Chair's Summary: Global Summit to End Sexual Violence in Conflict."

184 Wood, "Conflict-related sexual violence and the policy implications of recent research," 476.

185 House of Lords, "Select Committee on Sexual Violence in Conflict: Report of Session 2015-16: Sexual Violence in Conflict: A War Crime," 8.

186 Niklas K. Steffens, S. Alexander Haslam, and Stephen D. Reicher, "Up close and personal: Evidence that shared social identity is a basis for the 'special' relationship that binds followers to leaders," *The Leadership Quarterly* 25 (2015).

187 Guy, L. Siebold, "The Essence of Military Group Cohesion," *Armed Forces & Society* 33(2) (2007): 286-295 and Anthony King, "The Existence of Group Cohesion in the Armed Forces: A Response to Guy Siebold," *Armed Forces & Society* 33(4) (2007): 638-645.

188 S.A. Haslam, and S. Reicher, "Beyond the banality of evil: three dynamics of an interactionist social psychology of terrorism," *Personality and Social Psychology Bulletin*, 33(5) (2007): 620.

189 Wood, "Conflict-related sexual violence and the policy implications of recent research," 478.

190 Wood, "Sexual violence during war: toward an understanding of variation," in *Order, Conflict and Violence*, eds. Stathis N. Kalyvas, Ian Shapiro and Tarek Masoud (New York and Cambridge: Cambridge University Press, 2008), 347.

into the effect of leaders and groups on behaviour could result in additional preventive measures being developed in the future. In particular, targeting leaders, who most closely resonate with their members, altering a group's social identity and exploiting military group cohesion as ways of changing behavioural norms.

Finally, the potential of social media should be considered. By 2020, smartphone ownership is forecast to be around 70% globally, with most of the new owners living in the developing world.[191] Analysis of open sources, such as social media sites, is already being used to detect crises and gain rapid situational awareness. For instance, citizen journalists, such as the 'Bell¿ngcat' team, fused social media sites to understand what was happening in the Ukrainian conflict zone.[192] The introduction of smartphones to some of the most remote and conflict-prone regions of the world in the next four-five years could be transformative in helping to prevent this traditionally hidden crime. The sense of impunity, which was covered earlier in the literature review as one of the main reasons for the use of sexual violence in conflict, could be eroded, if 'disruptive technologies' such as social media were exploited to provide situational awareness and early warning. Where it is not possible to prevent sexual violence being perpetrated, social media could contribute to the provision of data on its extent to provide a military/policing response, to help target medical assistance, and, potentially, support the evidence-gathering process.

This concludes the review of possible additional preventive measures, covering: the application of lessons from those groups which have chosen not to use sexual violence; the role of civil society actors and soft power; leader and group influence; and social media. It has sought to highlight that there is scope for academics and practitioners on preventing sexual violence in conflict to collaborate with their counterparts in other fields to consider alternative prevention approaches. It seems unlikely that any single measure could prevent the use of sexual violence in war, but a bespoke combination of the preventive measures could be adopted which takes into account the context and specifics of each armed conflict.

---

191 The Mobile Economy 2015), <http://gsmamobileeconomy.com/global/> (accessed May 12, 2016), 2.

192 Bell¿ngcat, "Confirming the Location of the Same Msta-S in Russia and Ukraine," Bell¿ngcat May 2015), <https://www.bellingcat.com/resources/case-studies/2015/05/29/confirming-the-location-of-the-same-msta-s-in-russia-and-ukraine/> (accessed May 12, 2016).

## Conclusion

In conclusion, this paper has examined whether it is possible to prevent sexual violence as a weapon of war against women, men and children or only to manage the after-effects. The literature review analysed five aspects of the issue: the reasons why sexual violence is used in conflicts; how men and boys can be victims, and women perpetrators; the manifold challenges in managing the after-effects; the risks from securitising the issue and negating progress on women's roles in peace and security; and, the evidence that sexual violence in conflict is not inevitable. Four existing prevention approaches were assessed, concerning: understanding; high-level support; training; and legislation. This paper concluded that they provided a solid foundation on which to build, but that improvements were needed, which would require long-term financial support and sustained effort. The specific case of Daesh was examined against the literature findings. This paper suggested that Daesh's use of sexual violence reflected much of the literature research, but that there were also distinctive elements, particularly their strategy for publicising their use of sexual violence through social media. The Daesh case study illustrated the shortcomings of current prevention approaches (especially the lack of deterrence from legislation) and an urgent requirement to identify other methods. Thus, alternative preventive measures were considered, which concluded that a broader and imaginative approach to prevention, in collaboration with experts in other fields, could yield results. Ultimately, the challenges of preventing sexual violence as a weapon of war, managing the after-effects and dealing with the generational impact, require all appropriate measures to be fully harnessed.

This paper has sought to provide evidence that it is possible to prevent sexual violence as a weapon of war. However, it has emphasised that the challenges of preventing sexual violence systematically and comprehensively are considerable. The literature review findings and the Daesh example indicated that the current prevention strategies need to be improved and additional measures introduced. The findings suggested a requirement for a coordinated and streamlined approach, involving health-care, police and judiciary experts, locally-led, but with external support, and which must be sustained for the long-term. In particular, each conflict necessitates a deep understanding of the context, actors and methods to ensure a tailored, sufficiently-resourced and multi-layered response that takes into account the different needs of women, men and children.

Additionally, the literature findings revealed that managing the after-effects effectively is an immense undertaking, which involves immediate and long-term physical and psychological care to be given to individuals. The after-effects for societies also need addressing to reduce the spread of STDs, deter retribution and re-build community cohesion. Somehow, the cycle of sexual violence has to be broken. Women and men – perpetrators, victims and witnesses – have to be reintegrated, and children, born of sexual violence, accepted into society. Survivors need recognition. Those who have committed sexual violence need to be brought to justice – fairly and expeditiously. The costs of long-term medical care, legal undertakings, education and reconstruction are incalculable and probably beyond the means of most war-torn countries to provide. However, effective management of the after-effects would contribute to the prevention of future outbreaks of sexual violence in conflict by helping to stop the cycle of violence.

If the prevention challenges seem insurmountable, the evidence of the non-inevitability of sexual violence as a weapon of war should be recalled. It is a choice, not an accident, as highlighted by the ICRC's research and experiences:

> It is no longer tenable to claim that sexual violence is simply an ugly facet of our worst human inclinations and an unfortunate companion of war; today it is widely acknowledged that sexual violence is not an inevitable consequence of armed conflict. This makes prevention efforts critical, legitimate and urgently needed.[193]

Gloria Steinem noted that: "the most significant characteristic of humans – the one that allows our species to survive – is that we're adaptable."[194] It is also notable that our predecessors have achieved the 'impossible' in war previously: for example, outlawing the use of child soldiers, cluster munitions and anti-personnel land mines. Even though such weapons of war still exist, it has to be hoped that with the passage of time they, and sexual violence, will disappear as strategies of war. Kerry recognised that: "we have banned the unconscionable before … sexual violence is a vile crime against humanity. It is not just an excusable, inevitable by-product of war."[195] In conclusion, preventing sexual violence as a weapon of war remains extremely demanding – and the magnitude of the undertaking should not be underestimated. However, the absence of sexual violence in many conflicts suggests that it is possible to prevent it systemically. It requires a determined effort, perhaps for generations, but it

193 ICRC, "Sexual Violence in Armed Conflict: E-Briefing," Part 4.

194 Lauren Wolfe, "Gloria Steinem on Rape in War, Its Causes, and How to Stop It," The Atlantic February 8, 2012), <http://www.theatlantic.com/international/archive/2012/02/gloria-steinem-on-rape-in-war-its-causes-and-how-to-stop-it/252470/> (accessed January 18, 2016).

195 Kerry, "Remarks at Global Summit to End Sexual Violence in Conflict".

seems that with improved understanding, high-level international support and action, training and legislation, positive developments are underway:

> we are determined to end the use of rape and sexual violence in conflicts around the world. ... the prevention of sexual violence in conflict is critical to peace, security and sustainable development ... Every individual has a moral responsibility to speak out ... to demand a change in how the world perceives and responds to these crimes.[196]

## Bibliography

Arieff, Alexis. "Sexual Violence in African Conflicts." *Congressional Research Service.* (November 2009). <http://web.a.ebscohost.com/ehost/pdfviewer/pdfviewer?sid=e00a61c4-d061-425e-9d6f-dac6e949281e%40sessionmgr4004&vid=15&hid=4212> (accessed May 17, 2016).

Al Achi, Dalia. "*Human Rights Day: Abuses rife in Central African Republic.*" UNHCR. (December 2015). <http://www.unhcr.org/5669a3a66.html> (accessed January 6, 2016).

Alcorn, Ted. "Responding to sexual violence in armed conflict." *The Lancet* Volume 383, No. 9934 2014): 2034-2037. <http://www.thelancet.com/journals/lancet/article/PIIS0140-6736(14)60970-3/fulltext> (accessed January 18, 2016).

Amnesty International. "Escape from Hell: Torture and Sexual Slavery in Islamic State Captivity in Iraq." Amnesty International. MDE 14/021/2014. (December 2014). <http://www.amnesty.org.uk/sites/default/files/escape_from_hell_-_torture_and_sexual_slavery_in_islamic_state_captivity_in_iraq_-_english_2.pdf> (accessed January 7, 2016).

Baaz, Maria Eriksson, and Maria Stern. *Sexual Violence as a Weapon of War? Perceptions, Prescriptions, Problems in the Congo and Beyond.* London: Zed Books Ltd, 2013. eBook Collection. <http://web.a.ebscohost.com/ehost/ebookviewer/ebook/bmxlYmtfXzU3NzU1OF9fQU41?sid=e00a61c4-d061-425e-9d6f-dac6e949281e@sessionmgr4004&vid=73&format=EK&rid=2> (accessed May 18, 2016).

Baker, Aryn. "War and Rape." *Time* 187, no. 14 (2016): 36-41. <http://web.a.ebscohost.com/ehost/pdfviewer/pdfviewer?sid=0e34b8af-4d52-4955-9dfa-eb6e4e3bae87%40sessionmgr4004&vid=20&hid=4107> (accessed May 23, 2016).

Bangura, Zainab. "Faith in Islam & Faith in Women: Why Gender Justice is Key to an Islam Without Extremes." International Crisis Group. (October 2015). <https://

196 Foreign & Commonwealth Office, "Statement of Action - Global Summit to End Sexual Violence in Conflict".

medium.com/the-future-of-conflict/faith-in-islam-faith-in-women-why-gender-justice-is-key-to-an-islam-without-extremes-8920277ef674#.dkjeoo8jg> (accessed January 6, 2016).

Bell¿ngcat. "Confirming the Location of the Same Msta-S in Russia and Ukraine." Bell¿ngcat. (May 2015). <https://www.bellingcat.com/resources/case-studies/2015/05/29/confirming-the-location-of-the-same-msta-s-in-russia-and-ukraine/> (accessed May 12, 2016).

Bernard, Vincent, and Durham, Helen. "Sexual violence in armed conflict: From breaking the silence to breaking the cycle." *International Review of the Red Cross* 96(894) (2014): 427-434. <doi:10.1017/S1816383115000442> (accessed January 11, 2016).

Bernard, Vincent, and Elvina Pothelet. "Through the eyes of a detention doctor: Interview with Raed Aburabi." *International Review of the Red Cross* 96(894) (2014): 479-484. <doi:10.1017/S1816383115000284> (accessed January 11, 2016).

Bouvier, Paul. "Sexual violence, health and humanitarian ethics: Towards a holistic, person-centred approach." *International Review of the Red Cross* 96(894) (2014): 565-584. <doi:10.1017/S1816383115000430> (accessed January 11, 2016).

Buckingham, Becks. "Rape and Sexual Violence: a Weapon of War?" Defence Research Paper, JSCSC, 2012.

Cannon, Patrick. "A Feminist Response to Rape as a Weapon of War in Eastern Congo." *Peace Review* 24, no. 4 (2012): 478-483. <http://web.a.ebscohost.com/ehost/pdfviewer/pdfviewer?sid=0e34b8af-4d52-4955-9dfa-eb6e4e3bae87%40sessionmgr4004&vid=30&hid=4107> (accessed May 23, 2016).

Carpenter, R. Charli. "Recognizing Gender-Based Violence Against Civilian Men and Boys in Conflict Situations." *Security Dialogue* 37(1) (2006): 83-103. <http://sdi.sagepub.com/content/37/1/83.full.pdf+html> (accessed May 19, 2016).

Carvajal, Doreen. "A Female Approach to Peacekeeping." New York Times. (March 5, 2010). <http://www.nytimes.com/2010/03/06/world/africa/06iht-ffpeace.html?_r=0> (accessed January 7, 2016).

Cohen, Dara Kay. "Female Combatants and the Perpetration of Violence: Wartime Rape in the Sierra Leone Civil War." *World Politics* 65, no. 3 (2013): 383-415. <doi: 10.1017/S0043887113000105> (accessed May 18, 2016).

Dammers, Tom. *"Paper commissioned for the EFA Global Monitoring Report 2011, The hidden crisis: Armed conflict and education".* United Nations Educational, Scientific and Cultural Organization. 2011/ED/EFA/MRT/PI/15. (2010). <http://unesdoc.unesco.org/images/0019/001907/190705e.pdf> (accessed May 23, 2016).

Davies, Mathew. "Women and Development, Not Gender and Politics: Explaining ASEAN's Failure to engage with the Women, Peace and Security agenda." *Contemporary Southeast Asia: A Journal of International & Strategic Affairs* 38, no. 1 (2016): 106-127. <http://web.a.ebscohost.com/ehost/pdfviewer/pdfviewer?vid=36&

sid=0e34b8af-4d52-4955-9dfa-eb6e4e3bae87%40sessionmgr4004&hid=4107> (accessed May 23, 2016).

de Jonge Oudraat, Chantal. "UNSCR 1325 – Conundrums and Opportunities." *International Interactions* 39, no. 4 (2013): 612-619. <http://web.a.ebscohost.com/ehost/pdfviewer/pdfviewer?sid=0e34b8af-4d52-4955-9dfa-eb6e4e3bae87%40sessionmgr4004&vid=48&hid=4107> (accessed May 23, 2016).

Dolan, Chris. "Letting go of the gender binary: Charting new pathways for humanitarian interventions on gender-based violence." *International Review of the Red Cross* 96(894) (2014): 485-501. <doi:10.1017/S1816383115000120> (accessed January 10, 2016).

Dolan, Chris. "Into the Mainstream: Addressing Sexual Violence against Men and Boys in Conflict." Briefing Paper prepared for the Overseas Development Institute. (2014) <https://www.warchild.org.uk/sites/default/files/Into-the-Mainstream.pdf> (accessed May 23, 2016).

Duroch, Françoise, and Catrin Schulte-Hillen. "Care for victims of sexual violence, an organization pushed to its limits: The case of Médecins Sans Frontières." *International Review of the Red Cross*, 96(894) (2014): 601-624. <doi:10.1017/S1816383115000107> (accessed January 11, 2016).

Edström Jerker, Alexa Hassink, Thea Shahrokh, and Erin Stern, eds. "Engendering Men: A Collaborative Review of Evidence of Men and Boys in Social Change and Gender Equality." EMERGE Evidence Review, Promundo-US, Sonke Gender Justice and the Institute of Development Studies. (September 2015). <http://opendocs.ids.ac.uk/opendocs/bitstream/handle/123456789/7059/EMERGE.pdf?sequence=1> (accessed January 22, 2016).

Ensler, Eve. "Bureau of Sex Slavery: for Yanar and my sisters in Iraq and Syria." *Nation* 301, no. 17 (2015): 4-6. <http://web.a.ebscohost.com/ehost/pdfviewer/pdfviewer?sid=e00a61c4-d061-425e-9d6f-dac6e949281e%40sessionmgr4004&vid=97&hid=4212> (accessed May 19, 2016).

Feeley, Rebecca, and Colin Thomas-Jensen. "Getting Serious about Ending Conflict and Sexual Violence in Congo." ENOUGH Strategy Paper #15. (2008). <http://www.enoughproject.org/files/CongoSerious.pdf> (accessed May 23, 2016).

Foreign & Commonwealth Office. "Foreign Secretary launches new Government initiative to prevent sexual violence in conflict." Foreign & Commonwealth Office. (May 2012).<https://www.gov.uk/government/speeches/foreign-secretary-launches-new-government-initiative-to-prevent-sexual-violence-in-conflict> (accessed March 21, 2016).

Foreign & Commonwealth Office. "The Foreign Secretary William Hague, Angelina Jolie and Zainab Hawa Bangura launch G8 Declaration on Preventing Sexual Violence in Conflict." Foreign & Commonwealth Office. (April 2013). <https://www.gov.uk/government/news/g8-declaration-on-preventing-sexual-violence-in-conflict> (accessed November 27, 2015).

Foreign & Commonwealth Office. "Declaration on Preventing Sexual Violence in Conflict." Foreign & Commonwealth Office. (April 2013). <https://www.gov.uk/government/uploads/system/uploads/attachment_data/file/185008/G8_PSVI_Declaration_-_FINAL.pdf> (accessed November 27, 2015).

Foreign & Commonwealth Office. "Statement of Action - Global Summit to End Sexual Violence in Conflict." Foreign & Commonwealth Office. (June 2014). <https://www.gov.uk/government/publications/statement-of-action-global-summit-to-end-sexual-violence-in-conflict> (accessed November 26, 2015).

Foreign & Commonwealth Office. "Chair's Summary - Global Summit to End Sexual Violence in Conflict." Foreign & Commonwealth Office. (June 2014). <https://www.gov.uk/government/publications/chairs-summary-global-summit-to-end-sexual-violence-in-conflict/chairs-summary-global-summit-to-end-sexual-violence-in-conflict> (accessed November 27, 2015).

Foreign & Commonwealth Office. "Angelina Jolie Pitt joins Baroness Anelay to chart next steps on tackling sexual violence." Foreign & Commonwealth Office. (June 2015). <https://www.gov.uk/government/news/angelina-jolie-pitt-joins-baroness-anelay-to-chart-next-steps-on-tackling-sexual-violence> (accessed January 12, 2016).

G7. "G7 Report on the Implementation of the G8 Declaration on Preventing Sexual Violence in Conflict." G7. (November 2015). <https://www.g7germany.de/Content/EN/_Anlagen/G7/2015-11-24-g7-erklaerung_svc_en.pdf?__blob=publicationFile&v=3> (accessed January 7, 2016).

G7. "G7 Foreign Ministers Meeting: Joint Communique." G7. (April 2016). <http://www.mofa.go.jp/files/000147440.pdf> (accessed May 13, 2016).

Gaggioli, Gloria. "Sexual violence in armed conflicts: A violation of international humanitarian law and human rights law." *International Review of the Red Cross* 96(894) (2014): 503-538. <doi:10.1017/S1816383115000211> (accessed January 11, 2016).

Geneva Call. <http://www.genevacall.org/> (accessed January 21, 2016).

Gingerich, Tara, and Jennifer Leaning. "The Use of Rape as a Weapon of War in the Conflict in Darfur, Sudan." 2004. <http://reliefweb.int/sites/reliefweb.int/files/resources/B119C9EFB7DCAA2DC1256F5F004FBEA9-hu-sud-310ct.pdf> (accessed May 25, 2016).

Global Peace Operations Review. "Female Participation in UN Peace Operations." <http://peaceoperationsreview.org/featured-data/> (accessed January 12, 2016).

Haslam, S.A., and S. Reicher. "Beyond the banality of evil: three dynamics of an interactionist social psychology of terrorism." *Personality and Social Psychology Bulletin*, 33(5) (2007): 615-622.

Henry, Marsha. "Ten Reasons Not to Write Your Master's Dissertation on Sexual Violence in War." *The Disorder of Things.* (June 4, 2013). <http://thedisorderofthings.

com/2013/06/04/ten-reasons-not-to-write-your-masters-dissertation-on-sexual-violence-in-war/> (accessed January 21 2016).

House of Lords. "Select Committee on Sexual Violence in Conflict: Report of Session 2015-16: Sexual Violence in Conflict: A War Crime." House of Lords. HL Paper 123. (April 12, 2016). <http://www.publications.parliament.uk/pa/ld201516/ldselect/ldsvc/123/123.pdf> (accessed April 15, 2016).

Human Rights Watch. "Rwanda: International Tribunal Closing Its Doors." HRW. (December 2015). <https://www.hrw.org/news/2015/12/23/rwanda-international-tribunal-closing-its-doors> (accessed January 6, 2016).

Human Security Report Project. *Human Security Report 2012: Sexual Violence, Education, and War: Beyond the Mainstream Narrative.* Vancouver: Human Security Press, 2012. <http://hsrgroup.org/human-security-reports/2012/text.aspx> (accessed May 23, 2016).

International Committee of the Red Cross. "Sexual Violence in Armed Conflict: E-Briefing." ICRC. (December 2015). <https://app.icrc.org/e-briefing/sexual-violence-armed-conflict/> (accessed January 7, 2016).

Jolie, Angelina. *In the Land of Blood and Honey.* (2011). DVD (accessed December 19, 2015).

Jones, Nicola, Janice Cooper, Elizabeth Presler-Marshall and David Walker. "The fallout of rape as a weapon of war: The life-long and intergenerational impacts of sexual violence in conflict." Overseas Development Institute. (2014). <http://www.odi.org/sites/odi.org.uk/files/odi-assets/publications-opinion-files/8990.pdf> (accessed May 23, 2016).

Justice Rapid Response. "Justice Rapid Response welcomes UN Women and Draper Richards Kaplan Foundation to its Executive Board." JRR. (November 2015). <http://www.justicerapidresponse.org/justice-rapid-response-welcomes-un-women-and-draper-richards-kaplan-foundation-to-its-executive-board/> (accessed January 7, 2016).

Kerry, John. "Remarks at The Global Summit to End Sexual Violence in Conflict." US Department of State. (June 2014). <http://www.state.gov/secretary/remarks/2014/06/227553.htm> (accessed November 27, 2015).

Kilcullen, David. *Out of the Mountains: the Coming of Age of the Urban Guerrilla.* London: C. Hurst & Co., 2013.

Kilmartin, Chris. "Men, Peace, and Security Symposium: Agents of Change." United States Institute of Peace. (October 29, 2013. Published November 13, 2013). <https://www.youtube.com/watch?v=rnXM8mvdzaw> (accessed January 22, 2016).

King, Anthony. "The Existence of Group Cohesion in the Armed Forces: A Response to Guy Siebold." *Armed Forces & Society* Vol 33, No. 4 (2007): 638-645.

Kirby, Paul. "How is rape a weapon of war? Feminist International Relations, modes of critical explanation and the study of wartime sexual violence." European Journal of

International Relations 19(4) (2013): 773-796. <doi:10.1177/1354066111426621> (accessed May 18, 2016).

Kirby, Paul. "Ending sexual violence in conflict: the Preventing Sexual Violence Initiative and its critics." *International Affairs*, 91(3) (2015): 457-472. <doi:10.1111/1468-2346.12283> (accessed October 8, 2015).

Kuehnast, Kathleen, Chantal de Jonge Oudraat, and Helga Hernes, eds. *Women and War: Power and Protection in the Twenty-First Century.* Washington, DC: United States Institute of Peace Press, 2011.

Leatherman, Janie. "Sexual Violence and Armed Conflict: Complex Dynamics of Re-Victimization." *International Journal of Peace Studies* 12, no. 1 (2007): 53-71. <http://web.a.ebscohost.com/ehost/pdfviewer/pdfviewer?sid=e00a61c4-d061-425e-9d6f-dac6e949281e%40sessionmgr4004&vid=92&hid=4212> (accessed May 18, 2016).

Leiby, Michele L. "Wartime Sexual Violence in Guatemala and Peru." *International Studies Quarterly* 53, no. 2 (2009): 445-468. <http://web.a.ebscohost.com/ehost/pdfviewer/pdfviewer?sid=e00a61c4-d061-425e-9d6f-dac6e949281e%40sessionmgr4004&vid=109&hid=4212> (accessed May 19, 2016).

Lewis, Stephen. "Against the war on women: V-day in the Congo." *Peace & Conflict Monitor.* (April 2008). <http://web.a.ebscohost.com/ehost/detail/detail?vid=29&sid=e00a61c4-d061-425e-9d6f-dac6e949281e%40sessionmgr4004&hid=4212&bdata=JnNpdGU9ZWhvc3QtbGl2ZQ%3d%3d#AN=32019173&db=tsh> (accessed May 18, 2016).

Magner, K, JE Desrosiers, I Blunt, T Hawken, and E Brick. *The role of faith based organisations in preventing and responding to sexual, intimate partner and gender-based violence in conflict settings: A modified critical interpretive synthesis.* University of Otago for the Sexual Violence Research Initiative. (2015). <http://svri.org.dedi6.cpt3.host-h.net/sites/default/files/attachments/2016-04-13/FBOreview.pdf> (accessed May 22, 2016).

Matfess, Hilary. "Boko Haram's War on Women." *Newsweek Global* 166, no. 7 (February 19, 2016): 12-15. <http://web.a.ebscohost.com/ehost/pdfviewer/pdfviewer?vid=55&sid=0e34b8af-4d52-4955-9dfa-eb6e4e3bae87%40sessionmgr4004&hid=4107> (accessed May 23, 2016).

Mehari, Zeresenay Berhane. *Difret.* (2014). DVD (accessed December 20, 2015).

MenEngage Alliance and United Nations Population Fund. "Sexual Violence in Conflict and Post-Conflict: Engaging Men and Boys." (July 2012). <http://menengage.org/resources/sexual-violence-conflict-post-conflict-engaging-men-boys/> (accessed January 12, 2016).

Mollmann, Marianne. "Rape in war: No more excuses." Human Rights Watch. (July 2011). <https://www.hrw.org/news/2011/07/22/rape-war-no-more-excuses> (accessed January 6, 2016).

Morgan, A.J. "Sexual Violence and Gender Roles: From Peace to Conflict and Back Again." Gender Across Borders. (November 2011). <http://www.genderacrossborders.com/2011/11/28/sexual-violence-and-gender-roles-from-peace-to-conflict-and-back-again/> (accessed May 22, 2016).

NATO. "Remarks by NATO Deputy Secretary General Alexander Vershbow at the United Nations Security Council Open Debate on the High-Level Review of UNSCR 1325 – Women, Peace and Security." NATO. Last modified October 14, 2015. <http://www.nato.int/cps/en/natohq/opinions_123768.htm?selectedLocale=en> (accessed January 12, 2016).

Nelaeva, Galina. "The Impact of Transnational Advocacy Networks on the Prosecution of Wartime Rape and Sexual Violence: The Case of the ICTR." *International Social Science Review* 85, no. 1/2 (2010): 3-27. <http://web.a.ebscohost.com/ehost/pdfviewer/pdfviewer?vid=31&sid=0e34b8af-4d52-4955-9dfa-eb6e4e3bae87%40sessionmgr4004&hid=4107> (accessed May 23, 2016).

Nordås, Ragnhild, and Siri C.A. Rustad. "Sexual Exploitation and Abuse by Peacekeepers: Understanding Variation." *International Interactions* 39, no. 4 (2013): 511-534. <http://web.b.ebscohost.com/ehost/pdfviewer/pdfviewer?vid=87&sid=d9b58e6f-f0a9-428e-86e5-c8fba15262df%40sessionmgr106&hid=105> (accessed May 23, 2016).

Office of the Special Representative of the Secretary-General for Sexual Violence in Conflict. Homepage. <http://www.un.org/sexualviolenceinconflict/> (accessed May 13, 2016).

Oxford Learner's Dictionary. "Prevent." Oxford Learner's Dictionary. <http://www.oxfordlearnersdictionaries.com/definition/english/prevent?q=prevent> (accessed May 15, 2016).

Parliament. "House of Commons Debates 29 June 2015: Tunisia, and European Council." Parliament. (June 2015). <http://www.publications.parliament.uk/pa/cm201516/cmhansrd/cm150629/debtext/150629-0001.htm#15062950000001> (accessed April 7, 2016).

Peterman, Amber, Dara Kay Cohen, Tia Palermo, and Amelia Hoov. "Rape reporting during war: Why the numbers don't mean what you think they do." *Foreign Affairs*. (August 1, 2011). <https://www.foreignaffairs.com/articles/2011-08-01/rape-reporting-during-war?page=show> (accessed May 23, 2016).

Rees, Madeleine and Christine Chinkin. "Why we support the PSVI." Women's International League for Peace and Freedom. (June 2015). <http://wilpf.org/why-we-support-the-psvi/> (accessed May 20, 2016).

Reicher, Stephen. "The Context of Social Identity: Domination, Resistance, and Change." *Political Psychology*. 259(6) (2004): 921-945. <doi:10.1111/j.1467-9221.2004.00403.x.> (accessed January 19, 2016).

Rowley, Elizabeth, Garcia Moreno, and Elizabeth Dartnall. *Executive Summary: A Research Agenda for Sexual Violence In Humanitarian, Conflict and Post-Conflict*

*Settings.* World Health Organization, UN Action, Sexual Violence Research Initiative and Medical Research Council South Africa. (2011). <https://www.researchgate.net/publication/233428122_Executive_Summary_A_Research_Agenda_for_Sexual_Violence_In_Humanitarian_Conflict_and_Post-Conflict_Settings> (accessed May 23, 2016).

Russell, Wynne. "Sexual violence against men and boys." *Forced Migration Review*, no. 27 (2007). <http://web.a.ebscohost.com/ehost/pdfviewer/pdfviewer?sid=e00a61c4-d061-425e-9d6f-dac6e949281e%40sessionmgr4004&vid=27&hid=4212> (accessed May 18, 2016).

Schuurman, Marriët. "NATO and the Women, Peace and Security Agenda: Time to Bring It Home." *Connections: The Quarterly Journal*, Vol XIV, No. 3 October 2015). <http://www.nato.int/cps/en/natohq/opinions_124032.htm?selectedLocale=en> (accessed January 12, 2016).

Shepherd, Laura J. and Jacqui True. "The Women, Peace and Security agenda and Australian leadership in the world: from rhetoric to commitment?" *Australian Journal of International Affairs*, Vol. 68, No. 3 (2014): 257-284. <http://dx.doi.org/10.1080/10357718.2014.903895> (accessed May 18, 2016).

Siebold, Guy, L. "The Essence of Military Group Cohesion." *Armed Forces & Society* Vol. 33, No. 2 (2007): 286-295.

Sivakumaran, Sandesh. "Lost in translation: UN responses to sexual violence against men and boys in situations of armed conflict." *International Review of the Red Cross*, 92(877) (2010): 259-277. <doi:10.1017/S1816383110000020> (accessed May 18, 2016).

Solangon, Sarah, and Preeti Patel. "Sexual violence against men in countries affected by armed conflict." *Conflict, Security and Development* 12(4) (2012): 417-42. <doi:10.1080/14678802.2012.724794> (accessed November 27, 2015).

Stauffer, Hilary and Erica Hall. "No Shame in Justice: addressing stigma against survivors to end sexual violence in conflict zones." World Vision UK. (December 2015). <http://9bb63f6dda0f744fa444-9471a7fca5768cc513a2e3c4a260910b.r43.cf3.rackcdn.com/files/1614/4888/7012/WVUK_No_Shame_in_Justice_low_res.pdf> (accessed May 19, 2016).

Steffens, Niklas K., S. Alexander Haslam, and Stephen D. Reicher. "Up close and personal: evidence that shared social identity is a basis for the 'special' relationship that binds followers to leaders." *The Leadership Quarterly* 25 (2015): 296-313.

The Mobile Economy. (2015). <http://gsmamobileeconomy.com/global/> (accessed May 12, 2016).

UNICEF (UK). "Sexual Violence in Conflict." (2014) <http://www.unicef.org.uk/Documents/Public-Affairs-Briefings/UNICEF-UK-Briefing-Sexual-Violence-in-Conflict.pdf> (accessed May 23, 2016).

United Kingdom Government. *National Security Strategy and Strategic Defence and Security Review 2015: A Secure and Prosperous United Kingdom.* Cm 9161. November 2015.

United Kingdom. Development, Concepts and Doctrine Centre. *UK Defence Doctrine.* Joint Doctrine Publication 0-01. 5th ed. Shrivenham: DCDC, 2014.

United Nations. "Report on the Protection of Civilians in the Armed Conflict in Iraq: 1 May – 31 October 2015." (January 2016). <http://www.uniraq.org/images/humanrights/UNAMI-OHCHR_%20POC%20Report_FINAL_01%20May-31%20October%202015_FINAL_11Jan2016.pdf> (accessed January 21, 2016).

United Nations Secretary General. "Conflict-related sexual violence: Report of the Secretary General." United Nations. S/2015/203 (March 23, 2015). <http://www.stoprapenow.org/uploads/advocacyresources/1428937312.pdf> (accessed January 6, 2016).

Verma, Baroness Sandip. "The UK firmly believes that the 15th anniversary must represent the start of a new era on Women, Peace and Security." UK Government. (October 13, 2015). <https://www.gov.uk/government/speeches/the-uk-firmly-believes-that-the-15th-anniversary-must-represent-the-start-of-a-new-era-on-women-peace-and-security> (accessed November 26, 2015).

Warner, Christopher H, George N. Appenzeller, Angela Mobbs, Jessica R. Parker, Carolynn M. Warner, Thomas Grieger, and Charles W. Hoge. "Effectiveness of battlefield-ethics training during combat deployment: a programme assessment." The *Lancet.* Vol 378 (2011): 915-924.

Watson, Callum. "Preventing and Responding to Sexual and Domestic Violence against Men: A Guidance Note for Security Sector Institutions." Democratic Control of the Armed Forces. 2014. <http://www.dcaf.ch/Publications/Preventing-and-Responding-to-Sexual-and-Domestic-Violence-against-Men-A-Guidance-Note-for-Security-Sector-Institutions> (accessed January 19, 2016).

Watson, Callum. "Bad apples or bad apple trees? An examination of the contexts in which sexual violence against men takes place." Paper presented at a workshop entitled, 'Sexual Violence Against Men during Conflicts: Bridging the Gap between Theory and Practice.' *The Graduate Institute of International and Development Studies*, Geneva February 26-27, 2015).

Wolfe, Lauren. "Gloria Steinem on Rape in War, Its Causes, and How to Stop It." *The Atlantic.* (February 8, 2012). <http://www.theatlantic.com/international/archive/2012/02/gloria-steinem-on-rape-in-war-its-causes-and-how-to-stop-it/252470/> (accessed January 18, 2016).

Women's International League for Peace and Freedom. "Women organising for change in Syria and Bosnia." WILPF. (2014). <http://wilpf.org/wp-content/uploads/2014/07/Women-Organising-for-Change-in-Bosnia-and-Syria.pdf> (accessed May 15, 2016).

Women's International League for Peace and Freedom. "WILPF reflects on the Global Summit to end Sexual Violence in Conflict." WILPF. (2014). <http://wilpf.org/wilpf-reflects-on-the-global-summit-to-end-sexual-violence-in-conflict/> (accessed May 20, 2016).

WomenPolice. "The Ongoing Fight to End Sexual Violence in Conflict." *WomenPolice.* (August 2015). <http://web.a.ebscohost.com/ehost/pdfviewer/pdfviewer?vid=9&sid=e00a61c4-d061-425e-9d6f-dac6e949281e%40sessionmgr4004&hid=4212> (accessed May 17, 2016).

Wood, Elizabeth Jean. "Sexual violence during war: toward an understanding of variation." in *Order, Conflict and Violence*, edited by Stathis N. Kalyvas, Ian Shapiro and Tarek Masoud. New York and Cambridge: Cambridge University Press, 2008.

Wood, Elizabeth Jean. "Armed Groups and Sexual Violence: When is Wartime Rape Rare?" *Politics and Society*, 37(1) (2009): 131-161.

Wood, Elizabeth Jean. "Conflict-related sexual violence and the policy implications of recent research." *International Review of the Red Cross* 96(894) (2014): 457-478. <doi:10.1017/S1816383115000077> (accessed January 7, 2016).

Zawati, Hilmi M., "Re-thinking rape law." *Journal of International Law and International Relations*, Vol. 102014): 31-43. <http://web.b.ebscohost.com/ehost/pdfviewer/pdf viewer?vid=58&sid=d9b58e6f-f0a9-428e-86e5-c8fba15262df%40sessionmgr 106&hid=105> (accessed May 23, 2016).

Zawati, Hilmi M., "The Challenge of Prosecuting Conflict-Related Gender-Based Crimes under Libyan Transitional Justice." *Journal of International Law & International Relations* Vol. 102014): 44-91. <http://web.b.ebscohost.com/ehost/pdf viewer/pdfviewer?sid=d9b58e6f-f0a9-428e-86e5-c8fba15262df%40sessionmgr106&vid=62&hid=105> (accessed May 23, 2016).

Zimbardo, Philip. *The Lucifer Effect: How Good People Turn Evil.* London: Rider, 2007.

# Verhinderung sexueller Gewalt als Kriegswaffe

Wir können sexuelle Kriegsführung, die sich gegen unschuldige Menschen richtet, beenden.
Wir können neue Normen etablieren, die Frauen, Mädchen, Männer und Jungen respektieren.
Wir können der Welt klarmachen, dass wir diese scheußlichen Taktiken nicht länger tolerieren.
Wir können offen sagen: „Jetzt nicht und niemals."[1]

∵

## Einführung

Wie die Geschichte nachweist, war sexuelle Gewalt als ein Kriegsmittel gegen Frauen, Männer und Kinder ein verborgenes Verbrechen, das die Opfer stillschweigend und ohne rechtlichen Schutz ausstehen mussten. Sie wurde über Jahrhunderte hinweg gegen beide Geschlechter angewandt: „Vom Raub der Sabinerinnen im alten Rom … bis hin zu … Kastration als eine Form des Sieges von chinesischen, persischen, amalekitischen, ägyptischen und altnordischen Armeen."[2] Regierungen und humanitäre Organisationen mit begrenzten Ressourcen priorisierten ihre Hilfe auf Fälle, in denen es um Leben und Tod ging. Überlebende, aus Scham, soziale Tabus zu brechen, wussten nicht genau an wen sie sich um Hilfe wenden sollten. Diejenigen, die versuchten, Friedens-

* Übersetzt von Gerta K. Valentine. Ursprünglicher Titel: "Is it possible to prevent sexual violence as a weapon of war against women, men and children or only to manage the after-effects?" Die in dieser Arbeit dargestellten Sichtweisen geben die der Autorin wieder und stellen nicht unbedingt die des britischen Verteidigungsministeriums noch eines anderen Ministeriums der Regierung Ihrer britischen Majestät, der Königin des Vereinigten Königreiches, dar. Des Weiteren können diese Sichtweisen nicht den Anspruch erheben, eine offizielle Bestätigung von sachlicher Genauigkeit, Meinungen, Schlussfolgerungen oder Empfehlungen des britischen Verteidigungsministeriums oder einer anderen Abteilung der Regierung Ihrer britischen Majestät des Vereinigten Königreichs wiederzugeben.

1 John Kerry, "Remarks at The Global Summit to End Sexual Violence in Conflict," US Department of State, Juni 2014, <http://www.state.gov/secretary/remarks/2014/06/227553.htm> (Zugriff: den 27. November 2015).

2 Sarah Solangon, and Preeti Patel, "Sexual violence against men in countries affected by armed conflict," *Conflict, Security and Development* 12(4) (2012), <doi:10.1080/14678802.2012.724794> (Zugriff: den 27. November 2015), 418-419.

 | DOI:10.1163/9789004396845_003

abkommen zu verhandeln, waren besorgt, dass sie das Vertrauen bewaffneter Gruppen verlieren würden, indem sie „heikle“ Themen anschnitten, die mit religiösen oder traditionellen Gebräuchen verbunden waren. Folglich scheint es auf den ersten Blick, dass sexuelle Gewalt wieder nur eine weitere der unabwendbaren, grauenvollen Charakteristiken des Krieges ist, die immer existierten und es immer tun werden.

Diese Studie möchte jedoch untersuchen, ob es im einundzwanzigsten Jahrhundert möglich ist, sexuelle Gewalt als Kriegsmittel gegen Frauen, Männer und Kinder zu unterbinden oder ob nur die Folgeerscheinungen behandelt werden können. Sie beginnt, indem sie kurz den Hintergrund des Themas erklärt und die Schlüsselbegriffe bespricht, bevor sie sich der aktuellen Literatur zuwendet. Danach analysiert sie vorhandene Ansätze zur Verhütung, untersucht den speziellen Fall von Daesh[3], und zum Schluss bespricht sie mögliche zusätzliche Verhütungsmaßnahmen, zusammen mit dem hoffnungsvollen Einsatz zusätzlicher fachübergreifender Werkzeuge, die für jeden Konflikt speziell konstruiert und finanziert werden können und die nachhaltig sind. Trotz immenser Herausforderungen wird gefolgert, dass es möglich ist, die Anwendung sexueller Gewalt als Kriegsmittel zu verhüten.

Um den Hintergrund zu erklären, so wurde die „Preventing Sexual Violence Initiative“ (PSVI) [Initiative zur Verhinderung sexueller Nötigung] von dem damaligen britischen Außenminister, William Hague, in 2012 eingeführt, der sagte: „Wenn mit den schlimmsten Grausamkeiten unserer Zeit konfrontiert, ist es nur zu leicht, gefühlsmäßig überwältigt zu sein und sich abzuwenden. Aber keiner der Fortschritte, die wir im Bereich der Menschenrechte gemacht haben, wäre ohne die absolute Entschlossenheit das hohe Ziel anzustreben, möglich gewesen.“[4] Im folgenden Jahr förderte Großbritannien seine PSVI-Planung, indem es den G8-Vorsitz benutzte, um eine G8-Erklärung zu vereinbaren und einen UN-Sicherheitsratsbeschluss (UN-Resolution 2106) zu befürworten. Außerdem übernahm Großbritannien die Leitung für einen von der Generalversammlung der Vereinten Nationen befürworteten „Aufruf zur Beipflichtung, um sexuelle Gewalt als Kriegsmittel zu beenden“, der seitdem

3 Spelling in accordance with Hansard: Parliament, “House of Commons Debates 29 Juni 2015: Tunisia, and European Council,” Parliament Juni 2015), <http://www.publications.parliament.uk/pa/cm201516/cmhansrd/cm150629/debtext/150629-0001.htm#15062953000001> (Zugriff: den 7. April 2016), Column 1182.

4 Foreign & Commonwealth Office, “Foreign Secretary launches new Government initiative to prevent sexual violence in conflict,” Foreign & Commonwealth Office Mai 2012), <https://www.gov.uk/government/speeches/foreign-secretary-launches-new-government-initiative-to-prevent-sexual-violence-in-conflict> (Zugriff: den 21. März 2016).

von 155 Ländern unterzeichnet wurde.[5] In 2014 veranstaltete Großbritannien ein globales Gipfeltreffen – das größte seiner Art. Hague wurde bei dieser Bestrebung von Zainab Bangura, dem Sonderbeauftragten des UN-Generalsekretärs für Sexuelle Gewalt als Kriegsmittel und Angelina Jolie Pitt, einer Sonderbeauftragten des UN-Hochkommissars für Flüchtlinge unterstützt. Es schien, dass Hague – der Biograf von William Wilberforce, der erfolgreich den Sklavenhandel im 19. Jahrhundert unterband – sich auf jeden Fall vor dem Niederlegen seines Amtes einen bestimmten Ruf schaffen wollte.

Bevor wir uns der aktuellen Literatur zu sexueller Gewalt zuwenden, müssen wir die Schlüsselbegriffe dieser Studie klarstellen: „Verhütung", „sexuelle Gewalt" und „Krieg". Die Literatur über sexuelle Gewalt hat keine theoretische oder praktische Definierung von „Verhütung" geboten, selbst nicht im Bereich der PSVI, folglich wird ein Wörterbucheintrag benutzt: "to stop somebody from doing something; to stop something from happening"[6] [um jemanden daran zu hindern, etwas zu tun; um ein Ereignis zu verhindern]. Im Gegensatz dazu erstellt der Generalsekretär der Vereinten Nationen (UNSG) einen jährlichen Bericht zu „Sexuelle Gewalt im Zuge von Konfliktsituationen", worin der Begriff „sexuelle Gewalt" offiziell wie folgt definiert wird:

> Vergewaltigung, Sexsklaverei, erzwungene Prostitution, erzwungene Schwangerschaft, erzwungene Sterilisierung und andere Formen sexueller Gewalt vergleichbarer Schwere, die gegen Frauen, Männer, Mädchen oder Jungen verübt werden, und die mit einer Konfliktsituation direkt oder indirekt (temporär, geografisch oder kausal) in Verbindung stehen.[7]

Das Internationale Komitee des Roten Kreuzes (IKRK) beschreibt diese Art von Handlungen mit ähnlichen Begriffen und erklärt: „Sexuelle Gewalt kann allgemein als ein Akt sexueller Art definiert werden, der mit Zwangsmitteln oder durch Nötigung oder durch Ausnutzung einer Zwangslage oder der Unfähigkeit einer Person, ihr echtes Einverständnis zu geben, aufgezwungen wird."[8]

5 Paul Kirby, "Ending sexual violence in conflict: the Preventing Sexual Violence Initiative and its critics," *International Affairs*, 91(3) (2015), <doi:10.1111/1468-2346.12283> (Zugriff: den 8. Oktober 2015), 457-458.

6 Oxford Learner's Dictionary, "Prevent," Oxford Learner's Dictionary, <http://www.oxfordlearnersdictionaries.com/definition/english/prevent?q=prevent> (Zugriff: den 15. Mai 2016).

7 United Nations Secretary General, "Conflict-related sexual violence: Report of the Secretary General," United Nations, S/2015/203 (März 23, 2015), <http://www.stoprapenow.org/uploads/advocacyresources/1428937312.pdf> (Zugriff: den 6. Januar 2016), 1/33.

8 International Committee of the Red Cross (ICRC), "Sexual Violence in Armed Conflict: E-Briefing," ICRC Dezember 2015) <https://app.icrc.org/e-briefing/sexual-violence-armed-conflict/> (Zugriff: den 7. Januar 2016), Part 3.

Die Rechtsprechung zur sexuellen Gewalt wird als Teil der Literaturauswertung angesprochen, aber wenn nicht legalistisch ausgedrückt, sieht man, dass die Terminologie des UN-Generalsekretärs und des IKRK sich leicht unterscheidet. In dieser Studie ist die Definition des UN-Generalsekretärs gültig – aufgrund der leitenden Position der UN in dieser Sache, ihrer Einbeziehung von „Frauen, Männer und Kinder" in ihre Definition und ihre Anerkennung, dass andere Aktivitäten in diesen Begriff eingeschlossen sein könnten. Mit Bezug auf den Gebrauch des Wortes „Krieg" im Titel, wird auch eine nicht zwingend gesetzliche Definition angenommen, die aus der „britischen Verteidigungslehre" stammt: „Krieg ist ein Zustand des bewaffneten Konflikts zwischen verschiedenen Ländern, oder verschiedenen Gruppen innerhalb eines Landes."[9] Aus diesem Grund sind „Kriegsmittel" im Titel eine symbolische Redewendung und sollte im Rahmen der britischen Verteidigungslehre als „Krieg" wie zuvor zitiert, verstanden werden.

Was die Parameter der Studie betrifft und in Anbetracht der vorgegebenen Wortzahl, befasst sich diese Studie nicht mit speziell britischen Richtlinien, sondern untersucht, wie diese Probleme von Akademikern, internationalen Organisationen, Regierungen und regierungsunabhängigen Organisationen (NGOs) angegriffen worden sind. Außerdem wird diese Studie keine Vergleichsbewertung der Vorzüge von PSVI und dem Plan für Women, Peace and Safety (WPS) [Frauen, Frieden und Sicherheit] durchführen, noch ist sie auf die Rolle der Frau in Wiederaufbausituationen in Nachkriegszeiten konzentriert. Allerdings sucht sie, die bedeutenden Ansprüche bei der Nachsorge darzustellen, für jene, die sexuelle Gewalt in Kriegssituationen erlebt haben, um die Herausforderungen zu betonen, die sich sowohl bei Verhütung als auch Abhilfe einstellen.

## Literaturauswertung

Der nächste Abschnitt wertet die derzeitige Literatur zum Thema aus, indem die wichtigsten Ergebnisse in fünf Bereichen untersucht werden: Erstens, die Gründe für den Einsatz von sexueller Gewalt in Konflikten; zweitens, der Nachweis, dass Männer und Jungen die Opfer und dass Frauen die Täterinnen sein können; drittens, die Herausforderung, mit den Nachwirkungen und Folgeerscheinungen fertig zu werden; viertens, die Risiken wegen der Versicherheitlichung und durch Ablenkung der Konzentration auf die WPS-Agenda;

9 United Kingdom, Development, Concepts and Doctrine Centre, *UK Defence Doctrine*, Joint Doctrine Publication 0-01. 5th ed. Shrivenham: DCDC, 2014), 18.

und schließlich der Nachweis, dass sexuelle Gewalt in Konfliktsituationen nicht unabwendbar ist.

### *Warum sexuelle Gewalt als Kriegsmittel eingesetzt wird*

Das erste wichtige Ergebnis im Rahmen der Literaturauswertung war eine Erklärung für die Gründe für sexuelle Gewalt im Einsatz als ein Kriegsmittel. Obwohl Wood durchgreifende Recherchen in diesem Bereich unternommen hat, schrieb sie noch in 2014, dass: „es immer noch vieles gibt, was wir in Hinsicht auf kriegsbezogene sexuelle Gewalt nicht verstehen."[10] Solangon und Patel waren sich einig in der Empfehlung einer detaillierteren Untersuchung der sexuellen Gewalt gegen Männer.[11] Trotz ihrer vorsichtigen Annäherung, legte die Literatur eine Reihe von Gründen nahe, die zu einem Großteil sexuelle Gewalt in Kriegssituationen erklärten. Watson schlug vor: „Das wichtigste Anzeichen sexueller Gewalt in allen Fällen ist, dass das Opfer sich in einer Umgebung befindet, in der der Täter Gewalt oder Missbrauch mit einem hohen Grad von Straflosigkeit begehen kann." [12] Solangon und Patel waren der gleichen Meinung: „Es ist ganz offensichtlich, dass eine Kultur der Straflosigkeit die Bereitschaft zur Gewalt fördert",[13] und sie betonten zudem, dass: „sozialwirtschaftlicher Verfall und schlechte Lebensbedingungen ... zu Straflosigkeit führen kann, aufgrund des Zusammenbruchs von Recht und Ordnung zum Schutz der Zivilisten." [14] Das IKRK stimmte überein: „In sehr vielen Zusammenhängen ist Straflosigkeit für sexuelle Gewalt der Kern des Problems." [15]

Hinzu betonten Solangon und Patel die Rolle sexueller Gewalt als eine: „Zurschaustellung von Macht, Vorherrschaft und Demütigung."[16] Dies wurde in einem UN-Bericht von 2016 versinnbildlicht, in dem ausgesagt wurde, dass die Zielgruppe der Terrormiliz Daesh die Stammesführer und religiösen

10 Elizabeth Jean Wood, "Conflict-related sexual violence and the policy implications of recent research," *International Review of the Red Cross* 96(894) (2014), <doi:10.1017/S1816383115000077> (Zugriff: den 7. Januar 2016), 477.

11 Solangon and Patel, "Sexual violence against men in countries affected by armed conflict," 435-436.

12 Callum Watson, "Preventing and Responding to Sexual and Domestic Violence against Men: A Guidance Note for Security Sector Institutions," Democratic Control of the Armed Forces 2014), <http://www.dcaf.ch/Publications/Preventing-and-Responding-to-Sexual-and-Domestic-Violence-against-Men-A-Guidance-Note-for-Security-Sector-Institutions> (Zugriff: den 19. Januar 2016), 14.

13 Solangon and Patel, "Sexual violence against men in countries affected by armed conflict," 426.

14 Ebd. 425-426.

15 ICRC, "Sexual Violence in Armed Conflict: E-Briefing," Part 3.

16 Solangon and Patel, "Sexual violence against men in countries affected by armed conflict," 425.

Oberhäupter, Ärzte, Journalisten, Juristen und Polizeikommissare[17] sind, als ein Mittel der Darstellung von ihrer Macht über Autoritäten und Respektspersonen. In anderen Konflikten werden auch Menschrechtler aus ähnlichem Grund angezielt, um die Kontrolle aller, die ihnen entgegenstehen, zu vernichten. Watson erklärte, dass sexuelle Gewalt benutzt wurde um: „Gemeinschaften zu zerstören",[18] und Menschen aus ihrer Heimat zu vertreiben und zukünftige Generationen mithilfe des Verlustes gesellschaftlichen Zusammenhalts zu vernichten.

Mit Bezug auf den geplanten Einsatz sexueller Gewalt von bewaffneten Gruppen, sagte Wood: „Es scheint am Beispiel in Bosnien, Guatemala und Ruanda eine Strategie zu sein."[19] Kirby meint: „Es ist besonders notorisch, dass serbische Kampfeinheiten mit dem Einsatz psychologischer Kriegsführung den Schluss zogen, dass Vergewaltigungen (einschließlich von Kindern) eine abträgliche Auswirkung auf die Feindmoral während des Bosnienkrieges haben würde und adoptierten somit eine Vergewaltigungsstrategie."[20] Wood erwähnte auch Michele Leibys Recherchen zu seinem Einsatz von staatlichen Militärs, einschließlich in Peru, als Aufstandsbekämpfungsoperationen, um Gemeinschaften, die Partisanen unterstützen, unter Kontrolle zu halten. Peruanische Streitkräfte benutzten sexuelle Gewalt an gefangenen Partisanen, um Informationen zu erhalten, Partisanen zu bestrafen und die Macht der Regierung unter Beweis zu stellen.[21] Solangon und Patel beschrieben, wie sie als: "Teil einer militärischen Strategie benutzt werden konnte, um die Zivilbevölkerung und Soldaten zu terrorisieren und zu demoralisieren."[22] Im Jahresbericht des UNSG des letzten Jahres über konfliktbezogene sexuelle Gewalt wurde angemerkt, dass Gruppen sexuelle Gewalt benutzten, um ihre: „strategischen Ziele, ihre Ideologie und ihre Finanzierung … [für] taktische Befehle zur Rekrutierung einzusetzen; wobei die Bevölkerung terrorisiert wurde, … Ge-

17 United Nations, "Report on the Protection of Civilians in the Armed Conflict in Iraq: 1 Mai – 31 Oktober 2015," (Januar 2016), <http://www.uniraq.org/images/humanrights/UNAMI-OHCHR_%20POC%20Report_FINAL_01%20Mai-31%20Oktober%202015_FINAL_11Jan2016.pdf> (Zugriff: den 21. Januar 2016), i.

18 Watson, "Preventing and Responding to Sexual and Domestic Violence against Men: A Guidance Note for Security Sector Institutions," 13.

19 Wood, "Conflict-related sexual violence and the policy implications of recent research," 472.

20 Kirby, "Ending sexual violence in conflict: Preventing Sexual Violence Initiative and its critics," 462.

21 Wood, "Conflict-related sexual violence and the policy implications of recent research," 472.

22 Solangon and Patel, "Sexual violence against men in countries affected by armed conflict," 425.

meinschaften aus strategischen Bereichen entfernt wurden, ... finanzielle Mittel erzeugt wurden, ... Folter eingesetzt wurde, um Informationen zu erzwingen ... [und] um verwandtschaftliche Beziehungen, die Gemeinschaften zusammenhalten, etablieren, zu ändern oder aufzulösen."[23]

Im Gegensatz dazu fasste Alcorn das Quellenstudium von Baaz und Stern über den Gebrauch von sexueller Gewalt der Streitkräfte in der Demokratischen Republik Kongo (DRC) zusammen, die sie zu der Schlussfolgerung führte, dass: „wenn überhaupt, dann ist es die gestörte Funktion der militärischen Hierarchie, die Raum für opportunistische sexuelle Gewalt geschaffen hat."[24] Solangon und Patel erkannten an, dass sexuelle Gewalt als eine militärische Strategie benutzt werden kann, aber akzeptierten auch, dass es: „eine Konsequenz schlechter Auswahlmechanismen der Kämpfer, mangelnder Disziplin, schlechter Lebensbedingungen, schlechter Schulung und schlechter Zusammenhalt zwischen den Mitgliedern"[25] sein könnte. Wood berief sich auf die Ergebnisse der Cohen-Forschung, in der: „sie nachweist, dass nicht-staatliche Streitkräfte, die erzwungene Rekrutierung durchführen, wahrscheinlich sexuelle Gewalt zu einem sehr hohen Grad anwenden."[26] Wood folgerte außerdem, dass sexuelle Gewalt unter irregulären Kampftruppen anbefohlen oder als Methode toleriert sein könnte.[27]

Um diese erste Schlüsselerkenntnis abzuschließen, bietet die Literatur eine Reihe von Erklärungen an, warum sexuelle Gewalt immer noch als ein Kriegsmittel benutzt wird. Die Begründung mag gelegentlich widersprüchlich klingen. Zum Beispiel könnte Teil einer definierten militärischen Strategie der Grund sein, oder zu anderen Zeiten eine Konsequenz des Zusammenbruchs der militärischen Prozederen darstellen. Allerdings spiegelt dies wahrscheinlich die verschiedenen Arten und Phasen eines jeden Konflikts wieder. Obgleich einige Akademiker die Notwendigkeit von weiteren Recherchen hervorheben, war die Literatur konsistent in der Identifizierung der Gründe für ihren Einsatz: die Kultur der Straflosigkeit, der Wille, Macht auszuüben,

---

23 UN Secretary General, "Conflict-related sexual violence: Report of Secretary General," 24/33.

24 Ted Alcorn, "Responding to sexual violence in armed conflict," *The Lancet* 383(9934) (2014), <http://www.thelancet.com/journals/lancet/article/PIIS0140-6736(14)60970-3/fulltext> (Zugriff: den 18. Januar 2016), 2036.

25 Solangon and Patel, "Sexual violence against men in countries affected by armed conflict," 429-430.

26 Elizabeth Jean Wood, "Rape is not inevitable during war," in: Kathleen Kuehnast, Chantal de Jonge Oudraat, and Helga Hernes, eds., *Women and War: Power and Protection in the Twenty-First Century* Washington, DC: US Institute of Peace Press, 2011), 58.

27 Wood, "Conflict-related sexual violence and the policy implications of recent research," 467 & 470.

und entweder als eine geplante Strategie oder als schlechtes militärisches Verhalten.

### *Männer und Jungen können Opfer und Frauen Täterinnen sein*

Die zweite Schlüsselerkenntnis aus der Literaturauswertung ist, dass Männer und Jungen Opfer und Frauen Täterinnen sein können. Solangon und Patel merkten an: „Das Ergebnis der Literaturauswertung weist auf, dass Nachweise und begriffliche Abhandlungen über an Männern verübte sexuelle Gewalt in Kriegssituationen ziemlich begrenzt sind."[28] Watson, der zwei Jahre später das Thema aufgriff, betonte, dass in akademischen Bereichen Fortschritte gemacht wurden, aber dass Informationen für Therapeuten noch immer in der Entwicklung nachhinkten.[29] Die Erfassung akkurater Daten war potenziell schwerer als bei Frauen, da sie für Männer häufig als „Folter" registriert wurden.[30] Andere Hindernisse bei der Datenerfassung waren das Ergebnis der Scham, die Männer aufgrund des Stigmas empfanden, den Bruch mit sozialen Tabus und möglichen lokalen Gesetzen, sowie auch die Demoralisation aufgrund der Unfähigkeit sich zu verteidigen. Historisch gesehen bestand hier auch ein Mangel an Verständnis oder Unterstützung im Bereich des Gesundheitswesens, Rechtswesens und der Medien. Skjelsboek deutete an, dass Fälle von Entmannung es manchen Männern schwer machte, sich Frauen mitzuteilen: „Um besseren Zugriff auf Daten zu erhalten, mag es erforderlich werden, mehr Männer in diesen Forschungsbereich einzubeziehen."[31] Dies wurde von Hagues Zusammenfassung auf dem globalen Gipfeltreffen in 2014 unterstützt: „Datensammlung sollte nicht geschlechtsneutral durchgeführt werden."[32]

Obwohl die Recherchen eingeschränkt sind, waren Gründe für sexuelle Gewalt gegen Männer in der Literatur nachweisbar, im Besonderen in den Studien von Solangon und Patel. Sie erklärten, dass sie als Einführung in eine Gruppe nach Einberufung in die Wehrpflicht oder bei Entführung stattfinden könnte, oder um eine Gruppenbindung zu brechen, oder als eine Form von:

---

28 Solangon and Patel, "Sexual violence against men in countries affected by armed conflict," 422.

29 Watson, "Preventing and Responding to Sexual and Domestic Violence against Men: A Guidance Note for Security Sector Institutions," 3.

30 Solangon and Patel, "Sexual violence against men in countries affected by armed conflict," 422-423.

31 Inger Skjelsboek, "Sexual violence in the post-Yugoslav wars," in: Kuehnast et al., eds., *Women and War: Power and Protection in Twenty-First Century*, 82.

32 Foreign & Commonwealth Office, "Statement of Action - Global Summit to End Sexual Violence in Conflict," Foreign & Commonwealth Office Juni 2014), <https://www.gov.uk/government/publications/statement-of-action-global-summit-to-end-sexual-violence-in-conflict> (Zugriff: den 26. November 2015).

„genozidaler sexueller Gewalt ...[mittels] genitaler Verstümmelung und Schlägen von Männern gewisser ethnischer Gruppen, oder um sie impotent zu machen."[33] Zudem identifizierten sie, dass: „die meisten Fälle von sexueller Gewalt gegen Männer in Lagern stattfinden ... beim Verhör und als Strafmaßnahmen."[34] Dr. Aburabi, ein Arzt des Internationalen Roten Kreuzes/ Halbmondes, erklärte, dass es möglich sei, jene, die in Lagern besonders gefährdet waren, zu identifizieren: „junge Häftlinge, erstmalige Häftlinge, solche mit gewissen äußeren Merkmalen, solche mit Lern- oder anderen Behinderungen, so wie auch Lesben, Schwule, Bisexuelle, Transgender- und Intersex-Personen."[35]

Die Schwierigkeiten des Themas wurden auch in der Literatur offenbar, wenn Frauen als Täterinnen genannt wurden. Wood sagte aus, dass amerikanische Soldatinnen für Handlungen sexueller Gewalt im Irak, in Afghanistan und in Guantánamo Bay verantwortlich waren.[36] In 2015 bestätigte das International Criminal Tribunal für Ruanda (ICTR) seinen Schuldspruch für Pauline Nyiramasuhuko, die frühere Ministerin für Familie und Frauenentwicklung, für ihre Beihilfe an der Organisation und dem Befehl, Vergewaltigungen während des Ruanda-Konflikts 1994 auszuüben. Weitere Literatur identifiziert Täterinnen in Sierra Leone,[37] Haiti[38] und der Demokratischen Republik Kongo.[39] Die Literatur betont, dass die Gründe für Frauen, die sexuelle Gewalt durchführen, weitere Untersuchungen benötigen, aber Edström et al. weisen darauf hin, dass: „einige Ursachen die Anpassung von Frauen an die Normen

33 Solangon and Patel, "Sexual violence against men in countries affected by armed conflict," 419 & 428-429.

34 Ebd. 429-430.

35 Vincent Bernard and Elvina Pothelet, "Through the eyes of a detention doctor: Interview with Raed Aburabi," *International Review of the Red Cross*, 96(894) (2014), <doi:10.1017/S1816383115000284> (Zugriff: den 11. Januar 2016), 482.

36 Wood, "Rape is not inevitable during war," in Kuehnast et al., eds., *Women and War: Power & Protection in Twenty-First Century*, 45.

37 Human Rights Watch, "Rwanda: International Tribunal Closing Its Doors," HRW December 2015), <https://www.hrw.org/news/2015/12/23/rwanda-international-tribunal-closing-its-doors> (accessed January 6, 2016) & Marianne Mollmann, "Rape in war: No more excuses," Human Rights Watch July 2011), <https://www.hrw.org/news/2011/07/22/rape-war-no-more-excuses> (accessed January 6, 2016).

38 Wood, "Rape is not inevitable during war," in Kuehnast et al., eds., *Women and War: Power & Protection in Twenty-First Century*, 45.

39 Jerker Edström, Alexa Hassink, Thea Shahrokh, and Erin Stern, eds.,"Engendering Men: A Collaborative Review of Evidence of Men and Boys in Social Change and Gender Equality," EMERGE Evidence Review, Promundo-US, Sonke Gender Justice and the Institute of Development Studies. (September 2015), <http://opendocs.ids.ac.uk/opendocs/bitstream/handle/123456789/7059/EMERGE.pdf?sequence=1> (Zugriff: den 22. Januar 2016), 142.

militarisierter Maskulinität, den Wunsch, sexuelle Gewalt umzulenken oder einen Feind zu demütigen, einschließen.“[40]

Betrachtet man das Ausmaß von Männern und Jungen als Opfer und Frauen als Täterinnen, werden die Schwierigkeiten beim Erhalt zuverlässiger Daten und der Mangel an Recherchen zu letzterem Thema in der Literatur offenbar. Solangon und Patel sagen aus, dass in einem der bosnischen Lager in den 90er Jahren 80% der fünftausend dort inhaftierten Männer vergewaltigt worden waren und sexuelle Gewalt gegen Männer wurde in 25 Kriegen unserer Zeit in der Welt ausgeübt.[41] Es kann vorausgesetzt werden, dass männliche Überlebende nur einen sehr geringen Anteil der Gesamtanzahl von Opfern ausmachen. Trotzdem, wenn man die Art dieser „verborgenen Verbrechen“ anschaut, sind weitere Recherchen und mehr Beweismaterial erforderlich, insbesondere die Berichterstattung über das „Foltern“ von Männern. Mit Hinsicht auf Täterinnen weist Cohens Forschungsarbeit daraufhin, dass: „Kämpferinnen zu 25 Prozent der RUF (Revolutionary United Front in Sierra Leone) an Gruppenvergewaltigungen teilnahmen.“[42] Trotzdem war das Hauptfazit der Literatur, dass: „entschieden gründlichere Forschungsarbeit erforderlich ist, um die wirkliche Anzahl von Täterinnen festzustellen, sowie auch die Ursachen und Konsequenzen von weiblicher Teilnahme an sexueller Gewalt.“[43]

Zum Abschluss dieser zweiten Schlüsselerkenntnis ging die Literatur das Vorurteil an, sexuelle Gewalt sei einzig und allein geschlechtsabhängig, d. h. Männer könnten ihre Herrschaft über Frauen straflos ausüben, indem dargestellt wird, dass Männer und Jungen Opfer und Frauen Täterinnen sein können. Die Literatur beschreibt die verschiedenen Ursachen und Zusammenhänge, in denen sexuelle Gewalt gegen Männer und Jungen benutzt werden. Im Gegensatz dazu scheint es, dass deutlich mehr Recherchen erforderlich wären, um die Gründe zu verstehen, weshalb Frauen sexuelle Gewalt ausüben. Das Ausmaß, in dem Männer und Jungen Opfer und Frauen Täterinnen sind – im Vergleich zur Anzahl von Frauen als Opfer und Männer als Täter – konnte der Literatur nur sehr schlecht entnommen werden. Trotzdem legt sie nahe, dass dies ein Aspekt der sexuellen Gewalt in Konfliktsituationen ist, der nicht ignoriert werden darf. Außerdem stellt sie dar, dass diese zweite Schlüsselerkenntnis der späteren Schlüsselerkenntnis (dass sexuelle Gewalt nicht

40 Ebd.

41 Solangon and Patel, “Sexual violence against men in countries affected by armed conflict,” 419.

42 Wood, “Rape is not inevitable during war,” in Kuehnast et al., eds., *Women and War: Power & Protection in Twenty-First Century*, 47.

43 Edström et al., eds.,“Engendering Men: Collaborative Review of Evidence of Men & Boys in Social Change and Gender Equality,” 142.

unabwendbar ist) nicht widerspricht, da man argumentieren könnte, dass ein besseres Verständnis des Themas dazu beitragen würde, seine Komplexitäten zu betonen. Wie später erklärt wird, wird sexuelle Gewalt nicht grundsätzlich immer angewandt, aber wenn, dann kann sie nicht nur gegen Frauen und Mädchen sondern auch gegen Männer und Jungen ausgeübt werden.

### *Bewerkstelligung der Nachsorge*

Diese dritte Schlüsselerkenntnis im Rahmen der Literaturauswertung befasst sich mit der Herausforderung, die Nachwirkungen anzusprechen und zu behandeln, einschließlich der Erstellung medizinischer und psychologischer Hilfe, Behandlung von Geschlechtskrankheiten und Ausbreitung sexuell übertragbarer Krankheiten, Adressierung des Themas Abtreibung und das Angebot von persönlich angepasster Unterstützung für Kinder und Männer. Nach Bouviers Aussage muss die medizinische Hilfe innerhalb von 72 Stunden geleistet werden: „damit Geschlechtskrankheiten, einschließlich HIV, vermieden werden und schnelle Schwangerschaftsverhütung stattfinden kann“[44]. Er brachte ein Beispiel der Schwierigkeiten aus einer Untersuchung im Kongo an, wo mehr als 95% der Überlebenden keinen Zugang zu medizinischer Nothilfe innerhalb dieses Zeitrahmens hatten.[45] Skjelsboek erkannte die Auswirkungen auf die reproduktive Gesundheit der einzelnen Personen, wie auch das zusätzliche Stigma einer Geschlechtskrankheit und legte nahe: „Wir müssen mehr darüber wissen, zu welchem Ausmaß sexuelle Gewalt in Kriegssituationen zur Ausbreitung von HIV/Aids beiträgt“.[46] Solangon und Patel stellen fest, dass: „eine dringende Anforderung von ... psychiatrischer Hilfe bei der Behandlung von psychologischen Traumata besteht“[47], und Bouvier betont die Notwendigkeit langfristiger Betreuung: „Fortbestehen der Betreuung und regelmäßige Nachuntersuchungen sind über längere Zeit hinweg unverzichtbar, einschließlich medizinischer Hilfe, geistiger Verfassung und psychosozialer Unterstützung.“[48] Andere Herausforderungen bei der Nachbetreuung schlossen die Abfertigung möglicher legaler Auswirkungen ein, z.B. wenn Vergewaltigung illegal und Abtreibung nicht gestattet ist. Bouvier betonte die Notwendigkeit,

44 Paul Bouvier, “Sexual violence, health and humanitarian ethics: Towards a holistic, person-centred approach,” *International Review of the Red Cross* 96(894) (2014), <doi:10.1017/S1816383115000430> (Zugriff: den 11. Januar 2016), 573.

45 Ebd., 574.

46 Skjelsboek, “Sexual violence in post-Yugoslav wars,” in Kuehnast et al., eds., *Women and War: Power & Protection in Twenty-First Century*, 81.

47 Solangon and Patel, “Sexual violence against men in countries affected by armed conflict,” 434.

48 Bouvier, “Sexual violence, health and humanitarian ethics: Towards a holistic, person-centred approach,” 576.

Frauen nach einer Abtreibung zu unterstützen, denn: „Sie haben Demütigung, Exklusion oder Stigmatisierung zu erwarten... Gewalt, selbst tödliche Gewalt ... (oder sie können) verfolgt und inhaftiert werden."[49]

Die Literaturauswertung ließ erkennen, dass Kinder besondere Bedürfnisse hatten, je nachdem ob sie sexuelle Gewalt erfahren haben, ausgeübt haben oder ein Ergebnis davon waren. Duroch und Schulte-Hillen beschrieben die Arbeit von Médecins Sans Frontières: „Die Betreuung von Kindern stellt eine zusätzliche Herausforderung dar, z.B. ... zeitweise mit schweren physischen und psychologischen Traumata fertig zu werden", wie auch die Notwendigkeit einer unbestreitbaren Patientenzustimmung, bevor medizinische Hilfe geleistet werden kann.[50] Solangon und Patel beschreiben: „die Komplexitäten bei der Wiederaufnahme von Kindern in die Gesellschaft, die vielleicht als Sexsklaven benutzt wurden, oder die gezwungen wurden, Handlungen sexueller Gewalt zu begehen."[51] Die MenEngage Alliance und UN Population Fund (UNFPA)[52] sagten aus, dass das Bedürfnis besteht: „Sonderstrategien und Spezialmethoden zu identifizieren, um mit Kindern und Jugendlichen zusammenzuarbeiten, die sexuelle Gewalt erfahren, gesehen und begangen haben".[53] Steinberg erinnert sich aus seiner Zeit als US-Botschafter in Angola während der 90er Jahre, dass es: „Jungen gab, die nie gelernt haben, mit Mädchen ihres Alters auf gleicher Ebene zu kommunizieren."[54] Bouvier identifizierte das Bedürfnis für frühe und langfristige Betreuung von Kindern, die das Produkt sexueller Gewalt sind: „sie sollten als gefährdete Kinder eingestuft werden, mit einem hohen Risiko negativer Folgen für ihre Gesundheit und Entwicklung."[55] Ein UN-Bericht aus 2015 befasste sich mit den Folgen, die in Bosnien und Herzegowina zwanzig Jahre nach dem Ende des Krieges erkennbar waren und bemerkten den Mangel an Unterstützung für: „Kinder, die aufgrund von

49 Ebd., 582.

50 Françoise Duroch, and Catrin Schulte-Hillen, "Care for victims of sexual violence, an organization pushed to its limits: The case of Médecins Sans Frontières," *International Review of the Red Cross*, 96(894) (2014), <doi:10.1017/S1816383115000107> (Zugriff: den 11. Januar 2016), 616 and 618-619.

51 Solangon and Patel, "Sexual violence against men in countries affected by armed conflict," 434.

52 Abbreviation conventionally adopted in accordance with its former name.

53 MenEngage Alliance and United Nations Population Fund, "Sexual Violence in Conflict and Post-Conflict: Engaging Men and Boys," (Juli 2012), <http://menengage.org/resources/sexual-violence-conflict-post-conflict-engaging-men-boys/> (Zugriff den 12. Januar 2016), 12.

54 Donald Steinberg, "Women and War: an Agenda for action," in Kuehnast et al., eds., *Women and War: Power and Protection in Twenty-First Century*, 121.

55 Bouvier, "Sexual violence, health and humanitarian ethics: Towards a holistic, person-centred approach," 582-583.

Kriegsvergewaltigungen geboren wurden und besonders gefährdet sind, dem Risiko von Stigmatisierung, Verlassen werden, Zurückweisung und niedrigem sozialwirtschaftlichem Status entgegenzusehen."[56]

Die Literatur offenbarte weiter, dass die Bedürfnisse von Männern sich bei der Nachsorge von denen der Frauen und Kinder unterscheiden. Solangon und Patel detaillieren die Herausforderungen jener, die sexuelle Gewalt erfahren haben, nicht zuletzt dort, wo Homosexualität illegal ist, aber auch, weil: „Männer oftmals sozial von ihren Gemeinschaften ausgegrenzt und als „Bush wives" tituliert, entmannt oder sonst wie gedemütigt werden, und manchmal wird ihnen die Schuld an dem Angriff zugeschrieben."[57] Sie förderten den Bedarf für sachgemäße Bildung und Kommunikationskampagnen und spezielle psychologische Hilfe.[58] Außerdem erkannten sie die verschiedenen Herausforderungen für die, die sexuelle Gewalt verübt hatten: „Männer und Jungen, die gezwungen wurden, ein Mitglied ihrer Familie oder Gemeinde zu vergewaltigen, wieder in die Gesellschaft zu integrieren, ist in vielen Gesellschaften maßlos problematisch."[59] Die MenEngage und UNFPA betonten die Bedürfnisse anderer Männer: „Verständnis dafür, dass das Miterleben von Gewalt gegen Angehörige eine direkte Erfahrung der Gewalt ist und zu der gleichen Art tieferem und bleibendem Traumata führen kann, wie bei Überlebenden von körperlichen Angriffen."[60] Ein weiterer Aspekt war der potenzielle Anstieg in häuslicher Gewalt, der von einer Reihe von Autoren identifiziert wurde, einschließlich Skjelsboek.[61] Steinberg beschrieb Männer, die aus einem Konflikt in Angola zurückkehrten, kaum Ausbildung hatten und dann in Gemeinschaften arbeitslos waren, wo Frauen gelernt hatten, ohne sie auszukommen. Dies führte zu einem Anstieg von Drogenkonsum und Alkoholismus, der oft in häusliche Gewalt ausartete: „In der Tat ließ das Ende des Zivilkrieges eine neue Ära von Gewalt gegen Frauen und Mädchen vom Stapel."[62] Edström et al. wiesen auf Forschungsergebnisse hin, die die: „Fortsetzung und Häufigkeit [sexu-

56 UN Secretary General, "Conflict-related sexual violence: Report of Secretary General," 20/33.

57 Solangon and Patel, "Sexual violence against men in countries affected by armed conflict," 421.

58 Ebd. 432-433 & 435.

59 Ebd. 421.

60 MenEngage Alliance and UNFPA, "Sexual Violence in Conflict and Post-Conflict: Engaging Men and Boys," 11.

61 Skjelsboek, "Sexual violence in post-Yugoslav wars," in Kuehnast et al., eds., *Women and War: Power & Protection in Twenty-First Century*, 81.

62 Steinberg, "Women and War: an Agenda for action," in Kuehnast et al., eds., *Women and War: Power and Protection in Twenty-First Century*, 121.

eller Gewalt] in Nachkriegssituationen“ [63] darstellten. Sie bezogen sich auf Recherchen, die in Ruanda angestellt wurden, wo Männer: „mit größerer Wahrscheinlichkeit sowohl physische als auch sexuelle Gewalt gegen ihre häuslichen Partner verübten, wenn sie in Völkermorden in diesem Krieg eingesetzt worden waren.“ [64]

Abschließend ist über die dritte Schlüsselerkenntnis aus der Literaturauswertung zu sagen, dass das Problem, mit den Nachwirkungen fertig zu werden, offensichtlich gravierend ist, sowohl kurz- als auch langfristig, mit Anforderungen für medizinische und psychologische Betreuung, der Eingrenzung der Ausbreitung sexuell übertragener Krankheiten, der Hilfe für Frauen, die Abtreibungen brauchen oder danach betreut werden müssen, und dem Erstellen von sachgemäßer Unterstützung für Kinder und Männer. Hinzu erwies sich aus der Literaturauswertung, dass eine Unterbrechung des Kreises der Gewalt ein wichtiges Element bei der Nachsorge ist, da sexuelle Gewalt in der Nachkriegszeit fortbesteht. Dies würde eine abschreckende Aussicht für die meisten Nationen sein, aber sie ist noch herausfordernder für im Krieg verwüstete Länder und solche, in denen eine solche Unterstützung noch nie existierte.

### *Die Risiken von Versicherheitlichung und Ablenkung von der Frauen-, Friedens- und Sicherheitsagenda*

Die vierte Schlüsselerkennung aus der Literaturauswertung befasste sich mit den Risiken der Versicherheitlichung des Problems, so wie auch der Ablenkung der Kenntnisnahme der „Women, Peace and Security“ [Frauen, Frieden und Sicherheit]-Agenda (WPS). Kirby sagte aus, dass: „ein politisches Projekt als Vordergrund von sexueller Gewalt … wenn es denn erfolgreich sein will, die entsprechende politische Auswirkung auf Regelung materieller Ressourcen haben muss“ und er warnte davor, dass das Potenzial bestünde, die Kenntnisnahme der dringenden Anforderungen zu verzerren, um sowohl andere Kriegsverbrechen wie auch häusliche Gewalt anzusprechen.[65] Zum Beispiel merkte er an, dass: „im Osten des Kongos (DRC), Haushaltsuntersuchungsdaten extrem hohe Fälle von sexueller Gewalt gegen *intime Partner* aufzeigen, trotz der allgemeinen Fixierung auf Gräueltaten bewaffneter Gruppen.[66] Wood stimmte zu: „In einigen Konfliktsituationen ist die Häufigkeit sexueller Gewalt

63 Edström et al., eds., “Engendering Men: Collaborative Review of Evidence of Men & Boys in Social Change and Gender Equality,” 141.

64 Ebd., 143.

65 Kirby, “Ending sexual violence in conflict: Preventing Sexual Violence Initiative and its critics,” 463.

66 Kirby, “Ending sexual violence in conflict: Preventing Sexual Violence Initiative and its critics,” 463.

bedeutend niedriger als zwischen intimen Partnern, Bekannten und Fremden",[67] wie auch Alcorn:

> Untersuchungen haben wiederholt dargestellt, dass Überlebende viel häufiger eine Vergewaltigung melden, wenn sie von einem Fremden begangen wurde, als wenn von einem Ehemann oder Freund. In Kriegs- und Nachkriegssituationen kann dieses unverhältnismäßige Underreporting von sexueller Gewalt innerhalb von Haushalten den Anteil der sexuellen Gewalt, die bewaffneten Gruppen angelastet werden, stark erhöhen.[68]

Die Ergebnisse der Literaturauswertung offenbarte gleichzeitig ein wachsendes Übereinkommen, dass, wenn Männer und Jungen Opfer sexueller Gewalt so wie auch Täter waren, dies von den schwer erkämpften Gewinnen der WPS-Agenda ablenken könnte. Kuehnast et al. schrieben, dass die UN-Resolution 135 in 2000 „internationalen Organisationen der Zivilgesellschaft und führenden Frauen in Friedensbewegungen einen wichtigen Sieg und ein maßgebendes Instrument für weitere Aktivierung gegeben hat"[69] und Alison fragte in 2007: „wenn Feministinnen nicht länger über Vergewaltigung sprechen, wer wird es dann tun?"[70] Kirbys kritische Betrachtung der Initiative für die Prävention sexueller Gewalt und ihre offene Interstützung für Männer und Jungen als Überlebende, schlossen die mögliche Folgerung ein, dass: „die UN und beitragende Staaten nicht energisch genug patriarchalische Machtverhältnisse und hierarchische Geschlechtsordnungen diagnostizieren und gegen sie vorgehen… [und] die Erwartung, dass vorhandene Programme die Ressourcen, die für Frauen und Mädchen zurückgelegt wurden, halbieren (oder bedeutend vermindern)."[71] Das IKRK schien jedoch das neue Konstrukt willkommen zu heißen: „der Blickpunkt hat sich von dem besonderen Schicksal von Frauen in Konfliktsituationen auf einen breiteren Aspekt konzentriert, der auf die Angreifbarkeit von sowohl von Männern wie auch Frauen aufgrund ihres Geschlechtes, basiert."[72] Dies wurde von Solangon und Patel bekräftigt: „sexuelle Gewalt gegen Männer muss in den Vordergrund gebracht werden, nicht als In-

67 Wood, "Conflict-related sexual violence and the policy implications of recent research," 460.

68 Alcorn, "Responding to sexual violence in armed conflict," 2035.

69 Kuehnast et al., eds., *Women and War: Power & Protection in Twenty-First Century*, 2.

70 Solangon and Patel, "Sexual violence against men in countries affected by armed conflict," 424.

71 Kirby, "Ending sexual violence in conflict: Preventing Sexual Violence Initiative and its critics," 471.

72 ICRC, "Sexual Violence in Armed Conflict: E-Briefing," Introduction.

fragestellung von Frauenrechten sondern als ein gleichwertiger Partner im Kampf gegen geschlechtsspezifische sexuelle Gewalt."[73] Obwohl einige Akademiker, Entscheidungstreffer und Fachleute sich nicht ganz wohl fühlen bei dieser Entwicklung, merkte Kirby an, dass es möglich sei, Änderungen in der Sprache festzustellen, wobei in den auf Frauen konzentrierten UN-Resolutionen 1888 und 1960 in 2008 und 2009 auf „Berater für Frauen und Gleichstellung" in UN-Resolution 2106 im Juni 2013 auf „Berater für Gleichstellung" in UN-Resolution 2122 in Oktober 2013 übergegangen wurde.[74] Das legt eine zunehmende Anerkennung und die Übereinstimmung der internationalen Gemeinschaft nahe, dass das Problem der sexuellen Gewalt in Konflikt- und Postkonfliktsituationen Auswirkungen auf Männer und Jungen, wie auch auf Frauen und Mädchen haben kann.

Um die vierte Schlüsselerkenntnis abzuschließen, stellten die Ergebnisse der Literaturauswertung dar, dass es wichtig war, sexuelle Gewalt als ein Kriegsmittel im Vergleich zu den potenziell häufigeren Fällen von *häuslicher* Gewalt in Konflikt-, Postkonflikt- und konfliktfreien Situationen nüchtern zu betrachten. Hinzu kommt, dass, obgleich diese Studie eine neutralere Analyse des Themas durchzuführen sucht, die Wichtigkeit die ist, die Rolle von Frauen in Angelegenheiten von Frieden und Sicherheit nicht zu unterschätzen – sowohl betreffs der effektiven Nachsorge aufgrund der Nachwirkungen als auch des Vermeidens künftiger Übergriffe durch sexuelle Gewalt in Konfliktsituationen.

### *Sexuelle Gewalt in Konfliktsituationen ist nicht unabwendbar*

Die fünfte Schlüsselerkenntnis aus der Literaturauswertung zeigt auf, dass sexuelle Gewalt in Konfliktsituationen nicht unabwendbar ist. Aus Woods eigenen Recherchen und einer Synthese anderer akademischer Forschungsergebnisse, identifiziert sie, dass das Ausmaß an sexueller Gewalt, die Art und Weise, in der sie verübt wurde, die Zeitspanne innerhalb des Konflikts, ihre Stellung innerhalb einer Auswahl gewalttätiger Methoden, und ob sie symmetrisch oder asymmetrisch war, von Konflikt zu Konflikt unterschiedlich ist. Außerdem erkannte sie, dass solche Schwierigkeiten nicht von der Art des Konflikts, oder den herrschenden traditionellen Normen, der praktizierten Religionen oder den vorhandenen Gelegenheiten abhingen, um sexuelle Gewalt auszuüben. Hinzu kam, dass Unterschiede nicht durch die Schwierigkeit des

73 Solangon and Patel, "Sexual violence against men in countries affected by armed conflict," 436.

74 Kirby, "Ending sexual violence in conflict: Preventing Sexual Violence Initiative and its critics," 470.

Erhaltens von verlässlichen Daten erklärt werden konnten.[75] Deshalb folgerte Wood: „Das vernachlässigte Faktum der Variation, einschließlich der relativen Abwesenheit von sexueller Gewalt in Kriegszeiten seitens einer oder mehrerer bewaffneten Gruppen, haben eine wichtige taktische Auswirkung: Vergewaltigung ist nicht so unabwendbar in Kriegen wie manchmal behauptet wird."[76] Wood brachte Beispiele einiger bewaffneten Gruppen an, die keine sexuelle Gewalt ausgeübt haben, z.B. in El Salvador, Israel/Palästina, Vietnam und Sri Lanka,[77] allerdings mit der Vorwarnung, dass "ich bei Abwesenheit von sexueller Gewalt die (relative) Abwesenheit von sexueller Gewalt meine. Sexuelle Gewalt, die von einer Gruppe angewandt wird, ist sehr selten (aber nicht vollständig abwesend)."[78]

In einem späteren Werk identifizierte Wood ein weiteres Variationselement: ob sexuelle Gewalt nur gegen Frauen oder gegen beide Geschlechter angewandt wurde.[79] Sie erstellte Daten aus anderen akademischen Forschungsstudien. Zum Beispiel zitierte sie Nordås, der behauptete dass: "von 59% der 177 bewaffneten Aktoren in den Zivilkriegen zwischen 2000 und 2009 in zwanzig afrikanischen Ländern nicht gemeldet wurde, dass sie Vergewaltigung oder andere Formen sexueller Gewalt benutzten."[80] Weiter bezog sie sich auf Cohens Ermittlung: „wo eine Partei des Konflikts sexuelle Gewalt fördert, während die andere das nicht tut, ein Muster, das auf fast 40% der Zivilkriege passt."[81] Zusätzlich folgerte sie aus der gemeinsamen Arbeit von Cohen and Nordås:

> Die besten, zur Verfügung stehenden supranationalen Datensätze bestätigen, dass sexuelle Gewalt (einschließlich Vergewaltigung) zwischen Staatsmilitärs, aufständischen Organisationen und regierungstreuen Bürgerwehren unterschiedlich sind; in der Tat, von allen drei Typen bewaffneter Akteure wurde zwischen 1989 und 2009 keine starke Mehrheit als Täter von sexueller Gewalt gemeldet.[82]

Solangon und Patel erkannten in ihren Recherchen über sexuelle Gewalt gegen Männer: „Sexuelle Gewalt wird nicht länger primär als eine biologische

75 Wood, "Rape is not inevitable during war," in Kuehnast et al., eds., *Women and War: Power & Protection in Twenty-First Century*, 37-39 and 43-45.

76 Ebd., 39.

77 Ebd., 40 & 43.

78 Ebd., 39.

79 Wood, "Conflict-related sexual violence and the policy implications of recent research," 461.

80 Ebd., 458.

81 Ebd., 462.

82 Ebd., 459.

sexuelle Begierde angesehen, sondern immer mehr als ein Beweis der Macht, Vorherrschaft und Demütigung".[83] Das IKRK stimmte überein: „Der Anspruch, dass sexuelle Gewalt ganz einfach ein hässlicher Aspekt unserer schlimmsten menschlichen Neigungen und eine unglückselige Begleiterscheinung von Krieg sein soll, ist nicht länger haltbar. Es wird heute weitgehend anerkannt, dass sexuelle Gewalt nicht eine unabwendbare Konsequenz eines bewaffneten Konflikts ist."[84] Dies war eine Schlüsselerkenntnis in der Literaturauswertung, die es nahe legte, dass, wenn sexuelle Gewalt nicht immer als ein Kriegsmittel benutzt wird, dann sollten vorbeugende Maßnahmen aus diesen Konflikten identifiziert und angewendet werden, um zukünftiges Ausbrechen sexueller Gewalt in Kriegssituationen zu verhindern.

### *Übersicht der Schlüsselerkenntnisse der Literaturauswertung*

Um die Auswertung der Literatur abzuschließen, erstellten Analysen von Akademikern und Fachleuten eine Reihe von Gründen für den Einsatz sexueller Gewalt in Konfliktsituationen und wiesen nach, dass Männer und Jungen Opfer und Frauen Täter sein konnten. Sie stellte die Abwendbarkeit von sexueller Gewalt in Konfliktsituationen dar – da sie nicht von allen bewaffneten Gruppen in allen Konfliktsituationen zu allen Zeiten eingesetzt wurde. Außerdem betonte sie die Herausforderungen in der Nachsorge bei den Opfern, das Risiko der Versicherheitlichung, aufgrund dessen dann andere Kriegsverbrechen und häusliche Gewalt nicht ausreichend finanziert werden, sowie das Risiko der Ablenkung von der WPS-Agenda.

## Derzeitige präventive Methoden

### *Verständnis*

Wenn wir uns nun einer Analyse vorhandener präventiver Vorgehen zuwenden, befassen wir uns mit vier Bereichen: Verständnis, Befürwortung auf hoher Ebene, Schulung und Gesetzgebung. Um zu verhüten, dass etwas stattfindet, muss man die Probleme verstehen. Der vorherige Abschnitt zu den Ergebnissen der Literaturauswertung versuchte darzustellen, dass das Verständnis der Probleme, die aus sexueller Gewalt als Kriegsmittel erwachsen sind, angestiegen ist. Obgleich die Literatur die Anforderung für weitere Recherchen unterstützte, scheint es jetzt eine solide Grundlage der Studien zu geben, die das

83 Solangon and Patel, "Sexual violence against men in countries affected by armed conflict," 425.

84 ICRC, "Sexual Violence in Armed Conflict: E-Briefing," Part 4.

Verständnis des Themas verbessert hat. Das IKRK bekundete, dass: „ihre Verbreitung und horrende Auswirkung auf einzelne Personen und Gesellschaften, sowie auch die Dynamik dahinter, während der letzten zwei Jahrzehnte immer besser verstanden wurde."[85] Zum Beispiel dauerte es bis 1999, bis Médecins Sans Frontières ihr erstes Behandlungspaket für überlebende Opfer sexueller Gewalt zusammenstellten, obgleich die Organisation bereits seit 1971 bestand.[86]

Die Literatur wies zusätzlich eine Kenntnisnahme der bekannten angreifbaren Standorte und Perioden nach, wo sexuelle Gewalt verübt werden konnte. Zum Beispiel beschrieben Solangon und Patel einige dieser angreifbaren Standorte, wie Internierungslager, Landesgrenzen, in isolierten Bereichen wie Felder und, im Gegensatz dazu, Märkte und einige Handelsrouten, auf die sich Gruppen von Leuten konzentriert zusammenfinden. Weiter legte sie die Gefahrensperioden nahe, z.B. wenn Wasser oder Holz gesammelt werden, auf dem Schulweg, des Nachts und während Wahlperioden.[87] Dr. Aburabi, ein IKRK-Internierungslagerlagerarzt, beschrieb die besonders für Männer bekannten gefährlichen Zeiten: „während der ersten Internierung, wenn der Häftling am stärksten desorientiert und isoliert von den gewohnten Unterstützungssystemen ist. Weiter ist die Gewalt auch in Verhörzentren weit verbreitet".[88] Skjelsboek weist auf ein Anzeichen hin, dass Leute für sexuelle Gewalt angreifbar sein können, wenn: „politische Debatten sexualisiert werden."[89] Watson merkte hierzu an, dass ein Element der Prävention von sexueller Gewalt gegen Männer (obgleich dies genauso gut auf Frauen und Kinder zutrifft) „die Reduktion der Anzahl vorhandener falscher Orte und falscher Zeiten, war."[90] Deshalb wird trotz der erforderlichen weiteren Recherchen nahegelegt, dass die aktuelle Ebene des Verständnisses der Probleme eine gute Grundlage für die Strategien sind, die für eine effektive Prävention konzipiert, implementiert und ausgewertet werden sollten.

---

85 ICRC, "Sexual Violence in Armed Conflict: E-Briefing," Introduction.

86 Duroch and Schulte-Hillen, "Care for victims of sexual violence, an organization pushed to its limits: case of Médecins Sans Frontières," 603.

87 Solangon and Patel, "Sexual violence against men in countries affected by armed conflict," 432.

88 Bernard and Pothelet, "Through eyes of a detention doctor: Interview with Raed Aburabi," 481.

89 Skjelsboek, "Sexual violence in post-Yugoslav wars," in: Kuehnast et al., eds., *Women and War: Power & Protection in Twenty-First Century*, 81.

90 Callum Watson, "Bad apples or bad apple trees? An examination of the contexts in which sexual violence against men takes place," paper presented at a workshop entitled, 'Sexual Violence Against Men during Conflicts: Bridging the Gap between Theory and Practice', *The Graduate Institute of International and Development Studies*, Geneva February 26-27, 2015), 9.

### *Unterstützung auf hoher Ebene*

Der zweite für seinen Beitrag zur derzeitigen Prävention untersuchte Bereich befasst sich mit dem Ausmaß der internationalen Unterstützung auf hoher Ebene. Im Rahmen der UN-Resolution 1888 wurde in 2009 die Ernennung eines „Sonderbeauftragten des Generalsekretärs für sexuelle Gewalt in Konfliktsituationen" etabliert. Ein Jahr später, mit der UN-Resolution 1960, wurde der UN-Generalsekretär beauftragt, einen Jahresbericht zu produzieren, in dem alle bewaffneten Gruppen, die sexuelle Gewalt in Konfliktsituation ausgeübt hatten, als Teil des „Naming and Shaming"-Programms aufgeführt waren. Dieser Bericht von 2015 erstellte Details von 45 staatlichen und nichtstaatlichen Gruppen, von denen dreizehn zum ersten Mal aufgeführt wurden.[91] Zusätzlich unternimmt „UN Action against Sexual Violence in Conflict" (UN-Aktivitäten gegen sexuelle Gewalt in Konfliktsituationen): „eine Reihe von strategischen Initiativen, um die systemweite Koordination, Weiterbildung, Verteidigung und technische Unterstützung auf Landesebene zu verbessern."[92] Seit 2013 haben 155 Länder eine Erklärung der UN-Generalversammlung befürwortet.[93] Während seiner Präsidentschaft der G8 in 2013, bewirkte Großbritannien eine Erklärung, gemäß der G8-Mitglieder vereinbarten, eine Reihe von Maßnahmen zu unterstützen. Diese waren u.a.: Finanzielle Unterstützung, Schulung, Beratung zur Dokumentierung von Beweismitteln, Anerkennung, dass sexuelle Gewalt zu einer schweren Verletzung der Genfer Abstimmungen führen kann (und somit international im Rahmen einer Universalrechtsprechung geahndet werden kann), die Notwendigkeit, sexuelle Gewalt in der ersten Phase jeglicher Stellungnahme zu adressieren, und dass in späteren Friedensvereinbarungen keine Amnestie für jene gebilligt wird, die sexuelle Gewalt ausgeübt haben.[94] Sie vereinbarten hinzu, einen Folgebericht unter der deutschen G8-Präsidentschaft in 2015 zu erstellen, um Fortschritte zu melden, die sie ordnungsgemäß durchführten (dann als G7 agierend).[95]

---

91 UN Secretary General, "Conflict-related sexual violence: Report of Secretary General," 1/33.

92 Ebd., 25/33.

93 G7, "G7 Report on the Implementation of the G8 Declaration on Preventing Sexual Violence in Conflict," G7 November 2015), <https://www.g7germany.de/Content/EN/_Anlagen/G7/2015-11-24-g7-erklaerung_svc_en.pdf?__blob=publicationFile&v=3> (Zugriff: den 7. Januar 2016), 2.

94 Foreign & Commonwealth Office, "The Foreign Secretary William Hague, Angelina Jolie and Zainab Hawa Bangura launch G8 Declaration on Preventing Sexual Violence in Conflict," Foreign & Commonwealth Office April 2013), <https://www.gov.uk/government/news/g8-declaration-on-preventing-sexual-violence-in-conflict> (Zugriff: den 27. November 2015).

95 G7, "G7 Report on the Implementation of the G8 Declaration on Preventing Sexual Violence in Conflict."

Im Juni 2014 veranstaltete Großbritannien ein Gipfeltreffen mit 120 Nationen[96] und Vertretern aller G7-Mitglieder, einschließlich 4 G7-Außenministern und dem hohen Vertreter der Europäischen Union für Außen- und Sicherheitspolitik.[97] Der damalige Außenminister der USA, John Kerry, der den Event abschloss, führte die Hilfe der USA auf, die die in 2013 angekündigte Initiative „Safe from the Start" (Sicherheit von Anfang an) beinhaltete, und bis zum November 2015 von der USA in der Höhe von 29 Millionen Dollar finanziell unterstützt wurde. Der britische Premierminister ernannte eine „Sonderbeauftragte für die Verhütung sexueller Gewalt in Konflikten", Baroness Anelay, und die Nationale Sicherheitsstrategie vom letzten Jahr verpflichtete sich: „die Reichweite und Umsetzung der Initiative zur Verhütung sexueller Gewalt in Konflikten (PSVI) auszuweiten."[98] Von dem Zeitpunkt an, an dem Großbritannien die PSVI in 2012 einführte, hatte die britische Regierung zu ihrer Unterstützung bis zum Ende von 2015 20 Millionen Pfund zugeteilt.[99] Die North Atlantic Treaty Organisation (NATO) schuf einen permanenten Posten der Sonderbeauftragten für WPS in 2014. Für ihren derzeitigen Einsatz in Afghanistan, Operation Resolute Support, schloss die NATO „Frauen, Frieden, Sicherheit" von vornherein in den Planungsprozess ein, und bewies: „dass diese Initiative nicht länger nur ein Nachtrag war: eine Geschlechtergleichstellung wurde von der Ebene der Entscheidungstreffung bis hinab zum Entwurf des Ausführungsplans für den Einsatz und der Bereitstellung von Truppen integriert."[100] Das IKRK änderte seine Arbeitsweise mit der Annahme, dass sexuelle Gewalt in einem Konflikt stattfand, bis Beweismittel für das Gegenteil vorgelegt werden.[101]

Es scheint also, dass es einen Grad der internationalen Unterstützung, von UN, G7, NATO, IKRK und einzelnen Ländern gibt, um sexuelle Gewalt als ein Kriegsmittel zu bekämpfen. Dies ist ein wichtiger Wegbereiter zur Bewerkstelligung der Verhütung und Hilfe anderer, um präventive Maßnahmen einzurichten. Bedenkt man allerdings die vorhandenen Herausforderungen, werden

96 Kirby, "Ending sexual violence in conflict: Preventing Sexual Violence Initiative and its critics," 457.

97 G7, "G7 Report on the Implementation of the G8 Declaration on Preventing Sexual Violence in Conflict," 2.

98 United Kingdom Government, *National Security Strategy and Strategic Defence and Security Review 2015: A Secure and Prosperous United Kingdom*, Cm 9161 November 2015), 63.

99 G7, "G7 Report on the Implementation of the G8 Declaration on Preventing Sexual Violence in Conflict," 5.

100 Marriët Schuurman, "NATO and the Women, Peace and Security Agenda: Time to Bring It Home." *Connections: The Quarterly Journal*, XIV(3) (2015), <http://www.nato.int/cps/en/natohq/opinions_124032.htm?selectedLocale=en> (Zugriff: den 12. Januar 2016).

101 ICRC, "Sexual Violence in Armed Conflict: E-Briefing," Part 2.

weitere Hilfsmittel erforderlich, sowie die nachhaltige Bereitschaft der Völkergemeinschaft, um die derzeitigen präventiven Maßnahmen zu stärken und Verbesserungen zu verankern. Außerdem muss die internationale Unterstützung sichtlich von nicht-westlich geprägten Organisationen kommen. Zum Beispiel ergaben Suchen auf den englischen Versionen der Webseiten der African Union (AU), der Commonwealth Arab League, des Gulf Cooperation Council, der Association of South East Asian Nations und der Organization of American States kaum, falls überhaupt, irgendwelche Informationen zu ihren Strategien, um sexuelle Gewalt als Kriegsmittel zu verhüten. Solche Organisationen müssen eigene Initiativen ergreifen, um klarzustellen, dass sie sexuelle Gewalt in Konflikten verurteilen und dies mit konkreten Maßnahmen bekräftigen. Ihre Bereitschaft, mit finanziellen und anderen Mitteln Unterstützung zu leisten, würde der restlichen internationalen Gemeinschaft, die selbst unter Druck steht, die Ressourcen zu finden, helfen und ihr beweisen, dass nicht-westliche Organisationen eine wirkliche Opposition zu sexueller Gewalt in Konflikten darstellen.

***Schulung***

Das dritte Thema, das für seinen Beitrag zur Verhütung konfliktbezogener sexueller Gewalt ausgewertet werden soll, befasst sich mit der derzeitigen Beschaffung von Schulung für militärische und zivile Streitkräfte. In 2010 entwikkelte die UN-Aktionskampagne eine „auf Szenario basierte Schulung vor dem Einsatz ..., um die einsatzfähige Bereitschaft von militärischen und polizeilichen Friedenssoldaten zu verbessern, damit sie schnell und angemessen reagieren können",[102] was weiterhin in UN-Schulungszentren ausgeführt wird. In 2014 vereinbarten Mitgliedsstaaten der NATO einen neuen Bildungs- und Schulungsplan für Geschlechtergleichheit in militärischen Einsätzen, der: „Geschlechterbildung und –schulung auf allen Ebenen zusammenführt und synchronisiert."[103] Im folgenden Jahr fand die hochrangigste politisch-militärische Krisenmanagementsübung der NATO statt: „die erste auf dieser Ebene ... [die] darauf hinwies, dass konfliktbezogene sexuelle Gewalt als eine Kriegstaktik stattfindet und prüfte, wie diese Hinweise strategische Entscheidungstreffungen beeinflussen könnten."[104] Im gleichen Jahr verkündete Großbritannien neue Finanzierungsmittel im Wert von £700.000, um AU-Friedenssoldaten

102 UN Secretary General, "Conflict-related sexual violence: Report of Secretary General," 26/33.

103 Schuurman, "NATO and Women, Peace and Security Agenda: Time to Bring It Home."

104 Ebd.

zu schulen, sexuelle Gewalt in Konflikten zu verhüten und zu maßregeln.[105] Weiter sagte Großbritannien aus, dass alle britischen Streitkräfte im internationalen Einsatz speziell für WPS und die PSVI bis November 2016 geschult würden.[106] Außerdem hat Großbritannien bis zum November 2015 mehr als 8.000 afrikanische Friedenssoldaten und Polizisten, 2.500 malische Streitkräfte und 800 Iraker Peschmerga-Truppen geschult.[107] Während es immer noch Fälle gibt, wo UN-Blauhelme und AU-Friedenssoldaten selbst sexuelle Gewalt ausüben, statt sie zu verhüten oder aufzuhalten, tendieren die aktuellen Ausbildungsmaßnahmen eher dazu, ein verbessertes Verhalten sicherzustellen. Deshalb kann Schulung als eine wichtige Maßnahme gesehen werden, Streitkräfte und Polizeibeamte mit den Fachkenntnissen und dem Verständnis auszurüsten, um mit Ausbrüchen sexueller Gewalt fertig zu werden und neue Auftritte zu verhüten. Hinzu werden sie als Rollenmodelle verstanden, um: „universale Begriffe, wie bewaffnete Akteure sich zu benehmen haben, formen zu helfen und welche Rolle und Aufgaben sie in Konflikten haben … selbst rebellische Gruppen könnten sie nachahmen, in der Hoffnung, eines Tages als legitime nationale Akteure anerkannt werden zu können."[108] Diese Ansicht wurde vom dem damaligen Außenminister William Hague in 2013 wiederholt: „Mitglieder der Militärs sind oft die ersten, die in Kontakt mit den Überlebenden geraten und könnten auch eine wichtige Rolle dabei spielen, die Einstellungen der Männer zu ändern."[109]

Es gibt also Beweismaterial, das nahelegt, dass Schulungspakete, die von der UN, NATO und einzelnen Ländern wie Großbritannien entwickelt wurden, für UN- und AU-Friedenssoldaten wie auch staatliche Militärs und Polizeibeamte eingeführt werden. Es ist wichtig, dass solche Schulung regelmäßig auf ihre Wirksamkeit ausgewertet (und verfeinert) und laufend an multinationale und

105 Foreign & Commonwealth Office, "Angelina Jolie Pitt joins Baroness Anelay to chart next steps on tackling sexual violence," Foreign & Commonwealth Office Juni 2015), <https://www.gov.uk/government/news/angelina-jolie-pitt-joins-baroness-anelay-to-chart-next-steps-on-tackling-sexual-violence> (Zugriff: den 12. Januar 2016).

106 Baroness Sandip Verma, "The UK firmly believes that the 15th anniversary must represent the start of a new era on Women, Peace and Security," UK Government Oktober 13, 2015), <https://www.gov.uk/government/speeches/the-uk-firmly-believes-that-the-15th-anniversary-must-represent-the-start-of-a-new-era-on-women-peace-and-security (accessed November 26, 2015).

107 G7, "G7 Report on the Implementation of the G8 Declaration on Preventing Sexual Violence in Conflict," 7.

108 Watson, "Bad apples or bad apple trees? Examination of contexts in which sexual violence against men takes place," 10.

109 FCO, "Foreign Secretary William Hague, Angelina Jolie and Zainab Hawa Bangura launch G8 Declaration on Preventing Sexual Violence in Conflict."

nationale Streitkräfte ausgegeben wird, und dass weiterführende Kurse verfügbar sind, sowie auch dass schnelle und bestrafende Maßnahmen getroffen werden, gegen solche, die sexuelle Gewalt ausüben, statt dass sie andere vor solcher Gewalt beschützen.

### *Rechtsprechung*

Das vierte und letzte Element, das für seinen Beitrag für die aktuelle Verhütung untersucht wird, befasst sich mit der Rechtsprechung und deckt das Gesetzeswerk, seine Umsetzung und seine abschreckende Wirkung. Zum Gesetz selbst überprüfte die Juristin und Akademikerin Gaggioli zuerst die derzeitigen gesetzlichen Bestimmungen innerhalb des internationalen Völkerrechts (International Humanitarian Law - IHL) und den internationalen Menschenrechten. Sie fand, dass: „Das IHL-Verbot von Vergewaltigung und anderen Formen sexueller Gewalt sowohl für internationale als auch nicht internationale bewaffnete Konflikte geltend und außerdem auch Teil des Gewohnheitsrechts ist. Die Menschenrechte verbieten sexuelle Gewalt in jeder Form und zu jeder Zeit."[110] Weiter identifizierte sie, dass: „Vergewaltigung und andere Formen sexueller Gewalt internationale Verbrechen darstellen können – Kriegsverbrechen, Verbrechen gegen die Menschlichkeit und Verübung von Völkermord – wenn die Umstände für solche Verbrechen ... vorhanden sind. Als solches ziehen sie individuelle Schuldfähigkeit mit sich."[111] Gaggioli folgerte, dass: „der internationale gesetzliche Rahmen ... deshalb außerordentlich robust, wenn auch nicht perfekt ist ... die verschiedenen internationalen Arme des Gesetzes (Humanitäres Völkerrecht, Menschenrechte, internationales Strafrecht) wiederholen und bestärken einander und ergänzen sich notwendigerweise."[112] Eine G8-Erklärung von 2013 stellte fest, dass: "internationale Menschenrechte ein langjähriges Verbot beinhalten ... und dass, ... wenn es einen Teil eines verbreiteten oder systematischen Angriffs auf eine Zivilbevölkerung darstellt, es ein Verbrechen gegen die Menschlichkeit und ein konstitutiver Akt mit Hinsicht auf Völkermord darstellen kann."[113] Eine jüngst erlassene Auswertung eines Sonderkomitees des House of Lords „überprüfte den Fall für weitere internationale

110 Gloria Gaggioli, "Sexual violence in armed conflicts: A violation of international humanitarian law and human rights law," *International Review of the Red Cross* 96(894) (2014), <doi:10.1017/S1816383115000211> (Zugriff: den 11. Januar 2016), 537

111 Ebd.

112 Ebd.

113 Foreign & Commonwealth Office, "Declaration on Preventing Sexual Violence in Conflict," Foreign & Commonwealth Office April 2013), <https://www.gov.uk/government/uploads/system/uploads/attachment_data/file/185008/G8_PSVI_Declaration_-_FINAL.pdf> (Zugriff: den 27. November 2015).

Rechtsprechung ... [aber] kam zu dem Schluss, dass die vorhandenen Bestimmungen ausreichend waren."[114] Deshalb scheint es der Fall zu sein, dass die rechtlichen Bestimmungen – zumindest auf dem Papier – robust genug sind.

Während die Literaturauswertung keine weitere Rechtsprechung forderte, betonte sie die Umsetzung. Zum Beispiel forderte Gaggioli: „Eine bessere Umsetzung vorhandener Regelungen auf lokaler Ebene und wirksame strafrechtliche Verfolgung von Straftätern sexueller Verbrechen auf lokaler und internationaler Ebene."[115] In 2013 unterstützten die G8-Staaten: „den Einsatz internationaler Experten, um die unparteiische, ermittelnde und rechtsfähige Gewalt anderer Länder aufzubauen."[116] Das IKRK empfahl: „Behörden müssen sicherstellen, dass zufriedenstellende Mechanismen eingesetzt sind, um es Opfern zu ermöglichen, die Gewalttaten in sicherer und vertraulicher Atmosphäre melden zu können."[117] Es forderte auch: „die entsprechende Sensibilisierung des juristischen Personals, technische Sonderanforderungen bezüglich Zeit und Ort der Vernehmen und genügend Rechtsbeistand für alle mutmaßlichen Straftäter."[118]

Obwohl es eine ungeheure Arbeit zu sein scheint, gab es Organisationen, die Ländern halfen, ihre Rechtsverfahren zu verbessern. Zum Beispiel betonte ein G7-Bericht in 2015 die Arbeit von „Justice Rapid Response" (JRR), eine zwischenstaatliche Organisation, die mit der UN zusammenarbeitet. Sie erklärt, dass JRR Listen schnell einsetzbarer Kriminaljustizexperten aufzählt (mehr als 500 Personen) und Ermittler (fast 150 Personen), letztere befassen sich mit den genaueren Untersuchungen.[119] JRRs eigene Webseite betont, dass die schnell einsetzbaren Experten 60 höhere Berufe repräsentieren und: „aus mehr als 95 Ländern stammen und über 80 Sprachen sprechen. JRRs Liste beträgt mehr als 40% vom globalen Süden und davon sind 50% Frauen."[120] In weniger als sechs

114 House of Lords, "Select Committee on Sexual Violence in Conflict: Report of Session 2015-16: Sexual Violence in Conflict: A War Crime," House of Lords, HL Paper 123 April 12, 2016), <http://www.publications.parliament.uk/pa/ld201516/ldselect/ldsvc/123/123.pdf> (Zugriff: den 15. April 2016), 8.

115 Gaggioli, "Sexual violence in armed conflicts: violation of international humanitarian law and human rights law," 533.

116 FCO, "Foreign Secretary William Hague, Angelina Jolie and Zainab Hawa Bangura launch G8 Declaration on Preventing Sexual Violence in Conflict."

117 ICRC, "Sexual Violence in Armed Conflict: E-Briefing," Part 3.

118 Ebd.

119 G7, "G7 Report on the Implementation of the G8 Declaration on Preventing Sexual Violence in Conflict," 7.

120 Justice Rapid Response, "Justice Rapid Response welcomes UN Women and Draper Richards Kaplan Foundation to its Executive Board," JRR November 2015), <http://www.justicerapidresponse.org/justice-rapid-response-welcomes-un-women-and-draper-richards-kaplan-foundation-to-its-executive-board/> (Zugriff: den 7. Januar 2016).

Jahren, hat JRR fast 70 Untersuchungen angestellt, einschließlich in Syrien und dem Irak.[121] Großbritannien hat auch sein eigenes Team von mehr als 70 Experten eingerichtet, und umfasst eine große Palette der Fachbereiche, einschließlich Polizei und Gerichtsmediziner,[122] die an 17 Projekten in 13 Ländern gearbeitet haben, einschließlich an der Grenze von Syrien u.a., um: „Untersuchungen zu verbessern und Strafverfolgungen für sexuelle Gewalt in Konflikten zu vermehren."[123] Außerdem haben G8-Außenminister in 2013 vereinbart, ein *Internationales Protokoll zur Dokumentierung und Untersuchung sexueller Gewalt in Konflikten* zu produzieren. Es wurde von britischen Beamten unter Expertenaufsicht zusammengestellt und auf dem Weltgipfeltreffen in 214 eingeführt, um: „die Basis der Beweismittel zur Strafverfolgung von Straftätern zu verstärken."[124] Seitdem hat Großbritannien ein Schulungspaket entwickelt und das Protokoll in andere Sprachen, einschließlich arabisch, übersetzt. Großbritannien hat auch verschiedenen Ländern geholfen, dieses Protokoll zu benutzen, einschließlich Bosnien, Kolumbien und Uganda.[125] Der Berufsstand der Ärzte hat außerdem anerkannt, dass er eine Rolle in der Beweismittelführung hat. Dies ist nicht unbedingt eine geradlinige Entwicklung, da es vor allem darum geht, Patienten zu behandeln, nicht Polizei zu spielen. Trotzdem haben seit 2011 „Ärzte für Menschenrechte" (PHR) Medizinalfachberufler und Juristen zusammengeführt, um ihre gemeinsamen Bemühungen zu verbessern: „[Krankenhausärzte] sind die ersten, die auf Beweismittel stoßen werden, folglich müssen sie beginnen, sie zu katalogisieren und zu präservieren, sodass sie später gesetzlich zulässig sind."[126] Auf diese Weise scheint es, dass die internationale Gemeinschaft erkannt hat, dass sie Ländern helfen muss, ihre gesetzlichen Prozedere zu verbessern und eine Reihe von Schritten unternommen hat, Änderungen zu unterstützen. Trotzdem verlangt dies ein nachhaltiges internationales und nationales Engagement, Schulung, Be-

121 Ebd. &G7, "G7 Report on the Implementation of the G8 Declaration on Preventing Sexual Violence in Conflict," 7.

122 FCO, "Foreign Secretary William Hague, Angelina Jolie and Zainab Hawa Bangura launch G8 Declaration on Preventing Sexual Violence in Conflict."

123 G7, "G7 Report on the Implementation of the G8 Declaration on Preventing Sexual Violence in Conflict," 7.

124 Foreign & Commonwealth Office, "Chair's Summary: Global Summit to End Sexual Violence in Conflict," Foreign & Commonwealth Office Juni 2014), <https://www.gov.uk/government/publications/chairs-summary-global-summit-to-end-sexual-violence-in-conflict/chairs-summary-global-summit-to-end-sexual-violence-in-conflict> (Zugriff: den 27. November 2015).

125 G7, "G7 Report on the Implementation of the G8 Declaration on Preventing Sexual Violence in Conflict," 5-6.

126 Alcorn, "Responding to sexual violence in armed conflict," 2037.

treuung und Ressourcen, um allgemein anerkannte Regeln einzubetten und bessere Anwendung der relevanten Gesetzgebung sicherzustellen, wenn sie denn eine wirkliche Auswirkung als eine präventive Maßnahme darstellen will. Dies scheint ein Bereich zu sein, der noch weiter anzusprechen ist. Wenn Staaten einmal akzeptiert haben, die relevante Gesetzgebung zu adoptieren, muss die internationale Gemeinschaft in der Lage sein, zu helfen und sicherzustellen, dass sie angewandt wird.

Der letzte Aspekt der Rechtsprechung, der zu untersuchen ist, ist ihre Wirksamkeit als abschreckendes Mittel. Eine der wichtigsten Kritiken von PSVI seitens Kirbys war, dass sie sich auf das Beenden von Straflosigkeit konzentrierte: „die hauptsächliche Hypothese der Straflosigkeit – nämlich, dass eine zunehmende Strafverfolgung von zukünftigen Gräueltaten abhalten würde, - steht der entschiedenen Herausforderung von Wirksamkeit, Kosten und Zweckmäßigkeit gegenüber."[127] Kirby zeigt auf, dass die durchschnittlichen Kosten der Überführung einer Person in den Internationalen Strafgerichten für das frühere Jugoslawien oder Ruanda (ICTY und ICTR) eine bestürzende Summe von je \$35M und £39M betrugen.[128] Er betonte zusätzlich, dass die: „Sieger und die Besiegten vor dem Gesetz nicht gleichwertig sind."[129] Human Rights Watch wies darauf hin, dass die Kritik des Internationalen Strafgerichtes (International Criminal Tribunal für Ruanda - ICTR), die Kosten, umständliche Verfahren, nur wenige Fälle, die vor Gericht gestellt wurden, die Dauer, während der die Überführten die Medien einspannen konnten, Mangel an Wiedergutmachung für die Überlebenden und Abstand von strafrechtlicher Verfolgung der „Gewinner" der Rwandan Patriotic Front einschloss.[130] Es scheint, dass die Aussicht auf langfristige Bestrafung zu Gunsten der kurzfristigen Gelegenheiten, einen Krieg zu gewinnen, zunichte gemacht werden kann.

Trotzdem überführte der Internationale Strafgerichtshof die frühere Premierministerin, Stabschefin der Armee und Stabschefin des Verteidigungsministeriums,[131] sowie auch die erste Frau, die an Völkermord, Kriegsverbrechen und Verbrechen gegen die Menschlichkeit beteiligt gewesen war, Pauline Nyiramasuhuko.[132] Weitere Meilensteine waren Duško Tadić, der als erster für

127 Kirby, "Ending sexual violence in conflict: Preventing Sexual Violence Initiative and its critics," 464.

128 Ebd., 465.

129 Ebd.

130 Human Rights Watch, "Rwanda: International Tribunal Closing Its Doors."

131 Ibid.

132 Mollmann, "Rape in war: No more excuses."

Kriegsverbrechen sexueller Gewalt gegen Männer in 1997 verurteilt wurde,[133] und in 2014 wurden General Kakwavu und „Colonel 106" für schuldig befunden, Verbrechen sexueller Gewalt in der Demokratischen Republik Kongo begangen zu haben, wozu die UN wie folgt vermerkte: „Diese Überführungen markieren einen Meilenstein in den Bemühungen, Offiziere hohen Ranges zur Verantwortung zu ziehen."[134] Im März 2016 sicherte der IStGH seine erste Verurteilung sexueller Gewalt in Konflikten (einschließlich gegen Männer) im Falle von Jean-Pierre Bemba. Es war auch das erste Mal, dass der IStGH erfolgreich eine Person für ihre „Vorgesetztenverantwortlichkeit" anklagte, und zwar für Bembas Rolle als Präsident und oberster Befehlshaber der „Mouvement de libération du Congo."[135] Der IStGH erwähnte besonders die symbolische Tragweite der Erhebung von Anklage gegen Personen, aufgrund der Botschaft, die sie anderen sendet, und dass sie Überlebenden eine Form der Anerkennung bietet.[136] Die Ergebnisse der Literaturauswertung anfangs weisen darauf hin, dass die Kultur der Straflosigkeit ein Schlüsselfaktor für die Heranziehung zur Verantwortung für sexuelle Gewalt als Kriegsmittel war. Deshalb ist die erfolgreiche Strafverfolgung von Politikern, Offizieren und Polizeibeamten in höchster und mittlerer Rangstellung und Mitglieder von staatlichen und nicht-staatlichen Gruppen eine notwendige Kondition, um zu verhindern, dass sexuelle Gewalt als Kriegsmittel in zukünftigen Konflikten eingesetzt wird. Allerdings scheint es, dass entschieden mehr in diesem Bereich erreicht werden muss, um eine effektive verhütende Maßnahme darzustellen.

### *Übersicht über aktuelle verhütende Maßnahmen*

Aus dieser Auswertung aktueller verhütender Maßnahmen geht hervor, dass effektive Maßnahmen in vollem Gang sind, aber es besteht die Notwendigkeit, sie zu verbessern. Positiv gesehen, wird das Thema sehr viel besser verstanden, was die Konzipierung und Implementierung präventiver Strategien ermöglicht hat, einschließlich Schulungspakete. Außerdem gibt es eine starke Befürwortung der Schwerpunkte in der Völkergemeinschaft, aufgrund der Ressourcen für dieses Problem verwendet werden und die die Umsetzung in Taten veranlasst hat. Tausende von bewaffneten und zivilen Streitkräften werden geschult und Maßnahmen ergriffen, wenn Friedenssoldaten Befehlen

133 Watson, "Bad apples or bad apple trees? Examination of contexts in which sexual violence against men takes place," 3.

134 UN Secretary General, "Conflict-related sexual violence: Report of Secretary General," 8/33.

135 House of Lords, "Select Committee on Sexual Violence in Conflict: Report of Session 2015-16: Sexual Violence in Conflict: A War Crime," 22.

136 ICRC, "Sexual Violence in Armed Conflict: E-Briefing," Part 3.

nicht gehorchen. Die rechtlichen Bestimmungen sind beträchtlich, Beweismittel werden gesammelt und Strafverfolgungen aufgenommen. Was die Verbesserungen betrifft, so sind weitere Recherchen erforderlich, um das Verständnis zu vertiefen, und zusätzliche verhütende Maßnahmen zu konstruieren (zum Beispiel, Frauen daran zu hindern, sexuelle Gewalt anzuwenden). Zusätzliche Ressourcen und nachhaltige Mitarbeit von der Völkergemeinschaft sind erforderlich. Internationale Unterstützung und Finanzierung muss sichtbar von nicht-westlichen Organisationen zur Verfügung gestellt werden, z.B. die AU, Arab League und Gulf Cooperation Council. Anbetracht der aktuellen Fälle von Ausübung sexueller Gewalt seitens der Friedenssoldaten und Gesetzeshüter, ist mehr Schulung anzubieten und eine weiterführende Schulung verfügbar zu machen (sowie auch gerichtliche Schritte). Die Auswirkung der Schulung muss ausgewertet und bei Bedarf muss sie geändert werden können. Schulung und Übungen sind auf komplexe Szenarien zu basieren, um das Verständnis und die Reaktionen der Auszubildenden zu prüfen. Weitere langfristige Hilfe ist in solchen Ländern zu leisten, die ein schwaches Rechtssystem und mangelhafte Prozedere haben, um Fälle der Strafverfolgung effektiv durchzuführen. Mehr Täter sollten schneller vor Gericht gebracht werden, einschließlich UN/AU-Friedenssoldaten und solche, die auf der gewinnenden Seite sind, um die Kultur (und die Kosten) der Straflosigkeit zu reduzieren. Deshalb wird ein solides Fundament vorgeschlagen, auf das aufgebaut werden kann. Aber die derzeitigen präventiven Maßnahmen benötigen eine weitere Entwicklung, wenn sie sexuelle Gewalt im Konflikt systematischer und umfassender verhüten sollen.

## Fallstudie: Daesh[137]

### *Verfahrensweise von Daesh*

Diese Studie wird nun den Fall Daesh und ihrem derzeitigen Einsatz sexueller Gewalt als Kriegsmittel im Irak und in Syrien untersuchen. Sie betrachtet die Daesh-Methoden im Licht der Forschungsergebnisse und bewertet die Wirksamkeit vorhandener verhütender Maßnahmen, wie zuvor beschrieben, als ein Mittel, um Daesh daran zu hindern, in Zukunft sexuelle Gewalt anzuwenden. Der Generalsekretär der Vereinten Nationen (UNSG) beschrieb: „Die ungeheuerlichen Formen konfliktbezogener sexueller Gewalt“[138], die von Daesh

137 Zur Rechtschreibung, siehe Fußnote 3.

138 UN Secretary General, “Conflict-related sexual violence: Report of Secretary General,” 24/33.

seit 2014 angenommen wurden, und ein G7-Bericht stimmte dem zu.[139] Der Jahresbericht des UN-Generalsekretärs mit der Aufstellung der bewaffneten Streitkräfte, die sexuelle Gewalt im Konflikt begehen, beschreibt die Daesh-Verfahrensweise im Irak wie folgt: „Sexuelle Gewalt wurde als Teil der ISIL-Strategie benutzt, um Terror zu verbreiten, ethnische und religiöse Minoritäten zu verfolgen und Gemeinschaften, die seine Ideologie nicht akzeptieren, zu unterdrücken."[140] In einem späteren Bericht, sagte die UN aus, dass Daesh sexuelle Gewalt als eine „Kriegstaktik"[141] benutzt. Dies wurde nach Woods Ansicht von Daesh als eine Gruppe unterstützt, die: „zweckmäßig ... sexuelle Gewalt in der Verfolgung der Ziele der Organisation adoptiert hat, und ist somit eine Strategie."[142] Dass Daesh sexuelle Gewalt anwendet, wurde auch in Internierungs- und Vertriebenenlagern sowie an Grenzkontrollen identifiziert.[143] Solche Eigenschaften stimmen mit den Ergebnissen der Literaturauswertung überein, dass sexuelle Gewalt benutzt werden kann, um Macht auszuüben, den Widerstand von Gemeinschaften zu neutralisieren, wehrpolitische Ziele zu unterstützen und Informationen zu erzwingen. Es scheint zudem, dass sie in wohlbekannt angreifbaren Bereichen eingesetzt wird.

Allerdings gibt es Elemente im Daesh-Einsatz von sexueller Gewalt, die sich von den Forschungsergebnissen unterscheiden oder in ihrer Form übertriebener sind. Zum Beispiel könnte man argumentieren, dass Dash sexuelle Gewalt durchführt, um Frauenrechte und ihren Wert in der Gesellschaft zu zerstören. Deshalb wies der Sonderbeauftragte des UN-Generalsekretärs darauf hin, dass: „die notorische Mount Sinjar-Offensive vom August 2014 ebenso sehr eine sexuelle Eroberung war ... wie auch ein Vorstoß auf Staatsgebiete."[144] In Städten wie ar-Raqqa, wurden Märkte eingerichtet, auf denen nackte Frauen mit einer „Daesh-Regelung" für Frauen und Mädchen gemäß ihrem Alter verkauft wur-

139 G7, "G7 Report on the Implementation of the G8 Declaration on Preventing Sexual Violence in Conflict," 1.

140 UN Secretary General, "Conflict-related sexual violence: Report of Secretary General," 9/33.

141 United Nations, "Report on Protection of Civilians in Armed Conflict in Iraq: 1 Mai – 31 Oktober 2015," 32.

142 Wood, "Conflict-related sexual violence and the policy implications of recent research," 472.

143 UN Secretary General, "Conflict-related sexual violence: Report of Secretary General," 18/33.

144 Zainab Bangura, "Faith in Islam & Faith in Women: Why Gender Justice is Key to an Islam Without Extremes," International Crisis Group Oktober 2015),<https://medium.com/the-future-of-conflict/faith-in-islam-faith-in-women-why-gender-justice-is-key-to-an-islam-without-extremes-8920277ef674#.dkjeo08jg> (Zugriff: den 6. Januar 2016).

den.[145] Ein weiteres Element der Daesh-Methode ist die Geiselnahme von Frauen und Mädchen, die die G7 als eine: „verstörende neue Dimension“ [146] beschrieben. Die Länder wiesen darauf hin, dass dies nicht nur auf Daesh zutraf und bezogen sich auf das Beispiel der 270 Schulmädchen, die im April 2014 aus Chibok in Nigeria entführt wurden.[147] Weiter identifizierte die UN die Verbindung der beiden Terrororganisationen: „die gleichen Ideologie und Ziele, die Boko Haram motivierten, Frauen und Mädchen in Nigeria zu entführen, treiben auch ISIL an, Frauen und Mädchen in Syrien, der Arabischen Republik und dem Irak zu versklaven."[148] Ein Bericht der Amnesty International vom Dezember 2014 stellte fest, dass Tausende von Frauen und Mädchen von Daesh gefangen gehalten wurden,[149] und ein UN-Bericht im Januar 2016 sagte aus, das dies Phänomen mit ca. 3.500 versklavten Jesiden und anderen Minoritätsgruppen fortgesetzt wurde.[150] Außerdem galt sexuelle Gewalt gegen Frauen als: „Teil der Nationalökonomie, ... mithilfe des illegalen Handels und der Geiselnahme von Frauen und Mädchen Einkommensquellen zu erbringen ... Frauen wurden Teil der ISIL-Finanzierung, um seine Macht zu festigen. Sie wurden als „Kriegsbeute“ zum Zahlungsmittel gemacht".[151] Zusätzlich wies der UN-Generalsekretär darauf hin, dass die Einrichtung von „Marriage Bureaux“, um Frauen an Mitglieder von Daesh zu verkaufen und die nächste Generation zu produzieren, eine Art von Staatenbildung war.[152] Auf diese Weise scheint Daesh sexuelle Gewalt zu benutzen, um seine strategischen, politischen und militärischen Ziele zu erreichen.

Die meisten ausgewerteten Berichte über die Verfahrensweisen von Daesh konzentrierten sich auf sexuelle Gewalt gegen Frauen und Mädchen. Aber ein UN-Bericht von 2016 identifizierte, dass 800 bis 900 Jungen in der Nähe von

145 UN Secretary General, "Conflict-related sexual violence: Report of Secretary General," 10/33.

146 G7, "G7 Report on the Implementation of the G8 Declaration on Preventing Sexual Violence in Conflict," 1.

147 Ibid.

148 UN Secretary General, "Conflict-related sexual violence: Report of Secretary General," 25/33.

149 Amnesty International, "Escape from Hell: Torture and Sexual Slavery in Islamic State Captivity in Iraq," Amnesty International, MDE 14/021/2014 Dezember 2014), <http://www.amnesty.org.uk/sites/default/files/escape_from_hell_-_torture_and_sexual_slavery_in_islamic_state_captivity_in_iraq_-english_2.pdf(Zugriff: den 7. Januar 2016), 5-6.

150 United Nations, "Report on Protection of Civilians in Armed Conflict in Iraq: 1 Mai – 31 Oktober 2015," 18.

151 Bangura, "Faith in Islam & Faith in Women: Why Gender Justice is Key to Islam without Extremes".

152 UN Secretary General, "Conflict-related sexual violence: Report of Secretary General," 25/33.

Mosul im Juni 2015 entführt worden sind, und jene, die: ‚sich weigerten, ISIL-Befehlen zu gehorchen, wurden ausgepeitscht, gefoltert oder vergewaltigt.“[153] Der gleiche Bericht behauptete auch, dass „UNAMI/OHCHR ebenfalls eine Reihe von Berichten über von ISIL wegen Homosexualität ermordeten Personen bestätigte (indem man sie von Gebäuden herunter stieß).“[154] Zudem registrierte der UN-Generalsekretär sexuelle Gewalt gegen „lesbische, homosexuelle, bisexuelle, transsexuelle und intersexuelle Menschen … als eine Form von „moralischer Säuberung"[155] und einer: „Form sozialer Kontrolle“ von Daesh in sowohl dem Irak als auch in Syrien.[156]

Abschließend ist ein weiteres wesentliches Merkmal der sexuellen Gewalt von Daesh, beschrieben vom Sonderbeauftragten des UN-Generalsekretärs, dass: „ISIL schamlos seine (sexuellen) Missbräuche veröffentlicht.“[157] Amnesty International stellte fest, dass: „mehr als jede andere Gruppe, hat er die größten Bemühungen angestellt, grausame Details der Gräueltaten zu veröffentlichen … ihnen weitreichende Resonanz über Videos und Aussagen zu verleihen, die umfangreich über die sozialen Medien, oftmals in mehreren Sprachen verbreitet wurden.“[158] Amnesty International glaubte, dass diese Methode angewandt wurde, um: „Furcht in seinen Feinden und jedem, der ihm im Weg stand, zu erzeugen."[159] Es ist möglich, dass dies umso einschüchternder ist, weil Daesh traditionelle religiöse und kulturelle Tabus herausfordert. Der UN-Generalsekretär legte nahe, dass „soziale Medien Brutalität in eine Form der Propaganda verwandelt haben, die Nachwuchs anfeuert, radikalisiert und anzieht."[160] Der Einsatz von sexueller Gewalt durch: „erzwungene Eheschließung mit ausländischen Kämpfern“ wurde im gleichen Bericht verzeichnet".[161] Es scheint, dass ein weiterer Grund für die Daesh-Strategie der sexuellen Gewalt die Ermutigung von Personen außerhalb des Iraks und von Syrien

153 United Nations, “Report on Protection of Civilians in Armed Conflict in Iraq: 1 Mai – 31 Oktober 2015,” 14.

154 Ibid., 17.

155 UN Secretary General, “Conflict-related sexual violence: Report of Secretary General,” 10/33.

156 Ibid., 2/33.

157 Bangura, “Faith in Islam & Faith in Women: Why Gender Justice is Key to Islam without Extremes”.

158 Amnesty International, “Escape from Hell: Torture and Sexual Slavery in Islamic State Captivity in Iraq,” 11.

159 Ibid.

160 UN Secretary General, “Conflict-related sexual violence: Report of Secretary General,” 25/33.

161 UN Secretary General, “Conflict-related sexual violence: Report of Secretary General,” 25/33.

anfeuert, der Gruppe beizutreten. Somit hat Daesh mit Vorbedacht die Ausübung von sexueller Gewalt gegen Frauen, Männer, Kinder, Homosexuelle und andere mitgeteilt, indem er die sozialen Medien ausnutzte, um eine globale Zielgruppe anzusprechen, mit dem dreifachen Ziel, seine Kernbotschaft durch Furcht, Anziehungskraft und Verschaffung von Schlagzeilen in den Medien voranzutreiben.

Während der Einsatz von sexueller Gewalt seitens Daesh mit den meisten der Forschungsergebnissen übereinstimmt, beinhaltet ihre Strategie außerdem: Erniedrigung von Frauen (zum Teil als ein Angriff auf westliche Wertvorstellungen), das Ausmerzen von Nicht-Heterosexuellen, sexuelle Gewalt als Finanzierungsmittel und Mittel zur externen Anwerbung und eine gezielte Informationskampagne zur sexuellen Gewalt. Daesh steht mit seiner Vorgehensweise nicht allein da, aber diese Fallstudie ließ besondere Aspekte seiner Methode erkennen.

### *Verhütende Maßnahmen gegen sexuelle Gewalt von Daesh*

Diese Studie wird nun die Wirksamkeit vorhandener verhütender Methoden auswerten, die bereits zuvor beschrieben wurden (Verständnis, Unterstützung auf hoher Ebene, Schulung und Rechtsprechung), als Mittel, um Daesh daran zu hindern, in Zukunft sexuelle Gewalt einzusetzen. Zuerst scheint eine Kenntnisnahme davon, wie und warum sexuelle Gewalt von Daesh benutzt wird, mit ausführlichen Berichten, z.B. von der UN, G7 und Amnesty International, vorhanden zu sein. Dies ist der Fall, obwohl die UN Schwierigkeiten meldete, präzise Statistiken zu erhalten,[162] aber dem wirkt scheinbar das offensichtliche Vorhaben von Daesh entgegen, ihren Einsatz sexueller Gewalt zu veröffentlichen, statt ihn zu verbergen oder zu leugnen, wie dies bei anderen Gruppen der Fall ist. Zweitens ist eine Unterstützung auf hoher Ebene vorhanden, um den von Daesh verbreiteten Gebrauch von sexueller Gewalt in Angriff zu nehmen. Zum Beispiel sagte die Nationale Sicherheitsstrategie aus, dass die PSVI besonders in Syrien und dem Irak ausgeweitet würde.[163] Ein G7-Bericht von 2015 zur Implementierung einer „G8-Erklärung" von 2013 zur PSVI schloss Details der Hilfeleistung für den Irak und Syrien ein. Zum Beispiel erstellte Großbritannien Peschmerga-Truppen Schulung zur Verfügung. Großbritannien schulte auch Menschenrechtler aus dem Irak und Syrien für Sammlung von Beweismitteln über das „Internationale Protokoll zur Dokumentierung und Untersuchung von sexueller Gewalt in Konflikten" und die USA finanzierten

162 Ibid.,18/33.

163 United Kingdom Government, *National Security Strategy and Strategic Defence and Security Review 2015: Secure and Prosperous United Kingdom*, 63.

syrische Ärzte für die gerichtsmedizinische Dokumentierung. Die Kanadier finanzierten Untersuchungen und Hilfe für Überlebende. Die Franzosen finanzierten „Gynäkologen ohne Grenzen", um syrischen Asylanten in Jordanien zu helfen. Die Deutschen finanzierten das „Berliner Zentrum für Opfer von Folter", um in sechs Bezirken im Irak Hilfe zu leisten, sowie einen irakischen Radiosender, der sich auf sexuelle Gewalt in Konflikten spezialisiert.[164] In ähnlicher Weise hat Großbritannien „Schulung von syrischen Medienaktivisten für den Einsatz des Radios finanziert, um Frauen mehr Macht zu geben und Männer zu engagieren, soziale Normen mit Hinsicht auf die Meldung von sexueller Gewalt zu ändern."[165] Der UN-Generalsekretär sagte: „Ich verdamme den Einsatz von sexueller Gewalt bei ISIL" und empfahl: „Programme, um die soziale Neuintegrierung von Frauen und Mädchen, die wieder freigelassen wurden, zu unterstützen."[166] Folglich sieht es aus, als ob Unterstützung auf hoher internationaler Ebene vorhanden ist, wie von einer Reihe von getroffenen Maßnahmen, einschließlich der Schulung von Peschmerga-Streitkräften, Menschenrechtlern, Ärzten und Medienaktivisten dargestellt wird.

Dies lässt nur die vierte verhütende Maßnahme offen, die in der Literaturauswertung untersucht wurde, nämlich die Rechtsprechung, vor allem die Aspekte von Abschreckung und Implementierung. Die Literaturauswertung bestätigte, dass: „sexuelle Gewalt gemäß internationalem Recht absolut und angemessen verboten ist".[167] Dies schien jedoch keinerlei Effekt auf die Strategie ihres Einsatzes von Daesh zu haben, was Kirbys Kritik der PSVI, bereits besprochen, unterstützt. Die Kultur der Straflosigkeit seitens Daesh scheint ungebrochen, obwohl er im internationalen Scheinwerferlicht steht und von höchster Ebene verdammt wird. Amnestie International behauptete, dass Daesh für Kriegsverbrechen und Verbrechen gegen die Menschlichkeit teilweise als Ergebnis des Ausübens von sexueller Gewalt im Irak verantwortlich ist.[168] Sie führte an, dass internationale Menschenrechte auf Daesh zutreffen und ihre zivilen und militärischen Anführer: „strafbar sind für Kriegsverbrechen", einschließlich der Maßnahmen ihrer Untergebenen durch eine Kommission,

---

164 G7, "G7 Report on the Implementation of the G8 Declaration on Preventing Sexual Violence in Conflict," 3-4, 6-7.

165 Foreign & Commonwealth Office, "Angelina Jolie Pitt joins Baroness Anelay to chart next steps on tackling sexual violence".

166 UN Secretary General, "Conflict-related sexual violence: Report of Secretary General," 19/33 & 10/33.

167 Gaggioli, "Sexual violence in armed conflicts: violation of international humanitarian law and human rights law," 505.

168 Amnesty International, "Escape from Hell: Torture and Sexual Slavery in Islamic State Captivity in Iraq," 4.

die solche Maßnahmen ausübt oder sie nicht verhütet.[169] Ein UN-Bericht, der in diesem Jahr herausgegeben wurde, stimmte zu, dass Daesh Kriegsverbrechen, Verbrechen gegen die Menschlichkeit und möglicherweise „Völkermord" verübt hatte."[170] Der UN-Oberkommissar für Menschenrechte, Zeid Ra'ad Al Hussein, sagte: „Die internationale Gemeinschaft ... sollte weiterhin die Situation im Irak beobachten, mit der Aussicht, sicherzustellen, dass die Täter grober Verletzungen und Missbrauch der Menschenrechte und ernsthafter Verletzungen des internationalen humanitären Völkerrechts zur Verantwortung gezogen werden."[171] Im gleichen Bericht drang die UN darauf, dass die Iraker Regierung ihre eigene Rechtsprechung änderte, sodass irakische Gerichtshöfe eine Gerichtsbarkeit für internationale Verbrechen haben können. Weiter hielt sie den Irak dazu an, solche Angelegenheiten sexueller Gewalt dem Internationalen Strafgerichtshof (IStGH) zu überantworten oder Teil des IStGHs[172] zu werden (was allerdings kaum geschehen wird, da der gleiche Bericht auch Anspruch darauf erhob, dass die irakischen staatlichen Streitkräfte internationale humanitäre und Menschrechte verletzt hatte).[173] Daesh scheint somit nicht von den Bemühungen der G7-Mitglieder, Beweismittel zu sammeln und zu dokumentieren, siehe oben, abgeschreckt zu werden, auch nicht von der Arbeit der Internationalen Untersuchungskommission in Syrien und dem Untersuchungsausschuss im Irak, die das Justice Rapid Response Team der Experten unterstützten.[174] Folglich scheint Daesh sich nicht beirren zu lassen, trotz aller Bemühungen. Beweismittel und glaubwürde Anklagen zu sammeln, dass Daesh sexuelle Gewalt Kriegsverbrechen, Verbrechen gegen die Menschlichkeit und möglicherweise Völkermord anwendet.

### *Schlussfolgerungen zu Daesh*

Als Schlussfolgerung dieser Auswertung von Daesh als Fallstudie stellt sich heraus, dass sie sowohl typisch als auch charakteristisch ist. Viele Gründe für den Gebrauch von sexueller Gewalt als ein Kriegsmittel spiegeln die Forschungsergebnisse wieder: eine Kultur der Straflosigkeit, das Ziel, Macht auszuüben und den Widerstand in der Gemeinschaft zu neutralisieren, und Teil einer geplanten militärischen Strategie, um Land zu erobern. Sexuelle Gewalt

169 Ibid., 15.

170 United Nations, "Report on Protection of Civilians in Armed Conflict in Iraq: 1 Mai – 31 Oktober 2015," i.

171 Ibid., start of report (no page number).

172 Ibid., ii.

173 Ibid.

174 G7, "G7 Report on the Implementation of the G8 Declaration on Preventing Sexual Violence in Conflict," 7.

scheint sich hauptsächlich gegen Frauen und Mädchen gerichtet zu haben, vor allem bei religiösen und ethnischen Minoritäten. Es wurde jedoch auch sexuelle Gewalt gegen Männer und Jungen eingesetzt, um Informationen zu erzwingen und Widerstand zu brechen. Sie wurde in als besonders gefährdet bekannten Zonen verübt, zum Beispiel in Internierungs- und Sammellagern und an Kontrollstellen in Grenzgebieten. Andere Elemente, die die Forschungsergebnisse bestätigen, schließen die Scham ein, die die überlebenden Opfer empfinden und die bei der Leistung von Hilfe und dem Sammeln zuverlässiger Daten eine noch größere Herausforderung bedeutet. Amnesty International betonte die Anzahl von Jesiden-Familien, die leugnen, dass ihre eigenen Verwandten sexueller Gewalt ausgesetzt waren, aber darauf bestanden, dass sie systematisch gegen Mitglieder ihrer Gesellschaft verübt wurde.[175] Amnesty International beschrieb außerdem, die Schwierigkeiten für überlebende Opfer, aufgrund mangelnder Aufklärung, der geografischen Distanzen, Kosten und der Transport zu den Hilfeleistungsstellen medizinische und psychologische Hilfe zu erhalten,[176] – wiederum hat die Literaturauswertung solche Probleme als Teil der vielen Herausforderungen bei der Nachsorge der Nachwirkungen identifiziert.

Die Literaturauswertung betonte, dass jeder Konflikt anders ist, weshalb Verhütungsmethoden eine genaue Beurteilung des Kontexts und der angemessenen Reaktion erfordern. Die Strategie von Daesh, ihren Einsatz von sexueller Gewalt über die neuesten Kommunikationskanäle zu veröffentlichen, dient drei Zielen: Menschen im Irak und in Syrien Daesh unterzuordnen, Nachwuchs anzuwerben und sicherzustellen, dass ihre allgemeine Botschaft, ein islamisches Kalifat einzurichten, in aller Welt verkündet wird. Daesh scheint als Kernstück ihrer militärischen Kampagne einen Informationsbetrieb zu haben, und sexuelle Gewalt ist eine der wichtigsten Wiedergaben, um diese Botschaft zu verstärken. Andere Eigenschaften, die sich von den Hauptforschungsergebnissen unterscheiden, schließen eine ideologische und finanzielle Strategie für den Einsatz von sexueller Gewalt ein, um den Status von Frauen zu reduzieren und sie in eine Ware zu verwandeln, um seine Kriegsanstrengungen zu finanzieren. Er benutzt sexuelle Gewalt auch, um Nicht-Heterosexuelle zu eliminieren, was in der Literatur nur begrenzt erwähnt wurde.

Mit Hinsicht auf die aktuellen Präventionsmethoden, die in der Literatur identifiziert wurden, bestätigt die Daesh-Fallstudie die meisten Forschungsergebnisse. Es scheint ein gutes Verständnis seitens der UN, G7 und Amnesty

175 Amnesty International, "Escape from Hell: Torture and Sexual Slavery in Islamic State Captivity in Iraq," 13-14.

176 Ebd., 13.

International zu geben, warum und wie Daesh sexuelle Gewalt anwendet, mit Akademikern wie Wood, die bereits ihre Methoden untersuchen. Weiter besteht internationale Unterstützung auf höchster Ebene, einschließlich des UN-Generalsekretärs, seinem Sonderbeauftragten für sexuelle Gewalt in Konflikten und dem Oberkommissar für Menschenrechte der UN, sowie auch die G7-Mitglieder. Wie auch bei den Forschungsergebnissen, spiegelt diese internationale Unterstützung eine westliche Tendenz wieder und es wäre sehr nützlich, wenn sich andere Organisationen um das Problem kümmern würden, wie die Arab League und Gulf Cooperation Council. Trotzdem hat der Support auf hoher Ebene Ressourcen gefunden, die eine Reihe von Maßnahmen unterstützen, einschließlich der Schulung von Peschmerga-Streitkräften, Menschenrechtlern, Ärzten und Medienaktivisten. Doch der vierte Handlungsstrang vorhandener Präventionsstrategien – Abschreckung durch Gesetzgebung – scheint äußerst unzulänglich zu sein. Und dies trotz der Versuche der UN und von Amnesty International, Beweismittel und glaubhafte Anklagen zu sammeln, dass die von Daesh ausgeübte sexuelle Gewalt sich auf Kriegsverbrechen, Verbrechen gegen die Menschlichkeit und möglichem Völkermord beläuft. Daesh lässt sich nicht abschrecken.

Es gibt wenig andere Verhütungsmaßnahmen, die gegen den Einsatz von sexueller Gewalt als Kriegsmittel seitens Daesh getroffen werden. Journalisten haben sich ernsthaft bemüht, über die Aktivitäten von Daesh zu berichten – oftmals aufgrund der Bemühungen von Aktivisten der Gemeinschaft und gelegentlich von Familienmitgliedern. Vielleicht hat dies als ungewollte Konsequenz sich als ein negativer Druck auf überlebende Opfer ausgewirkt, mit der Presse zu sprechen. Aufgrund dessen rief Amnesty International für eine verantwortlichere Presse und für lokale Wortführer und Aktivisten zu größerer Rücksichtnahme auf.[177] Doch es ist weiterhin wichtig, dass die internationalen Medien engagiert bleiben, sodass die Aktivitäten sexueller Gewalt nicht vor den Weltpolitikern verborgen bleiben, die alle zukünftigen Verhütungsstrategien durchboxen müssen. Ein weiterer Aspekt ist die Rolle des geistigen Oberhauptes der Jesiden, Baba Sheikh, der im Februar 2015 öffentlich seine Gemeinschaft aufforderte, jesidische Frauen, die vor Daesh geflohen waren, zu unterstützen.[178] Obwohl dies vor allem darauf zielte, überlebenden Opfern bei der Neuintegration zu helfen, diente es auch der Herausforderung der Daesh-Politik, Frauen zu erniedrigen. Aber solche Botschaften müssen immer wieder regelmäßig von den geistigen und weltlichen Oberhäuptern erteilt werden, um

177 Ibid., 17.

178 Bangura, "Faith in Islam & Faith in Women: Why Gender Justice is Key to Islam without Extremes".

den festgeschalteten Kommunikationen von Daesh entgegen zu treten. Obgleich es noch zu früh ist, zu wissen, ob diese präventiven Maßnahmen irgendeine Wirkung haben, wird nahegelegt, dass andere verhütende Maßnahmen erforderlich sind, wenn Daesh weiterhin auf seiner Strategie der sexuellen Gewalt besteht. Dies scheint besonders dringend zu sein, wenn man sich die mangelnde Wirkung der in der Literatur beschriebenen vorhandenen präventiven Methoden ansieht, die zwar gegen Daesh eingesetzt sind, aber scheinbar bislang erfolglos bleiben.

## Zusätzliche verhütende Maßnahmen

Die Forschungsarbeit der Akademiker und Fachleute boten nur wenige praktische verhütende Maßnahmen, abgesehen von den in dieser Studie beschriebenen, mit den Grenzen dieser vorhandenen Methoden, die in der gerade untersuchten Fallstudie von Daesh identifiziert wurden. Dieser letzte Abschnitt wird deshalb kurz mögliche zusätzliche präventive Werkzeuge betrachten. Es ist keine vollständige Liste, sondern sie konzentriert sich darauf: von Gruppen zu lernen, die sich geweigert haben, sexuelle Gewalt einzusetzen, die Rolle der Akteure der zivilen Gesellschaft und Soft Power (Kultur und Ideologie), den Einsatz von Recherchen in anderen militärischen Bereichen und die Ausnutzung der Fähigkeiten der sozialen Medien.

Zuerst einmal trat das IKRK dafür ein, das es wichtig war, von solchen Truppen zu lernen, die keine sexuelle Gewalt in Konflikten angewandt hatten.[179] Bei der Untersuchung individueller Fälle merkte Wood an: „Die militärischen Anführer können sexuelle Gewalt aus strategischen, normativen oder praktischen Gründen verbieten."[180] Wood identifizierte die hauptsächlichen Gründe für das Verbot sexueller Gewalt wie folgt: Vermeidung des Kontrollverlusts über Untergeordnete, Beibehaltung der moralischen Überlegenheit, Finanzierung und Ressourcen von anderen Quellen und ebenso den Frieden, wie auch den Krieg gewinnen, um in Zukunft an die Macht zu kommen.[181] Es ist möglich, dass solche Argumente bewaffnete Truppen überreden, sexuelle Gewalt zu vermeiden oder nicht länger auszuüben, indem die militärstrategischen Vorteile auf einsatzbereiter Ebene betont werden, die andere bewaffneten Truppen bereits erkannt haben. Eine angepasste Kombinationen von Ansporn

179 ICRC, "Sexual Violence in Armed Conflict: E-Briefing," Part 4.

180 Wood, "Rape is not inevitable during war," in Kuehnast et al., eds., *Women and War Power & Protection in Twenty-First Century*, 54.

181 Ebd. 54-55.

und Strafmaßnahmen, die ein gründliches Verständnis der militärischen Hierarchie, Akteure, Kultur und Methoden der Gewalt voraussetzen, könnten helfen, sexuelle Gewalt von dieser Truppe auszuschließen, besonders wenn die Vorteile von denen beschrieben werden, die bereits den Einsatz von sexueller Gewalt in ihren eigenen bewaffneten Kämpfen aufgegeben hatten.

Abgesehen von dem Einsatz glaubwürdiger militärischer Anführer, um positive Ergebnisse zu erhalten, könnte die Rolle der Zivilisten besser benutzt werden. Mit Fokussierung auf positive männliche Vorbilder (obgleich dies auch auf weibliche Vorbilder zutreffen könnte), betonten MenEngage Alliance und UNFPA, dass Dienstleister: „eine wichtige Rolle ... der Neubildung sozialer Normen" spielen könnten – nicht nur im Rahmen ihrer professionellen Rollen, sondern aufgrund ihres Status innerhalb dieser Gesellschaft.[182] In Hagues Zusammenfassung des Gipfeltreffens von 2014 bestätigte er die Rolle von religiösen Gruppen: „Durch ihre Netze haben sie oft Zugang zu und Einfluss auf lokale Gemeinschaften, wie sonst kein Akteur. Von daher befinden sie sich in einer einmaligen Position, Herzen und Sinne zu ändern."[183] Frauen- und Männerorganisationen können weitere Ressourcen anbieten, um ihre Bemühungen innerhalb ihrer eigenen Gesellschaft zu unterstützen. Der Gebrauch von „Soft Power" von Organisationen wie British Council, UN und NGOs, sowie auch einzelner Aktivisten, ist schon lange populär. Allerdings wurden nur wenige Beispiele innerhalb der Literatur mit Hinsicht auf praktische Maßnahmen, um sexuelle Gewalt zu verhüten, angegeben. Wood legte nahe, dass Lektionen von anderen Kampagnen identifiziert werden sollten, z.B. solche, die „Blutdiamanten", Kindersoldaten und Landminen blockieren, und sollten angewendet werden, um sexuelle Gewalt in Konflikten zu verhüten.[184] Eine jüngste Auswertung vom House of Lords zu diesem Thema beschloss: „Es spricht dringend dafür, dass Programme, die Verhalten und Einstellungen ändern, bei der Verhütung von sexueller Gewalt in Konflikten helfen können."[185]

Mit Bezug auf andere Spezialgebiete, stellten Steffens et al. Recherchen an, wie sich Gefolgschaft mit bestimmten Anführern identifiziert und die Wichtigkeit geteilter sozialer Identitäten, um Gruppenverhalten zu ermöglichen.[186]

---

182 MenEngage Alliance and UNFPA, "Sexual Violence in Conflict and Post-Conflict: Engaging Men and Boys," 7.

183 FCO, "Chair's Summary: Global Summit to End Sexual Violence in Conflict."

184 Wood, "Conflict-related sexual violence and the policy implications of recent research," 476.

185 House of Lords, "Select Committee on Sexual Violence in Conflict: Report of Session 2015-16: Sexual Violence in Conflict: A War Crime," 8.

186 Niklas K. Steffens, S. Alexander Haslam, and Stephen D. Reicher, "Up close and personal: Evidence that shared social identity is a basis for the 'special' relationship that binds followers to leaders," *The Leadership Quarterly* 25 (2015).

Andere Akademiker haben diese Faktoren vor dem Hintergrund militärischer Gruppenverhalten untersucht.[187] Im Gegensatz dazu untersuchte eine andere Forschungsgruppe, weshalb Gruppen Massenmord begehen, wie z.B. während des Holocaust. Haslam und Reicher, zum Beispiel, legten nahe: „dass Gruppen die einzelnen Personen, die ihnen beitreten, *umformen*, indem sie die Gesinnungen ihrer Mitglieder ändern."[188]

Zudem fragte sich Wood, ob Forschungsergebnisse bezüglich Vergewaltigung in Campus-Universtäten, Jugendgruppen, Sportvereinen und Gefängnissen für sexuelle Gewalt in Konflikten verwendet werden können.[189] Weiter überlegte sie, dass: „die Dynamik kleiner Gruppen, die zu Einheitsnormen führt, die das Vorkommen von sexueller Gewalt fördert oder behindert, ein vielversprechender Forschungszweig zu sein scheint."[190] Deshalb könnten weitere Recherchen zu der Wirkung von Anführern und Gruppen auf Verhalten zu zusätzlichen präventiven Maßnahmen für die Zukunft führen. Besonders ist es das Anzielen von Anführern, die ihre Mitglieder am meisten ansprechen, und so die soziale Identität einer Gruppe und den Zusammenhalt militärischer Gruppen ausnutzen, als eine Art, Verhaltensnormen zu ändern.

Zum Schluss ist das Potenzial der sozialen Medien zu berücksichtigen. Bis 2020 sollen global 70% der Menschen Eigentümer von Smartphones sein, die Großzahl von ihnen in den Entwicklungsländern.[191] Die Analyse öffentlicher Quellen, wie Websites sozialer Medien, wird bereits benutzt, um Krisen zu erkennen und rapide Übersicht über Situationen zu gewinnen. Zum Beispiel vereinigten Laienjournalisten wie das 'Bell¿ngcat'-Team, Websites sozialer Medien, um zu verstehen, was in der ukrainischen Konfliktzone geschehen war.[192] Die Einführung von Smartphones in einigen unserer entferntesten und

187 Guy, L. Siebold, "The Essence of Military Group Cohesion," *Armed Forces & Society* 33(2) (2007): 286-295 and Anthony King, "The Existence of Group Cohesion in the Armed Forces: A Response to Guy Siebold," *Armed Forces & Society* 33(4) (2007): 638-645.

188 S.A. Haslam, and S. Reicher, "Beyond the banality of evil: three dynamics of an interactionist social psychology of terrorism," *Personality and Social Psychology Bulletin*, 33(5) (2007): 620.

189 Wood, "Conflict-related sexual violence and the policy implications of recent research," 478.

190 Wood, "Sexual violence during war: toward an understanding of variation," in: *Order, Conflict and Violence*, eds. Stathis N. Kalyvas, Ian Shapiro and Tarek Masoud (New York and Cambridge: Cambridge University Press, 2008), 347.

191 The Mobile Economy 2015), <http://gsmamobileeconomy.com/global/> (Zugriff: den 12. Mai 2016), 2.

192 Bell¿ngcat, "Confirming the Location of the Same Msta-S in Russia and Ukraine," Bell¿ngcat Mai 2015), <https://www.bellingcat.com/resources/case-studies/2015/05/29/confirming-the-location-of-the-same-msta-s-in-russia-and-ukraine/> (Zugriff: den 12. Mai 2016).

konfliktgefährdesten Regionen der Welt in den nächsten vier/fünf Jahren könnte sich umgestaltend auswirken, wenn es darum geht, traditionell versteckt gehaltene Verbrechen zu verhüten. Die Kultur der Straflosigkeit, die wir zuvor in der Literaturauswertung als einen der Hauptgründe für den Einsatz von sexueller Gewalt in Konflikten besprochen haben, könnte unterminiert werden, falls „störende Technologien“ wie soziale Medien ausgenutzt werden, um situationsbedingte Erkenntnis und Frühwarnung zu erstellen. Wo es nicht möglich ist, sexuelle Gewalt zu verhüten, könnten die sozialen Medien zur Erstellung von Daten über ihre Ausbreitung erstellen, um eine militärische/polizeiliche Reaktion zu erhalten, um medizinische Hilfe zu leisten und, möglicherweise, beim Sammeln von Beweismittel zu unterstützen.

Dies schließt die Übersicht möglicher zusätzlicher verhütender Maßnahmen ab und deckt: die Anwendung von Lektionen von solchen Gruppen, die gewählt haben, keine sexuelle Gewalt zu anzuwenden, die Rolle der Zivilisten und Soft Power, der Einfluss von Anführern und Gruppen und sozialen Medien. Sie versuchte zu betonen, dass es Raum für Akademiker und Fachleute gibt, um sexuelle Gewalt in Konflikten zu verhüten, mit ihren Kollegen in anderen Bereichen zusammenzuarbeiten, um alternative Präventionsmittel in Betracht zu ziehen. Es scheint unwahrscheinlich, dass irgendeine einzelne Maßnahme den Einsatz von sexueller Gewalt im Krieg verhüten könnte, aber eine angepasste Kombination präventiver Maßnahmen könnte adoptiert werden, die den Kontext und die Besonderheiten eines jeden bewaffneten Konflikts mitberücksichtigt.

## Konklusion

Zum Abschluss untersuchte diese Studie, ob es möglich ist, sexuelle Gewalt als ein Kriegsmittel gegen Frauen, Männer und Kinder zu verhüten oder ob nur die Nachwirkungen behandelt werden können. Diese Literaturauswertung analysierte fünf Aspekte dieses Themas: die Gründe dafür, sexuelle Gewalt in Konflikten anzuwenden, wie Männer und Jungen zu Opfern und Frauen zu Täterinnen werden können, die vielfältigen Herausforderungen der Nachsorge, die Risiken der Versicherheitlichung des Problems und den Fortschritt der Rolle von Frauen in Frieden und Sicherheit zunichte zu machen, sowie die Beweismittel, dass der Einsatz sexueller Gewalt in Konflikten nicht unabwendbar ist. Vier vorhandene Verhütungsmethoden wurden ausgewertet: Verständnis, Unterstützung auf hoher Ebene, Schulung und Rechtsprechung. Diese Untersuchung kam zu dem Schluss, dass sie eine solide Grundlage erstellen, auf die man aufbauen kann, aber dass Verbesserungen notwendig sind, die langfristige finanzielle Unterstützung und nachhaltige Bemühungen erfordern. Der spezielle Fall von Daesh wurde im Lichte dieser Forschungsergebnisse untersucht. Diese Studie legte nahe, dass der Einsatz sexueller Gewalt seitens Daesh vieles von ihnen belegte, aber dass es auch besondere Elemente gab, vor allem ihre Strategie, den Einsatz sexueller Gewalt über die sozialen Medien zu veröffentlichen. Die Daesh-Fallstudie stellte den Mangel aktueller Verhütungsmethoden dar (vor allem die mangelnde Abschreckung durch rechtliche Mittel) und eine dringende Notwendigkeit, andere Methoden zu identifizieren. Folglich wurden alternative verhütende Maßnahmen in Betracht gezogen, die zu dem Schluss kamen, dass eine breitere und einfallsreiche Methode der Verhütung in Verbindung mit Experten in anderen Bereichen Ergebnisse erreichen könnte. Letztlich erfordern die Aufgaben zur Prävention sexueller Gewalt als ein Kriegsmittel, die Nachsorge und der Umgang mit der allgemeinen Auswirkung, alle geeigneten Maßnahmen voll nutzbar zu machen.

Diese Studie versuchte nachzuweisen, dass es möglich ist, sexuelle Gewalt als ein Kriegsmittel zu verhindern. Allerding betonte sie, dass die Herausforderung, sexuelle Gewalt systematisch und umfassend zu verhüten, sehr stark ist. Die Forschungsergebnisse und das Beispiel von Daesh wiesen auf, dass die aktuellen Präventionsstrategien verbessert und dass zusätzliche Maßnahmen getroffen werden müssen. Die Ergebnisse legten nahe, dass ein Bedarf für eine koordinierte und geradlinige Methode erforderlich ist, die das Gesundheitswesen, polizeiliche und gesetzliche Experten auf lokaler Ebene mit zusätzlicher Unterstützung einbeziehen und die nachhaltig langfristig erhalten bleiben müssen. Im Besonderen benötigt jeder Krieg ein tiefschürfendes Verständnis des Kontexts, der Akteure und Methoden, um eine angepasste, zulänglich finanzierte und gestaffelte Reaktion zu sichern, die die verschiedenen Bedürfnisse von Frauen, Männern und Kindern berücksichtigt.

Außerdem legten die Forschungsergebnisse offen, dass der Umgang mit der Nachsorge ein riesiges Unterfangen ist, das sofortige und langfristige physische und psychologische Behandlung der einzelnen Personen verlangt. Die Nachwirkungen auf Gesellschaften müssen ebenfalls angesprochen werden, um die Ausbreitung von Geschlechtskrankheiten zu reduzieren, vor Racheakten zu schützen und den Zusammenhalt von Gemeinschaften wieder aufzubauen. Irgendwie muss der Zyklus der sexuellen Gewalt gebrochen werden. Frauen und Männer – Täter, Opfer und Zeugen – müssen wieder integriert und Kinder, die als Produkt sexueller Gewalt geboren werden, müssen von der Gesellschaft akzeptiert werden. Überlebende Opfer brauchen Beachtung. Diejenigen, die sexuelle Gewalt angewandt haben sind zur Rechenschaft zu ziehen – ordentlich und schnell. Die Kosten langfristiger medizinischer Behandlung, rechtlicher Prozesse, Bildung und Neuaufbau sind unabsehbar und wahrscheinlich von nicht von Kriegen zerrissenen Ländern zu erstellen. Aber die effektive Nachsorge würde zur Verhütung zukünftiger sexueller Gewalt in Konflikten beitragen, indem sie helfen, den Zyklus der Gewalt zu brechen.

Sollte die Herausforderung der Prävention unüberwindbar scheinen, sollte man sich den Nachweis, dass sexuelle Gewalt als ein Kriegsmittel nicht unabwendbar ist, ins Gedächtnis rufen. Es ist eine Wahl, kein Zufall, wie von den Recherchen und Erfahrungen des IKRKs hervorgehoben wird:

> Es ist nicht länger vertretbar, zu behaupten, dass sexuelle Gewalt einfach eine hässliche Tatsache unserer schlimmsten menschlichen Neigungen darstellt und eine unvermeidliche Folge des Krieges ist. Heute wird weitgehend bestätigt, dass sexuelle Gewalt nicht eine unabwendbare Konsequenz des bewaffneten Konflikts ist. Dies macht Präventionsbemühungen kritisch, legitim und dringend erforderlich.[193]

Gloria Steinem fügte an: „die wichtigste Eigenschaft der Menschen – die, die es unserer Gattung ermöglicht, zu überleben – ist, das wir anpassungsfähig sind."[194] Es ist auch bemerkenswert, dass unsere Vorgänger das „Unmögliche“ in früheren Kriegen erreicht haben: zum Beispiel, die Ausgrenzung des Einsatzes von Kindersoldaten, Streumunition und Landminen. Obwohl diese Kriegsmittel noch existieren, muss man hoffen, dass sie, sowie auch sexuelle Gewalt im Laufe der Zeit aus den Kriegsstrategien verschwinden. Kerry erkannte: „wir haben das Gewissenlose bereits zuvor verbannt ... sexuelle Gewalt ist ein gräuliches Verbrechen gegen die Menschlichkeit. Es ist nicht nur ein entschuldbares, unabwendbares Nebenprodukt des Krieges."[195] Zum Abschluss ist zu sagen, dass die Verhütung von sexueller Gewalt als ein Kriegsmittel äußerst schwierig ist – und die Herausforderung dieses Unterfangens ist nicht zu unterschätzen. Allerdings legt die Abwesenheit von sexueller Gewalt in vielen Konflikten nahe, dass es möglich ist, sie systematisch zu verhüten. Es erfordert eine resolute Bemühung, vielleicht über Generationen hinweg, aber es scheint, dass mit verbessertem Verständnis, internationaler Befürwortung auf hoher Ebene und Maßnahmen, Schulung und Rechtsprechung, positive Entwicklungen im Gange sind:

193 ICRC, "Sexual Violence in Armed Conflict: E-Briefing," Part 4.

194 Lauren Wolfe, "Gloria Steinem on Rape in War, Its Causes, and How to Stop It," The Atlantic 8. Februar, 2012), <http://www.theatlantic.com/international/archive/2012/02/gloria-steinem-on-rape-in-war-its-causes-and-how-to-stop-it/252470/> (Zugriff: den 18. Januar, 2016).

195 Kerry, "Remarks at Global Summit to End Sexual Violence in Conflict".

Wir sind entschlossen, den Gebrauch von Vergewaltigung und sexueller Gewalt in Konflikten in aller Welt zu beenden ... die Verhütung von sexueller Gewalt in Konflikten ist kritisch für den Frieden, die Sicherheit und nachhaltige Entwicklung ... Jede einzelne Person hat eine moralische Verantwortung, dagegen ihre Stimme zu erheben ... um eine Änderung zu fordern, wie die Welt diese Verbrechen wahr nimmt und wie sie darauf reagiert.[196]

## Bibliographie

Arieff, Alexis. "Sexual Violence in African Conflicts." *Congressional Research Service.* (November 2009). <http://web.a.ebscohost.com/ehost/pdfviewer/pdfviewer?sid=e00a61c4-d061-425e-9d6f-dac6e949281e%40sessionmgr4004&vid=15&hid=4212> (accessed May 17, 2016).

Al Achi, Dalia. "*Human Rights Day: Abuses rife in Central African Republic.*" UNHCR. (December 2015). <http://www.unhcr.org/5669a3a66.html> (accessed January 6, 2016).

Alcorn, Ted. "Responding to sexual violence in armed conflict." *The Lancet* Volume 383, No. 9934 2014): 2034-2037. <http://www.thelancet.com/journals/lancet/article/PIIS0140-6736(14)60970-3/fulltext> (accessed January 18, 2016).

Amnesty International. "Escape from Hell: Torture and Sexual Slavery in Islamic State Captivity in Iraq." Amnesty International. MDE 14/021/2014. (December 2014). <http://www.amnesty.org.uk/sites/default/files/escape_from_hell_-_torture_and_sexual_slavery_in_islamic_state_captivity_in_iraq_-_english_2.pdf> (accessed January 7, 2016).

Baaz, Maria Eriksson, and Maria Stern. *Sexual Violence as a Weapon of War? Perceptions, Prescriptions, Problems in the Congo and Beyond.* London: Zed Books Ltd, 2013. eBook Collection. <http://web.a.ebscohost.com/ehost/ebookviewer/ebook/bmxlYmtfXzU3NzU1OF9fQU41?sid=e00a61c4-d061-425e-9d6f-dac6e949281e@sessionmgr4004&vid=73&format=EK&rid=2> (accessed May 18, 2016).

Baker, Aryn. "War and Rape." *Time* 187, no. 14 (2016): 36-41. <http://web.a.ebscohost.com/ehost/pdfviewer/pdfviewer?sid=0e34b8af-4d52-4955-9dfa-eb6e4e3bae87%40sessionmgr4004&vid=20&hid=4107> (accessed May 23, 2016).

Bangura, Zainab. "Faith in Islam & Faith in Women: Why Gender Justice is Key to an Islam Without Extremes." International Crisis Group. (October 2015). <https://medium.com/the-future-of-conflict/faith-in-islam-faith-in-women-why-gender-

196 Foreign & Commonwealth Office, "Statement of Action - Global Summit to End Sexual Violence in Conflict".

justice-is-key-to-an-islam-without-extremes-8920277ef674#.dkjeo08jg> (accessed January 6, 2016).

Bell¿ngcat. “Confirming the Location of the Same Msta-S in Russia and Ukraine.” Bell¿ngcat. (May 2015). <https://www.bellingcat.com/resources/case-studies/2015/05/29/confirming-the-location-of-the-same-msta-s-in-russia-and-ukraine/> (accessed May 12, 2016).

Bernard, Vincent, and Durham, Helen. “Sexual violence in armed conflict: From breaking the silence to breaking the cycle.” *International Review of the Red Cross* 96(894) (2014): 427-434. <doi:10.1017/S1816383115000442> (accessed January 11, 2016).

Bernard, Vincent, and Elvina Pothelet. “Through the eyes of a detention doctor: Interview with Raed Aburabi.” *International Review of the Red Cross* 96(894) (2014): 479-484. <doi:10.1017/S1816383115000284> (accessed January 11, 2016).

Bouvier, Paul. “Sexual violence, health and humanitarian ethics: Towards a holistic, person-centred approach.” *International Review of the Red Cross* 96(894) (2014): 565-584. <doi:10.1017/S1816383115000430> (accessed January 11, 2016).

Buckingham, Becks. “Rape and Sexual Violence: a Weapon of War?” Defence Research Paper, JSCSC, 2012.

Cannon, Patrick. “A Feminist Response to Rape as a Weapon of War in Eastern Congo.” *Peace Review* 24, no. 4 (2012): 478-483. <http://web.a.ebscohost.com/ehost/pdfviewer/pdfviewer?sid=0e34b8af-4d52-4955-9dfa-eb6e4e3bae87%40sessionmgr4004&vid=30&hid=4107> (accessed May 23, 2016).

Carpenter, R. Charli. “Recognizing Gender-Based Violence Against Civilian Men and Boys in Conflict Situations.” *Security Dialogue* 37(1) (2006): 83-103. <http://sdi.sagepub.com/content/37/1/83.full.pdf+html> (accessed May 19, 2016).

Carvajal, Doreen. “A Female Approach to Peacekeeping.” New York Times. (March 5, 2010). <http://www.nytimes.com/2010/03/06/world/africa/06iht-ffpeace.html?_r=0> (accessed January 7, 2016).

Cohen, Dara Kay. “Female Combatants and the Perpetration of Violence: Wartime Rape in the Sierra Leone Civil War.” *World Politics* 65, no. 3 (2013): 383-415. <doi:10.1017/S0043887113000105> (accessed May 18, 2016).

Dammers, Tom. *“Paper commissioned for the EFA Global Monitoring Report 2011, The hidden crisis: Armed conflict and education”.* United Nations Educational, Scientific and Cultural Organization. 2011/ED/EFA/MRT/PI/15. (2010). <http://unesdoc.unesco.org/images/0019/001907/190705e.pdf> (accessed May 23, 2016).

Davies, Mathew. “Women and Development, Not Gender and Politics: Explaining ASEAN’s Failure to engage with the Women, Peace and Security agenda.” *Contemporary Southeast Asia: A Journal of International & Strategic Affairs* 38, no. 1 (2016): 106-127. <http://web.a.ebscohost.com/ehost/pdfviewer/pdfviewer?vid=36&sid=0e34b8af-4d52-4955-9dfa-eb6e4e3bae87%40sessionmgr4004&hid=4107> (accessed May 23, 2016).

de Jonge Oudraat, Chantal. "UNSCR 1325 – Conundrums and Opportunities." *International Interactions* 39, no. 4 (2013): 612-619. <http://web.a.ebscohost.com/ehost/pdfviewer/pdfviewer?sid=0e34b8af-4d52-4955-9dfa-eb6e4e3bae87%40sessionmgr4004&vid=48&hid=4107> (accessed May 23, 2016).

Dolan, Chris. "Letting go of the gender binary: Charting new pathways for humanitarian interventions on gender-based violence." *International Review of the Red Cross* 96(894) (2014): 485-501. <doi:10.1017/S1816383115000120> (accessed January 10, 2016).

Dolan, Chris. "Into the Mainstream: Addressing Sexual Violence against Men and Boys in Conflict." Briefing Paper prepared for the Overseas Development Institute. (2014) <https://www.warchild.org.uk/sites/default/files/Into-the-Mainstream.pdf> (accessed May 23, 2016).

Duroch, Françoise, and Catrin Schulte-Hillen. "Care for victims of sexual violence, an organization pushed to its limits: The case of Médecins Sans Frontières." *International Review of the Red Cross*, 96(894) (2014): 601-624. <doi:10.1017/S1816383115000107> (accessed January 11, 2016).

Edström Jerker, Alexa Hassink, Thea Shahrokh, and Erin Stern, eds. "Engendering Men: A Collaborative Review of Evidence of Men and Boys in Social Change and Gender Equality." EMERGE Evidence Review, Promundo-US, Sonke Gender Justice and the Institute of Development Studies. (September 2015). <http://opendocs.ids.ac.uk/opendocs/bitstream/handle/123456789/7059/EMERGE.pdf?sequence=1> (accessed January 22, 2016).

Ensler, Eve. "Bureau of Sex Slavery: for Yanar and my sisters in Iraq and Syria." *Nation* 301, no. 17 (2015): 4-6. <http://web.a.ebscohost.com/ehost/pdfviewer/pdfviewer?sid=e00a61c4-d061-425e-9d6f-dac6e949281e%40sessionmgr4004&vid=97&hid=4212> (accessed May 19, 2016).

Feeley, Rebecca, and Colin Thomas-Jensen. "Getting Serious about Ending Conflict and Sexual Violence in Congo." ENOUGH Strategy Paper #15. (2008). <http://www.enoughproject.org/files/CongoSerious.pdf> (accessed May 23, 2016).

Foreign & Commonwealth Office. "Foreign Secretary launches new Government initiative to prevent sexual violence in conflict." Foreign & Commonwealth Office. (May 2012).<https://www.gov.uk/government/speeches/foreign-secretary-launches-new-government-initiative-to-prevent-sexual-violence-in-conflict> (accessed March 21, 2016).

Foreign & Commonwealth Office. "The Foreign Secretary William Hague, Angelina Jolie and Zainab Hawa Bangura launch G8 Declaration on Preventing Sexual Violence in Conflict." Foreign & Commonwealth Office. (April 2013). <https://www.gov.uk/government/news/g8-declaration-on-preventing-sexual-violence-in-conflict> (accessed November 27, 2015).

Foreign & Commonwealth Office. "Declaration on Preventing Sexual Violence in Conflict." Foreign & Commonwealth Office. (April 2013). <https://www.gov.uk/gov-

ernment/uploads/system/uploads/attachment_data/file/185008/G8_PSVI_Declaration_-_FINAL.pdf> (accessed November 27, 2015).

Foreign & Commonwealth Office. "Statement of Action - Global Summit to End Sexual Violence in Conflict." Foreign & Commonwealth Office. (June 2014). <https://www.gov.uk/government/publications/statement-of-action-global-summit-to-end-sexual-violence-in-conflict> (accessed November 26, 2015).

Foreign & Commonwealth Office. "Chair's Summary - Global Summit to End Sexual Violence in Conflict." Foreign & Commonwealth Office. (June 2014). <https://www.gov.uk/government/publications/chairs-summary-global-summit-to-end-sexual-violence-in-conflict/chairs-summary-global-summit-to-end-sexual-violence-in-conflict> (accessed November 27, 2015).

Foreign & Commonwealth Office. "Angelina Jolie Pitt joins Baroness Anelay to chart next steps on tackling sexual violence." Foreign & Commonwealth Office. (June 2015). <https://www.gov.uk/government/news/angelina-jolie-pitt-joins-baroness-anelay-to-chart-next-steps-on-tackling-sexual-violence> (accessed January 12, 2016).

G7. "G7 Report on the Implementation of the G8 Declaration on Preventing Sexual Violence in Conflict." G7. (November 2015). <https://www.g7germany.de/Content/EN/_Anlagen/G7/2015-11-24-g7-erklaerung_svc_en.pdf?__blob=publicationFile&v=3> (accessed January 7, 2016).

G7. "G7 Foreign Ministers Meeting: Joint Communique." G7. (April 2016). <http://www.mofa.go.jp/files/000147440.pdf> (accessed May 13, 2016).

Gaggioli, Gloria. "Sexual violence in armed conflicts: A violation of international humanitarian law and human rights law." *International Review of the Red Cross* 96(894) (2014): 503-538. <doi:10.1017/S1816383115000211> (accessed January 11, 2016).

Geneva Call. <http://www.genevacall.org/> (accessed January 21, 2016).

Gingerich, Tara, and Jennifer Leaning. "The Use of Rape as a Weapon of War in the Conflict in Darfur, Sudan." 2004. <http://reliefweb.int/sites/reliefweb.int/files/resources/B119C9EFB7DCAA2DC1256F5F004FBEA9-hu-sud-31oct.pdf> (accessed May 25, 2016).

Global Peace Operations Review. "Female Participation in UN Peace Operations." <http://peaceoperationsreview.org/featured-data/> (accessed January 12, 2016).

Haslam, S.A., and S. Reicher. "Beyond the banality of evil: three dynamics of an interactionist social psychology of terrorism." *Personality and Social Psychology Bulletin*, 33(5) (2007): 615-622.

Henry, Marsha. "Ten Reasons Not to Write Your Master's Dissertation on Sexual Violence in War." *The Disorder of Things*. (June 4, 2013). <http://thedisorderofthings.com/2013/06/04/ten-reasons-not-to-write-your-masters-dissertation-on-sexual-violence-in-war/> (accessed January 21 2016).

House of Lords. "Select Committee on Sexual Violence in Conflict: Report of Session 2015-16: Sexual Violence in Conflict: A War Crime." House of Lords. HL Paper 123. (April 12, 2016). <http://www.publications.parliament.uk/pa/ld201516/ldselect/ldsvc/123/123.pdf> (accessed April 15, 2016).

Human Rights Watch. "Rwanda: International Tribunal Closing Its Doors." HRW. (December 2015). <https://www.hrw.org/news/2015/12/23/rwanda-international-tribunal-closing-its-doors> (accessed January 6, 2016).

Human Security Report Project. *Human Security Report 2012: Sexual Violence, Education, and War: Beyond the Mainstream Narrative.* Vancouver: Human Security Press, 2012. <http://hsrgroup.org/human-security-reports/2012/text.aspx> (accessed May 23, 2016).

International Committee of the Red Cross. "Sexual Violence in Armed Conflict: E-Briefing." ICRC. (December 2015). <https://app.icrc.org/e-briefing/sexual-violence-armed-conflict/> (accessed January 7, 2016).

Jolie, Angelina. *In the Land of Blood and Honey.* (2011). DVD (accessed December 19, 2015).

Jones, Nicola, Janice Cooper, Elizabeth Presler-Marshall and David Walker. "The fallout of rape as a weapon of war: The life-long and intergenerational impacts of sexual violence in conflict." Overseas Development Institute. (2014). <http://www.odi.org/sites/odi.org.uk/files/odi-assets/publications-opinion-files/8990.pdf> (accessed May 23, 2016).

Justice Rapid Response. "Justice Rapid Response welcomes UN Women and Draper Richards Kaplan Foundation to its Executive Board." JRR. (November 2015). <http://www.justicerapidresponse.org/justice-rapid-response-welcomes-un-women-and-draper-richards-kaplan-foundation-to-its-executive-board/> (accessed January 7, 2016).

Kerry, John. "Remarks at The Global Summit to End Sexual Violence in Conflict." US Department of State. (June 2014). <http://www.state.gov/secretary/remarks/2014/06/227553.htm> (accessed November 27, 2015).

Kilcullen, David. *Out of the Mountains: the Coming of Age of the Urban Guerrilla.* London: C. Hurst & Co., 2013.

Kilmartin, Chris. "Men, Peace, and Security Symposium: Agents of Change." United States Institute of Peace. (October 29, 2013. Published November 13, 2013). <https://www.youtube.com/watch?v=rnXM8mvdzaw> (accessed January 22, 2016).

King, Anthony. "The Existence of Group Cohesion in the Armed Forces: A Response to Guy Siebold." *Armed Forces & Society* Vol 33, No. 4 (2007): 638-645.

Kirby, Paul. "How is rape a weapon of war? Feminist International Relations, modes of critical explanation and the study of wartime sexual violence." European Journal of International Relations 19(4) (2013): 773-796. <doi:10.1177/1354066111426621> (accessed May 18, 2016).

Kirby, Paul. “Ending sexual violence in conflict: the Preventing Sexual Violence Initiative and its critics.” *International Affairs*, 91(3) (2015): 457-472. <doi:10.1111/1468-2346.12283> (accessed October 8, 2015).

Kuehnast, Kathleen, Chantal de Jonge Oudraat, and Helga Hernes, eds. *Women and War: Power and Protection in the Twenty-First Century.* Washington, DC: United States Institute of Peace Press, 2011.

Leatherman, Janie. “Sexual Violence and Armed Conflict: Complex Dynamics of Re-Victimization.” *International Journal of Peace Studies* 12, no. 1 (2007): 53-71. <http://web.a.ebscohost.com/ehost/pdfviewer/pdfviewer?sid=e00a61c4-d061-425e-9d6f-dac6e949281e%40sessionmgr4004&vid=92&hid=4212> (accessed May 18, 2016).

Leiby, Michele L. “Wartime Sexual Violence in Guatemala and Peru.” *International Studies Quarterly* 53, no. 2 (2009): 445-468. <http://web.a.ebscohost.com/ehost/pdfviewer/pdfviewer?sid=e00a61c4-d061-425e-9d6f-dac6e949281e%40sessionmgr4004&vid=109&hid=4212> (accessed May 19, 2016).

Lewis, Stephen. “Against the war on women: V-day in the Congo.” *Peace & Conflict Monitor.* (April 2008). <http://web.a.ebscohost.com/ehost/detail/detail?vid=29&sid=e00a61c4-d061-425e-9d6f-dac6e949281e%40sessionmgr4004&hid=4212&bdata=JnNpdGU9ZWhvc3QtbGl2ZQ%3d%3d#AN=32019173&db=tsh> (accessed May 18, 2016).

Magner, K, JE Desrosiers, I Blunt, T Hawken, and E Brick. *The role of faith based organisations in preventing and responding to sexual, intimate partner and gender-based violence in conflict settings: A modified critical interpretive synthesis.* University of Otago for the Sexual Violence Research Initiative. (2015). <http://svri.org.dedi6.cpt3.host-h.net/sites/default/files/attachments/2016-04-13/FBOreview.pdf> (accessed May 22, 2016).

Matfess, Hilary. “Boko Haram’s War on Women.” *Newsweek Global* 166, no. 7 (February 19, 2016): 12-15. <http://web.a.ebscohost.com/ehost/pdfviewer/pdfviewer?vid=55&sid=0e34b8af-4d52-4955-9dfa-eb6e4e3bae87%40sessionmgr4004&hid=4107> (accessed May 23, 2016).

Mehari, Zeresenay Berhane. *Difret.* (2014). DVD (accessed December 20, 2015).

MenEngage Alliance and United Nations Population Fund. “Sexual Violence in Conflict and Post-Conflict: Engaging Men and Boys.” (July 2012). <http://menengage.org/resources/sexual-violence-conflict-post-conflict-engaging-men-boys/> (accessed January 12, 2016).

Mollmann, Marianne. “Rape in war: No more excuses.” Human Rights Watch. (July 2011). <https://www.hrw.org/news/2011/07/22/rape-war-no-more-excuses> (accessed January 6, 2016).

Morgan, A.J. “Sexual Violence and Gender Roles: From Peace to Conflict and Back Again.” Gender Across Borders. (November 2011). <http://www.genderacrossbor

ders.com/2011/11/28/sexual-violence-and-gender-roles-from-peace-to-conflict-and-back-again/> (accessed May 22, 2016).

NATO. "Remarks by NATO Deputy Secretary General Alexander Vershbow at the United Nations Security Council Open Debate on the High-Level Review of UNSCR 1325 – Women, Peace and Security." NATO. Last modified October 14, 2015. <http://www.nato.int/cps/en/natohq/opinions_123768.htm?selectedLocale=en> (accessed January 12, 2016).

Nelaeva, Galina. "The Impact of Transnational Advocacy Networks on the Prosecution of Wartime Rape and Sexual Violence: The Case of the ICTR." *International Social Science Review* 85, no. 1/2 (2010): 3-27. <http://web.a.ebscohost.com/ehost/pdfviewer/pdfviewer?vid=31&sid=0e34b8af-4d52-4955-9dfa-eb6e4e3bae87%40sessionmgr4004&hid=4107> (accessed May 23, 2016).

Nordås, Ragnhild, and Siri C.A. Rustad. "Sexual Exploitation and Abuse by Peacekeepers: Understanding Variation." *International Interactions* 39, no. 4 (2013): 511-534. <http://web.b.ebscohost.com/ehost/pdfviewer/pdfviewer?vid=87&sid=d9b58e6f-f0a9-428e-86e5-c8fba15262df%40sessionmgr106&hid=105> (accessed May 23, 2016).

Office of the Special Representative of the Secretary-General for Sexual Violence in Conflict. Homepage. <http://www.un.org/sexualviolenceinconflict/> (accessed May 13, 2016).

Oxford Learner's Dictionary. "Prevent." Oxford Learner's Dictionary. <http://www.oxfordlearnersdictionaries.com/definition/english/prevent?q=prevent> (accessed May 15, 2016).

Parliament. "House of Commons Debates 29 June 2015: Tunisia, and European Council." Parliament. (June 2015). <http://www.publications.parliament.uk/pa/cm201516/cmhansrd/cm150629/debtext/150629-0001.htm#15062950000001> (accessed April 7, 2016).

Peterman, Amber, Dara Kay Cohen, Tia Palermo, and Amelia Hoov. "Rape reporting during war: Why the numbers don't mean what you think they do." *Foreign Affairs*. (August 1, 2011). <https://www.foreignaffairs.com/articles/2011-08-01/rape-reporting-during-war?page=show> (accessed May 23, 2016).

Rees, Madeleine and Christine Chinkin. "Why we support the PSVI." Women's International League for Peace and Freedom. (June 2015). <http://wilpf.org/why-we-support-the-psvi/> (accessed May 20, 2016).

Reicher, Stephen. "The Context of Social Identity: Domination, Resistance, and Change." *Political Psychology.* 259(6) (2004): 921-945. <doi:10.1111/j.1467-9221.2004.00403.x.> (accessed January 19, 2016).

Rowley, Elizabeth, Garcia Moreno, and Elizabeth Dartnall. *Executive Summary: A Research Agenda for Sexual Violence In Humanitarian, Conflict and Post-Conflict Settings.* World Health Organization, UN Action, Sexual Violence Research Initiative and Medical Research Council South Africa. (2011). <https://www.researchgate.net/

publication/233428122_Executive_Summary_A_Research_Agenda_for_Sexual_Violence_In_Humanitarian_Conflict_and_Post-Conflict_Settings> (accessed May 23, 2016).

Russell, Wynne. “Sexual violence against men and boys.” *Forced Migration Review*, no. 27 (2007). <http://web.a.ebscohost.com/ehost/pdfviewer/pdfviewer?sid=e00a61c4-d061-425e-9d6f-dac6e949281e%40sessionmgr4004&vid=27&hid=4212> (accessed May 18, 2016).

Schuurman, Marriët. “NATO and the Women, Peace and Security Agenda: Time to Bring It Home.” *Connections: The Quarterly Journal*, Vol XIV, No. 3 October 2015). <http://www.nato.int/cps/en/natohq/opinions_124032.htm?selectedLocale=en> (accessed January 12, 2016).

Shepherd, Laura J. and Jacqui True. “The Women, Peace and Security agenda and Australian leadership in the world: from rhetoric to commitment?” *Australian Journal of International Affairs*, Vol. 68, No. 3 (2014): 257-284. <http://dx.doi.org/10.1080/10357718.2014.903895> (accessed May 18, 2016).

Siebold, Guy, L. “The Essence of Military Group Cohesion.” *Armed Forces & Society* Vol. 33, No. 2 (2007): 286-295.

Sivakumaran, Sandesh. “Lost in translation: UN responses to sexual violence against men and boys in situations of armed conflict.” *International Review of the Red Cross*, 92(877) (2010): 259-277. <doi:10.1017/S1816383110000020> (accessed May 18, 2016).

Solangon, Sarah, and Preeti Patel. “Sexual violence against men in countries affected by armed conflict.” *Conflict, Security and Development* 12(4) (2012): 417-42. <doi:10.1080/14678802.2012.724794> (accessed November 27, 2015).

Stauffer, Hilary and Erica Hall. “No Shame in Justice: addressing stigma against survivors to end sexual violence in conflict zones.” World Vision UK. (December 2015). <http://9bb63f6dda0f744fa444-9471a7fca5768cc513a2e3c4a260910b.r43.cf3.rackcdn.com/files/1614/4888/7012/WVUK_No_Shame_in_Justice_low_res.pdf> (accessed May 19, 2016).

Steffens, Niklas K., S. Alexander Haslam, and Stephen D. Reicher. “Up close and personal: evidence that shared social identity is a basis for the ‘special’ relationship that binds followers to leaders.” *The Leadership Quarterly* 25 (2015): 296-313.

The Mobile Economy. (2015). <http://gsmamobileeconomy.com/global/> (accessed May 12, 2016).

UNICEF (UK). “Sexual Violence in Conflict.” (2014) <http://www.unicef.org.uk/Documents/Public-Affairs-Briefings/UNICEF-UK-Briefing-Sexual-Violence-in-Conflict.pdf> (accessed May 23, 2016).

United Kingdom Government. *National Security Strategy and Strategic Defence and Security Review 2015: A Secure and Prosperous United Kingdom*. Cm 9161. November 2015.

United Kingdom. Development, Concepts and Doctrine Centre. *UK Defence Doctrine.* Joint Doctrine Publication 0-01. 5th ed. Shrivenham: DCDC, 2014.

United Nations. "Report on the Protection of Civilians in the Armed Conflict in Iraq: 1 May – 31 October 2015." (January 2016). <http://www.uniraq.org/images/human rights/UNAMI-OHCHR_%20POC%20Report_FINAL_01%20May-31%20 October%202015_FINAL_11Jan2016.pdf> (accessed January 21, 2016).

United Nations Secretary General. "Conflict-related sexual violence: Report of the Secretary General." United Nations. S/2015/203 (March 23, 2015). <http://www.sto prapenow.org/uploads/advocacyresources/1428937312.pdf> (accessed January 6, 2016).

Verma, Baroness Sandip. "The UK firmly believes that the 15th anniversary must represent the start of a new era on Women, Peace and Security." UK Government. (October 13, 2015). <https://www.gov.uk/government/speeches/the-uk-firmly-believes -that-the-15th-anniversary-must-represent-the-start-of-a-new-era-on-women-peace-and-security> (accessed November 26, 2015).

Warner, Christopher H, George N. Appenzeller, Angela Mobbs, Jessica R. Parker, Carolynn M. Warner, Thomas Grieger, and Charles W. Hoge. "Effectiveness of battle-field-ethics training during combat deployment: a programme assessment." The *Lancet.* Vol 378 (2011): 915-924.

Watson, Callum. "Preventing and Responding to Sexual and Domestic Violence against Men: A Guidance Note for Security Sector Institutions." Democratic Control of the Armed Forces. 2014. <http://www.dcaf.ch/Publications/Preventing-and-Respon ding-to-Sexual-and-Domestic-Violence-against-Men-A-Guidance-Note-for-Securi ty-Sector-Institutions> (accessed January 19, 2016).

Watson, Callum. "Bad apples or bad apple trees? An examination of the contexts in which sexual violence against men takes place." Paper presented at a workshop entitled, 'Sexual Violence Against Men during Conflicts: Bridging the Gap between Theory and Practice.' *The Graduate Institute of International and Development Studies*, Geneva February 26-27, 2015).

Wolfe, Lauren. "Gloria Steinem on Rape in War, Its Causes, and How to Stop It." *The Atlantic.* (February 8, 2012). <http://www.theatlantic.com/international/archive/ 2012/02/gloria-steinem-on-rape-in-war-its-causes-and-how-to-stop-it/252470/> (accessed January 18, 2016).

Women's International League for Peace and Freedom. "Women organising for change in Syria and Bosnia." WILPF. (2014). <http://wilpf.org/wp-content/uploads/2014/07/ Women-Organising-for-Change-in-Bosnia-and-Syria.pdf> (accessed May 15, 2016).

Women's International League for Peace and Freedom. "WILPF reflects on the Global Summit to end Sexual Violence in Conflict." WILPF. (2014). <http://wilpf.org/wilpf-reflects-on-the-global-summit-to-end-sexual-violence-in-conflict/> (accessed May 20, 2016).

WomenPolice. “The Ongoing Fight to End Sexual Violence in Conflict.” *WomenPolice.* (August 2015). <http://web.a.ebscohost.com/ehost/pdfviewer/pdfviewer?vid=9&sid=e00a61c4-d061-425e-9d6f-dac6e949281e%40sessionmgr4004&hid=4212> (accessed May 17, 2016).

Wood, Elizabeth Jean. “Sexual violence during war: toward an understanding of variation.” in *Order, Conflict and Violence,* edited by Stathis N. Kalyvas, Ian Shapiro and Tarek Masoud. New York and Cambridge: Cambridge University Press, 2008.

Wood, Elizabeth Jean. “Armed Groups and Sexual Violence: When is Wartime Rape Rare?” *Politics and Society,* 37(1) (2009): 131-161.

Wood, Elizabeth Jean. “Conflict-related sexual violence and the policy implications of recent research.” *International Review of the Red Cross* 96(894) (2014): 457-478. <doi:10.1017/S1816383115000077> (accessed January 7, 2016).

Zawati, Hilmi M., “Re-thinking rape law.” *Journal of International Law and International Relations,* Vol. 102014): 31-43. <http://web.b.ebscohost.com/ehost/pdfviewer/pdfviewer?vid=58&sid=d9b58e6f-f0a9-428e-86e5-c8fba15262df%40sessionmgr106&hid=105> (accessed May 23, 2016).

Zawati, Hilmi M., “The Challenge of Prosecuting Conflict-Related Gender-Based Crimes under Libyan Transitional Justice.” *Journal of International Law & International Relations* Vol. 102014): 44-91. <http://web.b.ebscohost.com/ehost/pdfviewer/pdfviewer?sid=d9b58e6f-f0a9-428e-86e5-c8fba15262df%40sessionmgr106&vid=62&hid=105> (accessed May 23, 2016).

Zimbardo, Philip. *The Lucifer Effect: How Good People Turn Evil.* London: Rider, 2007.

# Prévenir la violence sexuelle en tant qu'arme de guerre

> Nous pouvons en finir avec les guerres sexuelles menées contre des innocents.
> Nous pouvons établir de nouvelles normes pour le respect des femmes, des filles, des hommes et des garçons…
> Nous pouvons afficher aux yeux du monde notre détermination à ne plus tolérer ces tactiques abjectes…
> Nous pouvons dire « plus maintenant, plus jamais. »[1]

∴

## Introduction

Historiquement, la violence sexuelle en tant qu'arme de guerre contre les femmes, les hommes et les enfants est un crime tabou, dont les victimes se résignent à souffrir dans le silence et l'injustice. Il est perpétré contre les deux sexes durant des siècles : «  depuis les viols des Sabines dans la Rome antique […] aux […] castrations perpétrées par les armées chinoise, perse, amalécite, égyptienne et nordique à des fins de conquête ».[2] Les gouvernements et organisations humanitaires, avec des ressources limitées, se sont donné pour priorité de porter assistance aux questions de vie ou de mort. Les survivants, honteux de briser des tabous sociaux, ne savent vers qui se tourner pour se faire aider. Ceux cherchant à négocier des accords de paix craignent de perdre

* Traduit par Aurélia Boennec. Titre original: "Is it possible to prevent sexual violence as a weapon of war against women, men and children or only to manage the after-effects?" Les points de vue exprimés dans cet ouvrage sont ceux de l'auteur et ne reflètent pas nécessairement ceux du Ministère de la Défense britannique ou d'aucun autre ministère du Gouvernement de Sa Majesté du Royaume-Uni. De tels points de vue ne doivent en outre pas être considérés comme approuvant de manière officielle une précision des faits, une opinion, une conclusion ou une recommandation du Ministère de la Défense britannique ou d'aucun autre ministère du Gouvernement de Sa Majesté du Royaume-Uni.

1 John Kerry, "Remarks at The Global Summit to End Sexual Violence in Conflict,' Département d'État américain, juin 2014, <http://www.state.gov/secretary/remarks/2014/06/227553.htm> (consulté le 27 novembre 2015).

2 Sarah Solangon, et Preeti Patel, "Sexual violence against men in countries affected by armed conflict," *Conflict, Security and Development* 12(4) (2012), <doi:10.1080/14678802.2012.724794> (consulté le 27 novembre 2015), 418-419.

la confiance des groupes armés en traitant des sujets « difficiles » mêlés de coutumes religieuses ou traditionnelles. Ainsi, il apparaît de prime abord que la violence sexuelle n'est seulement qu'un aspect sombre de la guerre, qui a toujours existé et perdurera.

Toutefois, cette thèse étudie s'il est possible, au XXIè siècle, d'empêcher la violence sexuelle en tant qu'arme de guerre contre les femmes, les hommes et les enfants, ou seulement d'en prévenir les conséquences. Nous commencerons par expliquer brièvement l'arrière-plan du sujet et en expliciter les termes-clés, avant de passer en revue les travaux actuels. Nous analyserons ensuite les approches préventives existantes, examinerons le cas spécifique de Daech,[3] et nous nous pencherons enfin sur les mesures de prévention supplémentaires pouvant être mises en place. Ce travail s'efforcera de démontrer que la prévention peut être menée à bien grâce à des améliorations apportées aux mesures existantes, conjointement à un usage inventif d'outils pluridisciplinaires, quantifiés et maintenus, et établis sur mesure pour chaque conflit. Il conclura qu'en dépit de challenges importants, il est possible d'empêcher que la violence sexuelle ne soit utilisée en tant qu'arme de guerre.

En guise d'arrière-plan, l'Initiative de prévention des violences sexuelles (PSVI : Preventing Sexual Violence Initiative) est créée en mai 2012 par le Ministre des Affaires Etrangères britannique de l'époque, William Hague, qui a déclaré : « Lorsque nous sommes confrontés aux plus grands maux de notre monde, il est aisé, en se sentant submergé, de détourner le regard. Mais aucune des grandes avancées en droits de l'homme n'aurait pu être possible sans de hautes ambitions et une détermination constante ».[4] L'année suivante, le Royaume Uni promeut le programme de la PVSI en se servant de la présidence du G8 pour adhérer à une Déclaration du G8, et en soutenant une résolution du Conseil de Sécurité de l'ONU (UNSCR 2106). Le Royaume-Uni est aussi une figure de proue dans l'adoption d'une « Déclaration d'Engagement contre les violences sexuelles dans les conflits », ratifiée par l'Assemblée Générale de l'ONU, qui a depuis été signée par 155 pays.[5] En 2014, le Royaume-Uni organise

---

3 Traduction française de l'orthographe anglaise Daesh, en accord avec Hansard: Parliament, "House of Commons Debates 29 June 2015: Tunisia, and European Council," Parliament juin 2015), <http://www.publications.parliament.uk/pa/cm201516/cmhansrd/cm150629/debtext/150629-0001.htm#15062950000001> (consulté le 7 avril 2016), colonne 1182.

4 Bureau des Affaires étrangères et du Commonwealth, "Foreign Secretary launches new Government initiative to prevent sexual violence in conflict," Foreign & Commonwealth Office mai 2012), <https://www.gov.uk/government/speeches/foreign-secretary-launches-new-government-initiative-to-prevent-sexual-violence-in-conflict> (consulté le 21 mars 2016).

5 Paul Kirby, "Ending sexual violence in conflict: the Preventing Sexual Violence Initiative and its critics," *International Affairs*, 91(3) (2015), <doi:10.1111/1468-2346.12283> (consulté le 8 octobre 2015), 457-458.

un sommet mondial, le plus grand jamais tenu dans sa catégorie, pour lequel Hague est appuyé par Zainab Bangura, représentante spéciale du Secrétaire Général de l'ONU dans le cadre de la campagne contre la violence sexuelle en période de conflit, et Angelina Jolie Pitt, envoyée spéciale pour le Haut-Commissariat des Nations unies pour les réfugiés. Il semble que Hague, biographe de William Wilberforce ayant aboli l'esclavage au XIXè siècle, soit déterminé à laisser son propre héritage avant de quitter le pouvoir.

Avant de passer en revue la littérature actuelle sur la violence sexuelle, il est important de clarifier les termes-clés utilisés dans la présente étude : « empêcher », « violence sexuelle », et « guerre ». Les travaux sur la violence sexuelle ne fournissant aucune définition théorique ou pratique du terme « empêcher », y compris dans le domaine du PVSI, une définition du dictionnaire sera donc employée : « ne pas permettre à quelqu'un de faire quelque chose ; faire en sorte que quelque chose ne se produise pas ».[6] Par contre, le Secrétaire Général de l'ONU (SGONU) publie une Rapport annuel sur les violences sexuelles liées aux conflits, où le terme « violence sexuelle » est formellement défini comme :

> le viol, l'esclavage sexuel et la prostitution, la grossesse, l'avortement, la stérilisation et le mariage forcés, ainsi que toute autre forme de violence sexuelle de gravité comparable, perpétrés contre des femmes, des hommes, des filles ou des garçons, et ayant un lien direct ou indirect avec un conflit.[7]

Le Comité International de la Croix-Rouge (CICR) reconnaît ces types d'activités en des termes semblables, et explique : « La violence sexuelle peut être définie au sens large comme un ensemble d'actes de nature sexuelle imposés par la force, la menace ou la coercition, ou perpétrés en profitant d'un environnement coercitif ou de l'incapacité d'un individu à donner son consentement véritable».[8] La législation sur la violence sexuelle sera passée en revue au même titre que les articles spécialisés ; cependant, il apparaît qu'en des termes non-légaux, les terminologies du SGONU et du CICR diffèrent légèrement.

6 Oxford Learner's Dictionary, "Prevent," Oxford Learner's Dictionary, <http://www.oxfordlearnersdictionaries.com/definition/english/prevent?q=prevent> (consulté le 15 mai 2016).

7 Secrétaire Général des Nations Unies, "Conflict-related sexual violence Report of the Secretary General," United Nations, S/2015/203 (23 mars 2015), <http://www.stoprapenow.org/uploads/advocacyresources/1428937312.pdf> (consulté le 6 janvier 2016), 1/33.

8 Comité international de la Croix-Rouge (CICR), "Sexual Violence in Armed Conflict: E-Briefing," CICR décembre 2015) <https://app.icrc.org/e-briefing/sexual-violence-armed-conflict/> (consulté le 7 janvier 2016), Partie 3.

Dans le cadre de cette thèse, nous adhèrerons à la définition du SGONU, en raison du rôle de leader tenu par l'ONU sur ce sujet et de son inclusion des « femmes, hommes et enfants » dans sa définition, ainsi que sa reconnaissance d'autres activités pouvant être comprises par cette expression. Concernant l'usage du terme « guerre » dans le titre, nous opterons également pour une définition non-légale, tirée de la doctrine militaire britannique (UK Defence Doctrine) : « La guerre est une situation de conflit armé entre différents pays ou différents groupes au sein d'un même pays ».[9] Par conséquent, l'expression « arme de guerre » employée dans le titre est symbolique et doit être appréhendée dans le cadre de la définition de la guerre sus-citée.

Au vu des facteurs d'étude et en raison de la limite de mots imposée, ce travail ne tentera pas d'évaluer les politiques britanniques en la matière, mais il examinera la façon dont les universitaires, les organisations internationales, les gouvernements et les Organisations Non Gouvernementales (ONG) ont abordé le problème. Par ailleurs, ce travail ne présentera pas d'étude comparative des mérites du PVSI et de l'agenda Femmes, Paix et Sécurité (FPS) ni ne se concentrera sur le rôle des femmes dans les questions de reconstruction post-conflits. Cependant, il s'efforcera de démontrer les exigences considérables dans la gestion des répercussions auxquelles sont confrontées les victimes de violence sexuelle durant un conflit, pour mettre en relief les challenges en matière de prévention et de remède.

## Revue de littérature

La section suivante passe en revue la littérature actuelle sur le sujet en analysant les découvertes clés dans cinq domaines : premièrement, les raisons de l'usage de la violence sexuelle en situation de conflit ; deuxièmement, le principe selon lequel les hommes et les garçons peuvent en être les victimes, et les femmes les auteurs ; troisièmement, les challenges de la gestion des répercussions ; quatrièmement, les risques posés par la titrisation et l'attention détournée du programme FPS, et enfin, les preuves que la violence sexuelle en situation de conflit n'est pas inéluctable.

### *Pourquoi la violence sexuelle est-elle utilisée comme arme de guerre ?*

La première conclusion d'importance de la revue de littérature est une explication des raisons pour lesquelles la violence sexuelle est utilisée comme arme

9 United Kingdom, Development, Concepts and Doctrine Centre, *UK Defence Doctrine*, Joint Doctrine Publication 0-01. 5th ed. (Shrivenham: DCDC, 2014), 18.

de guerre. Bien que Wood ait mené des recherches étendues dans ce domaine, elle écrit en 2014 qu' « il y a encore beaucoup à comprendre de la violence sexuelle liée aux conflits ».[10] Solangon et Patel approuvent et recommandent une étude plus approfondie de la violence sexuelle faite aux hommes.[11] En dépit de leurs précautions, la littérature présente un certain nombre d'explications menant à une meilleure compréhension des raisons de l'utilisation de la violence sexuelle en situation de conflit. Watson propose que « le plus important facteur pouvant prédire la violence sexuelle en tous les cas est que la victime soit dans un environnement où l'auteur peut user de violence et commettre un abus avec un haut degré d'impunité ».[12] Solangon et Patel en conviennent : « il est clair qu'une culture de l'impunité favorise la propension à la violence »,[13] et de souligner que « la détérioration de la situation socio-économique et de piètres conditions de vie [...] peuvent conduire à l'impunité en raison de l'effondrement de la loi et l'ordre garantissant la sécurité civile »,[14] Le CICR adhère à ces remarques : « L'impunité des violences sexuelles demeure au cœur du problème dans bien des circonstances ».[15]

En outre, Solangon et Patel mettent l'accent sur le rôle des violences sexuelles comme une « démonstration de pouvoir, de domination et d'humiliation ».[16] Ceci est caractérisé dans un rapport de l'ONU de 2016 qui affirme que Daech cible les leaders religieux et tribaux iraquiens, les médecins, journalistes, avocats et officiers de police[17] dans le but de manifester le pouvoir de l'organisation sur l'autorité et les figures de respect. Dans d'autres conflits, les

---

10 Elizabeth Jean Wood, "Conflict-related sexual violence and the policy implications of recent research," *International Review of the Red Cross*, 96(894) (2014), <doi:10.1017/S1816383115000077> (consulté le 7 janvier 2016), 477.

11 Solangon et Patel, "Sexual violence against men in countries affected by armed conflict," 435-436.

12 Callum Watson, "Preventing and Responding to Sexual and Domestic Violence against Men: A Guidance Note for Security Sector Institutions," Democratic Control of the Armed Forces 2014), <http://www.dcaf.ch/Publications/Preventing-and-Responding-to-Sexual-and-Domestic-Violence-against-Men-A-Guidance-Note-for-Security-Sector-Institutions> (consulté le 19 janvier 2016), 14.

13 Solangon et Patel, "Sexual violence against men in countries affected by armed conflict," 426.

14 Ibid., 425-426.

15 CICR, "Sexual Violence in Armed Conflict: E-Briefing," Partie 3.

16 Solangon et Patel, "Sexual violence against men in countries affected by armed conflict," 425.

17 Nations Unies, "Report on the Protection of Civilians in the Armed Conflict in Iraq: 1 May – 31 October 2015," (janvier 2016), <http://www.uniraq.org/images/humanrights/UNAMI-OHCHR_%20POC%20Report_FINAL_01%20May-31%20October%202015_FINAL_11Jan2016.pdf> (consulté le 21 janvier 2016), i.

défenseurs des droits de l'homme sont également pris pour cible par leurs opposants pour des logiques similaires de contrôle. Watson explique que la violence sexuelle sert à « défaire les liens communautaires »,[18] déplacer les populations par la force et détruire les générations futures au moyen de la perte de cohésion sociétale.

Concernant l'usage prémédité de violence sexuelle par les groupes armés, Wood déclare qu'il « semble avoir représenté une stratégie en Bosnie, au Guatemala et au Rwanda, par exemple ».[19] Kirby écrit : « Les unités d'opérations psychologiques serbes ont notoirement conclu que les viols (y compris d'enfants) auraient un effet délétère sur le moral de l'ennemi durant la guerre de Bosnie, et ont conformément adopté une politique de viol. »[20] Wood mentionne également les travaux de Michele Leiby sur son usage par les forces étatiques, y compris au Pérou, en tant que stratégie de contre-insurrection visant à exercer un contrôle sur les communautés soutenant les insurgés. Les forces étatiques péruviennes utilisent également la violence sexuelle à l'encontre de prisonniers afin de leur soutirer des informations, de les punir et de faire montre du pouvoir du gouvernement.[21] Solangon et Patel décrivent ses modes d'utilisation : « comme faisant partie d'une stratégie militaire pour terroriser et démoraliser les civils et les combattants ».[22] Le rapport du SGONU de l'année dernière sur la violence sexuelle liée aux conflits remarque que des groupes en faisaient usage pour servir leurs « objectifs stratégiques, leur idéologie et leur financement [...] à des fins tactiques telles que le recrutement, le maintien des populations dans la terreur, [...] le déplacement des communautés d'endroits stratégiques, [...] la création de revenu, [...] la pratique de la torture pour soutirer des informations [...] [et] établir, altérer ou détruire les liens de parenté sur lesquels reposent les communautés ».[23]

En revanche, Alcorn résume les recherches premières de Baaz et Stern sur l'usage de violences sexuelles par les forces étatiques en République Démocratique du Congo (RDC), ce qui les a menés à la conclusion que « le cas échéant,

18 Watson, "Preventing and Responding to Sexual and Domestic Violence against Men: A Guidance Note for Security Sector Institutions," 13.

19 Wood, "Conflict-related sexual violence and the policy implications of recent research," 472.

20 Kirby, "Ending sexual violence in conflict: Preventing Sexual Violence Initiative and its critics," 462.

21 Wood, "Conflict-related sexual violence and the policy implications of recent research," 472.

22 Solangon et Patel, "Sexual violence against men in countries affected by armed conflict," 425.

23 Secrétaire Général des Nations Unies, "Conflict-related sexual violence: Report of Secretary General," 24/33.

c'est le dysfonctionnement de la hiérarchie militaire qui a créé l'espace nécessaire à l'apparition de la violence sexuelle opportuniste ».[24] Solangon et Patel concèdent que le recours à la violence sexuelle peut faire partie d'une stratégie militaire, mais ils conviennent également que ce peut être « une conséquence d'une sélection médiocre des combattants, une mauvaise discipline, de piètres conditions de vie, un entraînement lacunaire et peu de cohésion entre les militaires ».[25] Wood se réfère aux résultats des recherches de Cohen, où « elle montre que les groupes armés non-étatiques qui pratiquent le recrutement forcé sont plus enclins à démontrer un usage important de violences sexuelles ».[26] Wood estime également que le recours à ce type de violence peut être commandé, ou toléré au sein d'un groupe armé.[27]

Pour conclure sur ce premier aspect clé, la littérature donne un certain nombre de raison expliquant pourquoi la violence sexuelle est toujours utilisée en tant qu'arme de guerre. Ce raisonnement peut parfois paraître contradictoire : par exemple, ce type de violence peut être considéré comme faisant partie d'une stratégie militaire définie, ou comme une conséquence de l'effondrement des procédures militaires. Cependant, cela constitue une représentation plausible de la nature et de la situation de chaque conflit. Bien que certains universitaires aient souligné le besoin d'approfondissement des recherches, la littérature est unanime quant à l'identification des raisons de l'usage de cette violence : un sentiment d'impunité, une détermination à exercer un certain pouvoir, et soit une stratégie militaire préméditée, soit des pratiques militaires indigentes.

### *Les hommes et les garçons peuvent être victimes, et les femmes auteurs*

Le second principe-clé de la revue de littérature postule que les hommes et les garçons peuvent être les victimes, et les femmes les auteurs. Solangon et Patel notent que : « les résultats de la revue de la litérature indiquent que les preuves et les concepts de violence sexuelle contre les hommes en situation de conflit

24 Ted Alcorn, "Responding to sexual violence in armed conflict," *The Lancet* 383(9934) (2014), <http://www.thelancet.com/journals/lancet/article/PIIS0140-6736(14)60970-3/fulltext(consulté le 18 janvier 2016), 2036.

25 Solangon et Patel, "Sexual violence against men in countries affected by armed conflict," 429-430.

26 Elizabeth Jean Wood, "Rape is not inevitable during war," in Kathleen Kuehnast, Chantal de Jonge Oudraat, and Helga Hernes, eds., *Women and War: Power and Protection in the Twenty-First Century* Washington, DC: US Institute of Peace Press, 2011), 58.

27 Wood, "Conflict-related sexual violence and the policy implications of recent research," 467 & 470.

sont assez limités ».[28] Quelques années plus tard, Watson met en évidence les progrès réalisés dans le milieu universitaire, mais aussi le manque de développement des informations pour les praticiens.[29] Le travail consistant à réunir des données exactes s'avère potentiellement plus exigeant que pour les femmes, car les violences sexuelles faites aux hommes rentrent fréquemment dans le cadre de la « torture ».[30] D'autres obstacles à la collecte de données sont dus à la honte éprouvée par les hommes résultant de la stigmatisation, la rupture de tabous sociaux ou de possibles lois du pays d'origine, mais également la démoralisation résultant de l'incapacité de se défendre soi-même. Historiquement, on remarque également un manque de sensibilisation et de soutien de la part des milieux médical, légal et journalistique. Skjelsboek propose que le sentiment d'émasculation éprouvé par certains hommes peut rendre leur témoignage auprès d'une femme difficile: « Afin de fournir un meilleur accès aux données, il serait peut-être nécessaire que davantage d'hommes s'impliquent dans ces recherches ».[31] Cet argument est appuyé par Hague, qui résume, lors du Sommet Mondial de 2014 : « La collecte de données ne doit pas ignorer celles concernant les hommes et les garçons ».[32]

Bien que les recherches en la matière soient limitées, les raisons des violences sexuelles faites aux hommes sont manifestes dans la littérature, en particulier dans les travaux de Solangon et Patel. Ils expliquent qu'elles peuvent représenter un rite initiatique au sein d'un groupe, à la suite de la conscription ou d'un enlèvement, ou pour briser la cohésion d'un autre groupe, ou encore en guise de « violence sexuelle génocidaire [...] [par] la mutilation ou les blessures génitales faites aux hommes appartenant à certains groupes ethniques, dans le but de les rendre impuissants ».[33] Ils remarquent également que « la plupart des cas de violences sexuelles perpétrées contre des hommes se produisent lorsque les victimes sont détenues [...] à des fins d'interrogation et de

---

28 Solangon et Patel, "Sexual violence against men in countries affected by armed conflict," 422.

29 Watson, "Preventing and Responding to Sexual and Domestic Violence against Men: A Guidance Note for Security Sector Institutions," 3.

30 Solangon et Patel, "Sexual violence against men in countries affected by armed conflict," 422-423.

31 Inger Skjelsboek, "Sexual violence in the post-Yugoslav wars," in Kuehnast et al., eds., *Women and War: Power and Protection in Twenty-First Century*, 82.

32 Bureau des Affaires Étrangères et du Commonwealth, "Statement of Action - Global Summit to End Sexual Violence in Conflict," Foreign & Commonwealth Office juin 2014), <https://www.gov.uk/government/publications/statement-of-action-global-summit-to-end-sexual-violence-in-conflict> (consulté le 26 novembre 2015).

33 Solangon et Patel, "Sexual violence against men in countries affected by armed conflict," 419 & 428-429.

punition ».[34] Dr. Aburabi, un médecin du CICR, explique qu'il est possible d'identifier les personnes à risque dans les camps de détention : « les jeunes détenus, les primo-délinquants, ceux qui montrent une apparence spéciale, ceux présentant un handicap cognitif ou autre, mais également les personnes homosexuelles, bisexuelles, transgenre ou intersexuées ».[35]

La complexité du sujet apparaît également dans la littérature traitant des femmes auteurs de violences. Wood déclare que des militaires féminines américaines étaient responsables d'actes de violence sexuelle en Irak, en Afghanistan et dans la baie de Guantanamo.[36] En 2015, le Tribunal International pénal pour le Rwanda maintient sa condamnation de Pauline Nyiramasuhuko, l'ancienne ministre de la famille et du développement des femmes, pour avoir aidé à organiser, et avoir contraint d'autres personnes à commettre des viols lors du conflit rwandais en 1994.[37] D'autres travaux identifient des auteurs féminins au Sierra Leone,[38] en Haïti et en République Démocratique du Congo.[39] La littérature met l'accent sur la nécessité de recherches plus poussées quant aux raisons pour lesquelles les femmes commettent des violences sexuelles, mais Edström et al. proposent que « certaines causes peuvent inclure l'adaptation des femmes à des normes de masculinité militarisée, le désir de rediriger la violence sexuelle, ou la volonté d'humilier un ennemi ».[40]

Concernant le nombre d'hommes et de garçons victimes, et celui de femmes auteurs, les difficultés à obtenir des chiffres fiables et le manque de recherche en la matière sont prégnants dans la littérature. Solangon et Patel affirment

---

34 Ibid., 429-430.

35 Vincent Bernard, et Elvina Pothelet, "Through the eyes of a detention doctor: Interview with Raed Aburabi," *International Review of the Red Cross*, 96(894) (2014), <doi:10.1017/S1816383115000284> (consulté le 11 janvier 2016), 482.

36 Wood, "Rape is not inevitable during war," in: Kuehnast et al., eds., *Women and War: Power & Protection in Twenty-First Century*, 45.

37 Human Rights Watch, "Rwanda: International Tribunal Closing Its Doors," HRW décembre 2015), <https://www.hrw.org/news/2015/12/23/rwanda-international-tribunal-closing-its-doors> (consulté le 6 janvier 2016) & Marianne Mollmann, "Rape in war: No more excuses," Human Rights Watch juillet 2011), <https://www.hrw.org/news/2011/07/22/rape-war-no-more-excuses> (consulté le 6 janvier 2016).

38 Wood, "Rape is not inevitable during war," in: Kuehnast et al., eds., *Women and War: Power & Protection in Twenty-First Century*, 45.

39 Jerker Edström, Alexa Hassink, Thea Shahrokh, et Erin Stern, eds.,"Engendering Men: A Collaborative Review of Evidence of Men and Boys in Social Change and Gender Equality," EMERGE Evidence Review, Promundo-US, Sonke Gender Justice and the Institute of Development Studies. (septembre 2015), <http://opendocs.ids.ac.uk/opendocs/bitstream/handle/123456789/7059/EMERGE.pdf?sequence=1> (consulté le 22 janvier 2016), 142.

40 Ibid.

que, dans les années 1990, 80% des cinq mille hommes emprisonnés dans un camp bosniaque ont été violés, et que l'on a enregistré des violences similaires commises contre des hommes dans 25 conflits du monde moderne.[41] Il est probable que les survivants masculins représentent une proportion extrêmement faible du nombre total de victimes. Cependant, étant donné la nature de ce « crime caché », davantage de preuves et de recherches sont nécessaires, en particulier dans les comptes-rendus de « torture » commise contre des hommes. En ce qui concerne les auteurs féminins, les recherches de Cohen suggèrent que « les combattantes ont participé à 25% des viols collectifs du RUF [Revolutionary United Front, Front révolutionnaire uni au Sierra Leone] ».[42] Néanmoins, la conclusion principale de littérature est que « bien davantage de recherches sont nécessaires pour déterminer le nombre exact de femmes auteurs de violences sexuelles, ainsi que les causes et conséquences de leur perpétration ».[43]

Pour conclure sur ce deuxième principe, la littérature nuance la préconception selon laquelle la violence sexuelle est une question de genre, où les hommes exercent impunément une domination sur les femmes, en démontrant que les hommes et les garçons peuvent en être victimes, et les femmes les auteurs. Les travaux détaillent les différents causes et contextes des violences sexuelles faites aux hommes et garçons. Par contre, il semble que bien plus de recherches seraient nécessaires pour comprendre les raisons de l'usage de violence sexuelle par les femmes. Le nombre d'hommes et de garçons victimes et de femmes auteurs, comparé au nombre de femmes victimes et d'hommes auteurs, est très imprécis dans la littérature. La revue a toutefois démontré que cela représente un aspect non négligeable de la violence sexuelle en période de conflit. Par ailleurs, il est suggéré que ce deuxième principe-clé n'en contredit pas un autre ci-après (selon lequel la violence sexuelle n'est pas inévitable), puisque l'on peut affirmer qu'une meilleure compréhension du problème met en lumière sa complexité. L'on expliquera plus loin que le recours à la violence sexuelle n'est pas systématique, mais le cas échéant, les victimes peuvent être des hommes et des garçons tout comme des femmes et des filles.

---

41 Solangon et Patel, "Sexual violence against men in countries affected by armed conflict," 419.

42 Wood, "Rape is not inevitable during war," in: Kuehnast et al., eds., *Women and War: Power & Protection in Twenty-First Century*, 47.

43 Edström et al., eds.,"Engendering Men: Collaborative Review of Evidence of Men & Boys in Social Change and Gender Equality," 142.

### *La gestion des répercussions*

Le troisième principe-clé de la revue de littérature concerne les challenges posés par la gestion des répercussions de ces actes de violences, entre autres : apporter de l'aide médicale et psychologique, faire face à la propagation d'infections sexuellement transmissibles (IST), aborder le problème de l'avortement, et adapter le soutien aux hommes et enfants. Bouvier décrit la nécessité d'offrir des soins médicaux dans les 72 heures : « dans le but de prévenir les infections sexuellement transmissibles, y compris le VIH, et d'assurer la contraception d'urgence ».[44] Il donne un exemple de ces difficultés dans une étude en RDC, où plus de 95% des survivants n'ont pas accès à une aide médicale d'urgence dans ce laps de temps.[45] Skjelsboek en constate les implications pour la santé reproductive des individus, ainsi que la stigmatisation résultant de la contraction d'une IST, et suggère : « Il est nécessaire d'en savoir plus sur la mesure dans laquelle la violence sexuelle en conflit armé contribue à la propagation du VIH/SIDA ».[46] Solangon et Patel écrivent qu'il y a un « besoin urgent de [...] prise en charge psychiatrique dans la gestion du traumatisme »,[47] et Bouvier souligne la nécessité d'un soutien sur le long terme : « Continuité des soins et suivi régulier, tels que soins médicaux et aide psychologique et psychosociale, sont indispensables sur une période »[48]. Les autres enjeux de la gestion des répercussions comprennent le traitement des prolongements légaux, lorsque le viol est illégal et que l'avortement est proscrit. Bouvier insiste sur le besoin de soutenir les femmes à la suite d'un avortement, alors qu' « elles peuvent être humiliées, exclues ou stigmatisées [...], violentées, parfois même à mort [...], [ou] poursuivies et emprisonnées ».[49]

La revue de littérature indique que les enfants montrent des besoins spécifiques, selon qu'ils aient commis ou été victimes, ou encore représentent le fruit, de violences sexuelles. Duroch et Schulte-Hillen décrivent ainsi le travail de Médecins Sans Frontières : « Soigner des enfants présente des enjeux supplémentaires, tels que [...] gérer parfois des traumatismes physiques et psychologiques sévères », mais également la nécessité d'obtenir le consentement

44 Paul Bouvier, "Sexual violence, health and humanitarian ethics: Towards a holistic, person-centred approach," *International Review of the Red Cross* 96(894) (2014), <doi:10.1017/S1816383115000430> (consulté le 11 janvier 2016), 573.

45 Ibid., 574

46 Skjelsboek, "Sexual violence in post-Yugoslav wars," in Kuehnast et al., eds., *Women and War: Power & Protection in Twenty-First Century*, 81.

47 Solangon et Patel, "Sexual violence against men in countries affected by armed conflict," 434.

48 Bouvier, "Sexual violence, health and humanitarian ethics: Towards a holistic, person-centred approach," 576.

49 Ibid., 582.

éclairé des patients avant d'apporter une aide médicale.[50] Solangon et Patel évoquent : « la difficulté de réintégrer des enfants soldats, qui peuvent avoir été utilisés comme esclaves sexuels ou forcés à commettre des actes de violence sexuelle ».[51] L'Alliance MenEngage et le Fonds des Nations Unies pour la population (FNUAP)[52] affirment qu'il est nécessaire de « Cibler des stratégies et techniques spécifiques pour travailler avec des enfants et adolescents qui ont vécu, commis ou été témoins d'actes de violence sexuelle ».[53] Steinberg, ambassadeur des États-Unis en Angola dans les années 1990, remarque qu'il y a « de jeunes garçons, qui n'ont jamais appris à interagir avec des filles de leur âge sur un même pied d'égalité ».[54] Bouvier identifie les prérequis des soins de courte ou longue durée aux enfants nés d'actes de violence sexuelle : « ces enfants doivent être considérés comme vulnérables, et présentant un risque fort de retombées négatives sur leur santé et développement ».[55] Un rapport de l'ONU de 2015 évaluant les conséquences de la guerre en Bosnie Herzégovine vingt après la fin du conflit note le manque de soutien aux « enfants nés de viols commis durant la guerre, qui sont particulièrement exposés à un risque de stigmatisation, d'abandon, de rejet et de faible statut socio-économique ».[56]

La littérature illustre également que les besoins des hommes dans la gestion des répercussions diffèrent de ceux des femmes et enfants. Solangon et Patel exposent les épreuves que doivent traverser les victimes de violences sexuelles, non moins que là où l'homosexualité est illégale, mais « Les hommes sont souvent mis au ban de la société, appelés « bush wives », émasculés, humiliés et parfois accusés d'avoir provoqué l'agression ».[57] Ils mettent en avant la néces-

50 Françoise Duroch, et Catrin Schulte-Hillen, "Care for victims of sexual violence, an organization pushed to its limits: The case of Médecins Sans Frontières," *International Review of the Red Cross*, 96(894) (2014), <doi:10.1017/S1816383115000107> (consulté le 11 janvier 2016), 616 and 618-619.

51 Solangon et Patel, "Sexual violence against men in countries affected by armed conflict," 434.

52 Abréviation adoptée par convention en accord avec sa précédente dénomination.

53 MenEngage Alliance et Fonds des Nations Unies pour la Population, "Sexual Violence in Conflict and Post-Conflict: Engaging Men and Boys," (juillet 2012), <http://menengage.org/resources/sexual-violence-conflict-post-conflict-engaging-men-boys/> (consulté le 12 janvier 2016), 12.

54 Donald Steinberg, "Women and War: an Agenda for action," in: Kuehnast et al., eds., *Women and War: Power and Protection in Twenty-First Century*, 121.

55 Bouvier, "Sexual violence, health and humanitarian ethics: Towards a holistic, person-centred approach," 582-583.

56 Secrétaire Général des Nations Unies, "Conflict-related sexual violence: Report of Secretary General," 20/33.

57 Solangon et Patel, "Sexual violence against men in countries affected by armed conflict," 421.

sité d'une éducation adaptée et de campagnes de communication, mais également d'une aide psychologique spécifique.[58] Ils reconnaissent également les épreuves que traversent les auteurs de violences sexuelles : « Réintégrer socialement des hommes et des garçons que l'on a forcés à violer une famille ou un membre de la communauté demeure extrêmement problématique dans beaucoup de sociétés ».[59] MenEngage et le FNUAP soulignent les besoins d'autres hommes : « Comprendre qu'être témoin de violences subies par leurs êtres chers est une expérience directe de l'agression et peut entraîner des traumatismes aussi profonds et durables que ceux qui y ont survécu ».[60] Un autre aspect réside dans l'augmentation potentielle des violences domestiques, qu'ont constatée nombre d'auteurs, dont Skjelsboek.[61] Steinberg parle également d'hommes qui, une fois rentrés du conflit en Angola et peu compétents, se retrouvent au chômage au sein de communautés où les femmes ont appris à vivre sans eux. Ceci entraîne un accroissement de la consommation de drogues et d'alcool, qui conduit à la violence domestique : « En fait, la fin de la guerre civile a tout bonnement marqué l'avènement d'une ère de violence contre les femmes et les filles ».[62] Edström et al. mettent en évidence des résultats, montrant « la perpétuation et la prévalence [de la violence sexuelle] dans des situations d'après-conflit ».[63] Ils se réfèrent aux recherches effectuées au Rwanda, où les hommes sont « plus enclins à user à la fois de violence physique et sexuelle contre leur conjoint » s'ils ont participé à des actes de génocide dans ce conflit.[64]

Pour résumer les conclusions de ce troisième aspect présenté par la revue de littérature, il apparaît évident que la gestion des répercussions pose des enjeux considérables, à la fois sur le court terme et le long terme, comprenant la nécessité de soins médicaux et psychologiques ; de mesures pour lutter contre la prolifération d'IST ; d'aider les femmes devant subir ou se remettre d'un avortement ; et d'apporter un soutien adapté aux enfants et aux hommes. De plus, la revue de littérature désigne le fait de briser l'engrenage de la violence comme une notion importante de la gestion des répercussions, qui plus est

58 Ibid., 432-433 & 435.

59 Ibid., 421.

60 MenEngage Alliance et FNUAP, "Sexual Violence in Conflict and Post-Conflict: Engaging Men and Boys," 11.

61 Skjelsboek, "Sexual violence in post-Yugoslav wars," in: Kuehnast et al., eds., *Women and War: Power & Protection in Twenty-First Century*, 81.

62 Steinberg, "Women and War: an Agenda for action," in: Kuehnast et al., eds., *Women and War: Power and Protection in Twenty-First Century*, 121.

63 Edström et al., eds.,"Engendering Men: Collaborative Review of Evidence of Men & Boys in Social Change and Gender Equality," 141.

64 Ibid., 143.

lorsque la violence sexuelle est toujours présente après le conflit. C'est une perspective inquiétante à gérer pour la plupart des nations, mais d'autant plus difficile pour les pays fortement touchés par un conflit, et où un tel soutien n'est pas préexistant.

### *Les risques de sécurisation ainsi que de détournement d'attention de l'agenda* Femmes, Paix et Sécurité

Le quatrième élément mis en évidence par la revue de littérature concerne les risques que présentent la sécurisation du problème et de détournement d'attention de l'agenda « Femmes, Paix et Sécurité » (FPS). Kirby écrit qu' « un projet politique mettant en évidence la violence sexuelle [...] doit, s'il rencontre un succès, pouvoir engendrer un effet politique qui allouera les ressources matérielles » à ce problème, et prévient qu'il existe un potentiel de transformation de la réflexion pour aborder à la fois d'autres crimes de guerre et la violence domestique.[65] Il remarque, par exemple, que « dans l'Est de la République Populaire de Chine, les données d'enquête auprès des ménages révèlent des taux extrêmement hauts de violence conjugale, en dépit de la fixation générale des atrocités commises par les groupes armés ».[66] Wood en convient : « Dans certaines situations de conflit, la fréquence des violences sexuelles commises par les acteurs armés est significativement moindre comparée aux violences commises par les partenaires, connaissances ou étrangers »,[67] de même qu'Alcorn :

> Des études ont montré de façon répétée que les survivants ont une propension nettement plus élevée à signaler un viol si un étranger en est l'auteur, que si un mari ou un petit-ami en sont les auteurs. Dans les situations de conflit et d'après-conflit, le sous-signalement de violences sexuelles au sein des ménages peut grandement augmenter la proportion des violences sexuelles imputées aux groupes armés.[68]

Les résultats de la revue de littérature ont également mis en évidence une reconnaissance croissante qu'étant donné que les hommes soient à la fois victimes et auteurs de violences sexuelles, cela pourrait réduire les acquis durement gagnés de l'agenda FPS. Kuehnast et al. déclarent que l'UNSCR 1325,

65 Kirby, "Ending sexual violence in conflict: Preventing Sexual Violence Initiative and its critics," 463.

66 Ibid., 462.

67 Wood, "Conflict-related sexual violence and the policy implications of recent research," 460.

68 Alcorn, "Responding to sexual violence in armed conflict," 2035.

passée en 2000, « attribue aux organisations de la société civile et aux militantes de la paix dans la monde une victoire décisive et un instrument de mobilisation faisant autorité »[69] et, en 2007, Alison demande : « si les féministes arrêtent de parler de viol, qui le fera ? »[70] La critique de Kirby de la PSVI et son soutien manifeste aux survivants hommes et garçons, pourrait éventuellement impliquer que « l'ONU et les états participants seront désormais moins efficaces dans le repérage et les réponses apportées aux relations de pouvoir patriarcales et *aux ordres hiérarchiques de genre* [...] [*et*] *l'on pourrait s'attendre à ce que les programmes* existants ne réduisent les ressources dédiées aux femmes et aux filles de moitié (ou de façon significative) ».[71] Cependant, le CICR semble faire bon accueil à cette nouvelle structuration : « l'attention est passée de la situation critique des femmes durant un conflit à une approche plus large, basée sur les vulnérabilités des femmes et des hommes en fonction de leur genre. »[72] Ce point de vue est soutenu par Solangon et Patel : « on doit attirer l'attention sur la violence sexuelle faite aux hommes, non comme une menace aux droits des femmes mais comme une lutte associée dans la guerre contre la violence sexuelle basée sur le genre ».[73] Bien que certains universitaires ne soient pas à l'aise avec cette remarque, Kirby note qu'il est possible de suivre les changements de termes dans les UNSCR 1888 et 1960 en 2008 et 2009 centrées sur les femmes, puis l'UNSCR 2106 de juin 2013 mentionnant « femmes et consultants en questions de genre » jusqu'aux « consultants en questions de genre » de l'UNSCR 2122 d'octobre 2013.[74] Ceci suggère une reconnaissance et une acceptation croissantes par la communauté internationale que le problème de violence sexuelle en conflit doit être abordé en termes d'impact sur les hommes et les garçons, au même titre que les femmes et les filles.

En conclusion de ce quatrième point-clé, les résultats de la revue de littérature montrent qu'il est important de placer la violence sexuelle commise en tant qu'arme de guerre dans une perspective de taux plus élevés de violence *domestique* en conflit, post-conflits et en absence de conflit. Par ailleurs, bien que cet ouvrage se veuille être une analyse impartiale du sujet, l'importance du rôle des femmes dans les questions de paix et de sécurité ne doit être

69 Kuehnast et al., eds., *Women and War: Power & Protection in Twenty-First Century*, 2.

70 Solangon et Patel, "Sexual violence against men in countries affected by armed conflict," 424.

71 Kirby, "Ending sexual violence in conflict: Preventing Sexual Violence Initiative and its critics," 471.

72 CICR, "Sexual Violence in Armed Conflict: E-Briefing," Introduction.

73 Solangon et Patel, "Sexual violence against men in countries affected by armed conflict," 436.

74 Kirby, "Ending sexual violence in conflict: Preventing Sexual Violence Initiative and its critics," 470.

sous-estimée, à la fois en termes de gestion efficace des répercussions et de prévention de futures occurrences de violences sexuelles en conflit.

### *La violence sexuelle en situation de conflit n'est pas inévitable*

Le cinquième point-clé de la revue de littérature démontre que la violence sexuelle perpétrée en situation de conflit n'est pas inévitable. D'après ses propres recherches et la synthèse des conclusions d'autres universitaires, Wood identifie des différences dans l'étendue et les modes de la violence sexuelle, son timing, sa place au sein d'un répertoire de modes opératoires violents et son caractère symétrique ou asymétrique au cours d'un conflit donné. Elle découvre en outre que ces différences ne peuvent être justifiées ni par le type de conflit, ni par les normes ou traditions dominantes, les religions pratiquées ou les occasions se présentant pour commettre des violences sexuelles. De plus, ces différences ne peuvent s'expliquer par la difficulté à obtenir des données fiables.[75] Wood conclut ainsi que « la variabilité omise, ainsi que l'absence relative de violences sexuelles en temps de guerre par un ou plusieurs groupes armés, ont d'importantes répercussions politiques : contrairement à ce qui est parfois avancé, le viol n'est pas inévitable en situation de guerre ».[76] Wood donne des exemples de groupes armés n'ayant pas employé la violence sexuelle au Salvador, en Israël ou Palestine, au Vietnam et au Sri Lanka[77]. Cependant, elle prévient également que « par absence de violence sexuelle, j'entends l'absence relative de violence sexuelle : celle commise par un groupe est très rare (mais pas inexistante) ».[78]

Dans un ouvrage ultérieur, Wood identifie un autre facteur de variation, lorsque la violence ne cible uniquement les femmes ou les deux sexes.[79] Elle donne également des chiffres provenant d'autres travaux de recherche académiques. Elle cite par exemple Nordås qui affirme que : « 59% des 177 acteurs armés dans les guerres civiles entre 2000 et 2009 dans vingt pays africains n'ont pas été signalés avoir commis des viols ou d'autres formes de violence sexuelle ».[80] Elle fait également allusion aux conclusions de Cohen : « lorsqu'un camp du conflit encourage la violence sexuelle et l'autre pas, une tendance qui

75 Wood, "Rape is not inevitable during war," in: Kuehnast et al., eds., *Women and War: Power & Protection in Twenty-First Century*, 37-39 and 43-45.

76 Ibid., 39.

77 Ibid., 40 & 43.

78 Ibid., 39.

79 Wood, "Conflict-related sexual violence and the policy implications of recent research," 461.

80 Ibid., 458.

se vérifie dans 40% des guerres civiles ».[81] De plus, elle se base sur les travaux conjoints de Cohen et Nordås :

> La meilleure base de données inter-nations confirme que les violences sexuelles (y compris les viols) varient selon les armées, les organisations d'insurgés et les milices pro-gouvernements. En effet, pour ces trois types d'acteurs armés, une grande majorité n'a pas perpétré d'actes de violence sexuelle entre 1989 et 2009.[82]

Dans leurs recherches sur les violences sexuelles faites aux hommes, Solangon et Patel reconnaissent que « la violence sexuelle n'est plus principalement considérée comme un désir sexuel biologique, mais de plus en plus comme une démonstration de force, de domination et d'humiliation ».[83] Le CICR en convient : « Il n'est plus défendable d'affirmer que la violence sexuelle représente simplement le côté sombre de nos pires pulsions humaines et un dommage collatéral de la guerre ; il est aujourd'hui largement admis que la violence sexuelle n'est pas une conséquence inévitable des conflits armés ».[84] C'est un point-clé de la revue de littérature, car cela implique que si la violence sexuelle n'est pas toujours utilisée comme arme de guerre, alors des mesures préventives doivent être dérivées de ces conflits et appliquées à de futurs faits de violence sexuelle en temps de guerre.

### *Résumé des points-clés de la revue de littérature*

Pour conclure cette revue de littérature, les analyses effectuées par les universitaires et les professionnels ont mis en évidence un certain nombre de raisons expliquant l'usage de la violence sexuelle en conflit, ainsi que des preuves indiquant que les hommes et les garçons peuvent en être victimes, et les femmes les auteurs. Ces études ont révélé son caractère non inévitable en situation de conflit, étant donné que tous les groupes armés n'en font pas toujours usage dans tous les conflits. Elles ont également souligné le défi que représente la gestion de ses répercussions ; les risques qu'entraîne la titrisation lorsque les ressources ne sont plus suffisantes pour lutter contre les crimes de guerre et les autres formes de violence domestique, et le danger de l'attention détournée par l'agenda FPS.

---

81 Ibid., 462.

82 Ibid., 459.

83 Solangon et Patel, "Sexual violence against men in countries affected by armed conflict," 425.

84 CICR, "Sexual Violence in Armed Conflict: E-Briefing," Partie 4.

## Approches préventives actuelles

### *La compréhension*

Intéressons-nous maintenant à l'analyse des approches préventives existantes, qui couvrent quatre domaines : la compréhension, le soutien de haut niveau, la formation, et la législation. Premièrement, il est nécessaire de comprendre un problème pour empêcher qu'il ne se reproduise. La partie précédente, portant sur les résultats de la revue de littérature, a cherché à montrer une compréhension accrue des problèmes concernant l'usage de violence sexuelle en tant qu'arme de guerre. Bien que ces travaux soulignent la nécessité d'approfondir ces recherches, il existe aujourd'hui une solide base de travail qui a fait progresser la compréhension de ce sujet. Le CICR note que « sa prévalence et ses graves répercussions sur les individus et les sociétés, ainsi que ses dynamiques sous-jacentes, ont progressivement fait l'objet d'une meilleure compréhension au cours des deux dernières décennies ».[85] Par exemple, bien que Médecins Sans Frontières ait été fondée en 1971, on doit attendre 1999 pour que l'organisation conçoive son premier plan de traitement pour les survivants de violences sexuelles.[86]

La littérature a également montré une appréhension des lieux et moments reconnus propices à la perpétration d'actes de violence sexuelle. Par exemple, Solangon et Patel font la description de certaines de ces zones où les personnes sont vulnérables, telles que des camps de réfugiés, des passages de frontières, des lieux isolés comme des champs, ou, au contraire, des marchés ou des routes commerciales où la concentration des personnes est importante. Ils font également référence à des moments où la victime est plus vulnérable : en allant chercher de l'eau ou du bois, en allant à l'école, la nuit ou en période d'élections.[87] En particulier pour les hommes, Dr. Aburabi, médecin en milieu carcéral et membre du CICR, décrit les moments connus de vulnérabilité : « lors d'une primo-incarcération, lorsque le détenu est désorienté et isolé des instances de secours habituelles. [...] La prédominance est également élevée dans les centres d'interrogatoire ».[88] Skjelsboek propose qu'un indicateur de vulnérabilité aux violences sexuelles apparaît lorsque que « le discours

85 CICR, "Sexual Violence in Armed Conflict: E-Briefing," Introduction.

86 Duroch et Schulte-Hillen, "Care for victims of sexual violence, an organization pushed to its limits: case of Médecins Sans Frontières," 603.

87 Solangon et Patel, "Sexual violence against men in countries affected by armed conflict," 432.

88 Bernard et Pothelet, "Through eyes of a detention doctor: Interview with Raed Aburabi," 481.

politique devient sexualisé »,[89] et Watson note qu'un élément de prévention des violences sexuelles faites aux hommes (quoique tout aussi applicable aux femmes et enfants) consiste à « réduire la proportion de mauvais endroits et mauvais moments ».[90] Par conséquent, bien que davantage de recherches soient nécessaires, il semble que le niveau actuel de compréhension des problèmes fournisse une base satisfaisante pour la conception, la mise en place et l'évaluation de stratégies de prévention efficaces.

### *Le soutien de haut niveau*

Le deuxième domaine à l'étude pour sa contribution aux approches préventives actuelles est le degré de soutien international de haut niveau. En 2009, la résolution 1888 du Conseil de Sécurité des Nations Unies crée le poste de Représentant spécial du Secrétaire Général chargé de la question des violences sexuelles en conflit. Un an plus tard, la résolution 1960 mandate le Secrétaire Général des Nations Unies pour produire un rapport où figurent les noms de tous les groupes armés ayant recours à la violence sexuelle en conflit, dans une stratégie de « naming and shaming », c'est-à-dire les nommer pour mieux les dévaloriser. Le rapport de 2015 détaille 45 groupes étatiques et non-étatiques, dont 13 listés pour la première fois.[91] De plus, « l'action de l'ONU contre la violence sexuelle en conflit » prend « des initiatives stratégiques visant à améliorer la coordination au sein du système, la construction de connaissances, la défense et le soutien technique à l'échelle nationale ».[92] Depuis 2013, 155 pays ont signé une Déclaration de l'Assemblée Générale des Nations Unies pour mettre fin à la violence sexuelle en conflit.[93] Lors de sa présidence du G8 en 2013, le Royaume-Uni a assuré la production d'une Déclaration selon laquelle les membres du G8 s'engagent à soutenir une série de mesures comprenant : aide financière, formation, conseils sur la documentation des preuves, la re-

---

89 Skjelsboek, "Sexual violence in post-Yugoslav wars," in: Kuehnast et al., eds., *Women and War: Power & Protection in Twenty-First Century*, 81.

90 Callum Watson, "Bad apples or bad apple trees? An examination of the contexts in which sexual violence against men takes place," paper presented at a workshop entitled, 'Sexual Violence Against Men during Conflicts: Bridging the Gap between Theory and Practice', *The Graduate Institute of International and Development Studies*, Genève 26-27 février 2015), 9.

91 Secrétaire Général des Nations unies, "Conflict-related sexual violence: Report of Secretary General," 1/33.

92 Ibid., 25/33.

93 G7, "G7 Report on the Implementation of the G8 Declaration on Preventing Sexual Violence in Conflict," G7 novembre 2015), <https://www.g7germany.de/Content/EN/_Anlagen/G7/2015-11-24-g7-erklaerung_svc_en.pdf?__blob=publicationFile&v=3(accessed January 7, 2016), 2

connaissance que la violence sexuelle peut sérieusement enfreindre la Convention de Genève (et par là même faire l'objet d'une condamnation internationale en vertu de la compétence universelle), le besoin d'aborder le problème de la violence sexuelle en première phase de toute réaction, et l'absence, prévue dans les accords de paix ultérieurs, de toute amnistie pour les auteurs de violence sexuelle.[94] Sous la présidence de l'Allemagne en 2015, les membres du G8 ont également convenu de produire un rapport de suivi pour évaluer les progrès, qu'ils ont dûment réalisé (alors en qualité de membres du G7).[95]

En juin 2014, le Royaume-Uni a accueilli un sommet mondial avec la participation de 120 nations,[96] ainsi que la représentation de tous les membres du G7, dont quatre ministres des Affaires étrangères et le Haut représentant de l'Union Européenne pour les affaires étrangères et la politique de sécurité.[97] Le Secrétaire d'État américain, John Kerry, qui a clôturé le sommet, a exposé les grandes lignes de l'aide qu'entendent apporter les États-Unis, notamment l'initiative « Safe from the Start » annoncée en 2013, financée à hauteur de 22 millions de dollars en novembre 2015. Le Premier ministre britannique a nommé une Représentante spéciale pour la prévention de la violence sexuelle en conflit, la baronne Anelay, et la Stratégie pour la sécurité nationale de 2016 s'est engagée, s'agissant de la PSVI, à « étendre sa portée et sa mise en œuvre »,[98] le gouvernement britannique y ayant alloué, depuis son lancement en 2012 jusque fin 2015, 29 millions de livres.[99] L'Organisation du Traité de l'Atlantique Nord (OTAN) a créé un poste permanent de Représentant spécial pour FPS en 2014. Pour sa mission Soutien Déterminé (Resolute Support) en cours en Afghanistan, l'OTAN a incorporé FPS dès le début dans le processus de planification, démontrant ainsi que ce n'est « plus une arrière-pensée : une perspective de genre a été intégrée, du processus de décision politique à la rédaction du plan opérationnel

---

94 Bureau des Affaires Étrangères et du Commonwealth, "The Foreign Secretary William Hague, Angelina Jolie and Zainab Hawa Bangura launch G8 Declaration on Preventing Sexual Violence in Conflict," Foreign & Commonwealth Office avril 2013), <https://www.gov.uk/government/news/g8-declaration-on-preventing-sexual-violence-in-conflict (consulté le 27 novembre 2015).

95 G7, "G7 Report on the Implementation of the G8 Declaration on Preventing Sexual Violence in Conflict."

96 Kirby, "Ending sexual violence in conflict: Preventing Sexual Violence Initiative and its critics," 457.

97 G7, "G7 Report on the Implementation of the G8 Declaration on Preventing Sexual Violence in Conflict," 2.

98 Gouvernement britannique, *National Security Strategy and Strategic Defence and Security Review 2015: A Secure and Prosperous United Kingdom*, Cm 9161 novembre 2015), 63.

99 G7, "G7 Report on the Implementation of the G8 Declaration on Preventing Sexual Violence in Conflict," 5.

de la mission et la constitution des troupes ».[100] Le CICR a modifié sa façon de fonctionner pour présumer, jusqu'à preuve du contraire, de l'existence de violences sexuelles au cours d'un conflit.[101]

Il semblerait donc qu'il existe un certain degré de soutien international de haut niveau émanant des Nations Unies, du G7, de l'OTAN, du CICR et de pays individuels, dans la lutte contre l'utilisation de la violence sexuelle comme arme de guerre. C'est un élément facilitateur important dans la conduite et l'aide à la mise en place de mesures préventives. Cependant, en raison des challenges que cela implique, davantage de ressources et un engagement durable de la communauté internationale seront nécessaires pour renforcer les mesures préventives actuelles et consolider les améliorations apportées. Par ailleurs, le soutien international venant d'organisations non-occidentales doit également être visible : par exemple, les recherches effectuées sur les versions en anglais des sites internet de l'Union Africaine (UA), le Commonwealth, la Ligue des États arabes, le Conseil de coopération du Golfe, l'Association des nations de l'Asie du Sud-Est, et l'Organisation des États américains ont renvoyé très peu de résultats contenant des informations sur leurs politiques de prévention de la violence sexuelle en tant qu'arme de guerre. De telles organisations doivent se montrer proactives dans leur condamnation de la violence sexuelle en conflit, qui doit être confortée par des actions concrètes. Leur engagement, financier ou autre, aiderait le reste de la communauté internationale, elle-même sous tension au niveau des ressources, et montrerait leur véritable opposition à la violence sexuelle en conflit.

### *La formation*

Le troisième élément à être évalué dans sa contribution à prévenir la violence sexuelle en conflit concerne la provision actuelle consistant à former les forces armées et civiles. En 2010, l'action des Nations Unies a développé « des activités de pré-déploiement basées sur des scénarios [...] pour améliorer les capacités opérationnelles des soldats de la paix et des forces de police visant à agir promptement et de manière adéquate »,[102] qui continuent d'être utilisées dans les centres d'entraînement des Nations Unies. En 2014, les pays membres de l'OTAN ont approuvé un nouveau Plan de Formation et d'entraînement pour les questions de genre dans les opérations militaires, « qui harmonise et

100 Marriët Schuurman, "NATO and the Women, Peace and Security Agenda: Time to Bring It Home." *Connections: The Quarterly Journal*, XIV(3) (2015), <http://www.nato.int/cps/en/natohq/opinions_124032.htm?selectedLocale=en> (consulté le 12 janvier 2016).

101 CICR, "Sexual Violence in Armed Conflict: E-Briefing," Part 2.

102 Secrétaire Général des Nations Unies, "Conflict-related sexual violence: Report of Secretary General," 26/33.

synchronise l'éducation aux questions de genre à tous les niveaux ».[103] L'année suivante, l'exercice OTAN de gestion de crise militaro-politique le plus avancé « était le premier à ce niveau [...] à inclure des indicateurs montrant que la violence sexuelle liée au conflit constitue une tactique de guerre, et à tester la façon dont ces indicateurs peuvent influer sur la prise de décision stratégique ».[104] La même année, la Royaume-Uni a annoncé la mise en œuvre d'un financement à hauteur de 700 000 livres pour entraîner les soldats de la paix de l'UA à prévenir et répondre aux violences sexuelles en conflit,[105] et également affirmé que toutes ses troupes déployées à l'étranger seraient entraînées par FPS et la PVSI pour novembre 2016.[106] En outre, le Royaume-Uni a formé à cette date plus de 8000 policiers et soldats de la paix africains, 2500 membres des forces armées maliennes et 800 membres des troupes Peshmerga irakiennes.[107] Alors que des cas ont été rapportés où des soldats de la paix de l'ONU ou de l'UA commettent eux-mêmes des violences sexuelles au lieu de les prévenir ou d'y mettre fin, les dispositifs de formation actuels contribuent à assurer de meilleurs comportements. Par conséquent, la formation peut être considérée comme une mesure importante donnant aux forces armées et policières les compétences et la compréhension nécessaires pour faire face aux cas de violence sexuelle et prévenir les occurrences ultérieures. Elle leur donne également le rôle de modèle pour « contribuer à définir des notions universelles sur le comportement, les rôles et les responsabilités que les acteurs des forces armées doivent avoir en conflit. Même les groupes rebelles peuvent en faire autant, dans l'attente qu'ils puissent un jour être reconnus comme acteurs nationaux légitimes ».[108] Cela fait écho à la vision du Secrétaire des Affaires Étrangères de l'époque, William Hague, qui a déclaré en 2013 : « les membres des forces armées sont souvent les premiers à établir un contact avec les

103 Schuurman, "NATO and Women, Peace and Security Agenda: Time to Bring It Home."

104 Ibid.

105 Bureau des Affaires Étrangères et du Commonwealth, "Angelina Jolie Pitt joins Baroness Anelay to chart next steps on tackling sexual violence," Bureau des Affaires étrangères et du Commonwealth juin 2015), <https://www.gov.uk/government/news/angelina-jolie-pitt-joins-baroness-anelay-to-chart-next-steps-on-tackling-sexual-violence> (consulté le 12 janvier 2016).

106 Baronne Sandip Verma, "The UK firmly believes that the 15th anniversary must represent the start of a new era on Women, Peace and Security," Gouvernement britannique 13 octobre 2015), <https://www.gov.uk/government/speeches/the-uk-firmly-believes-that-the-15th-anniversary-must-represent-the-start-of-a-new-era-on-women-peace-and-security> (consulté le 26 novembre 2015).

107 G7, "G7 Report on the Implementation of the G8 Declaration on Preventing Sexual Violence in Conflict," 7.

108 Watson, "Bad apples or bad apple trees? Examination of contexts in which sexual violence against men takes place," 10.

survivants, et pourraient également jouer un rôle important dans le changement des attitudes masculines ».[109]

### *La législation*

Le quatrième et dernier élément à l'étude pour sa contribution aux approches préventives actuelles concerne la législation, qui couvre le cadre légal, sa mise en œuvre et la dissuasion. Premièrement, s'agissant de la loi en elle-même, Gaggioli, avocate et universitaire, a examiné les dispositions légales actuelles en droit international humanitaire (DIH) et en droit international des droits de l'homme. Elle a mis en évidence que « La prohibition par le DIH du viol et d'autres formes de violence sexuelle s'applique à la fois aux conflits armés internationaux et non-internationaux et fait également partie du droit coutumier. En vertu des droits de l'homme, la violence sexuelle est interdite en tous temps ».[110] Elle souligne également que « Le viol et autres formes de violence sexuelle peuvent équivaloir à des crimes internationaux : crimes de guerre, crimes contre l'humanité et actes de génocide, lorsque les critères de ces crimes [...] sont remplis. À ce titre, ils engagent la responsabilité pénale individuelle ».[111] Gaggioli conclut : « Le cadre légal international [...] est par conséquent extrêmement fort, bien que perfectible [...] Les différentes branches du droit international (DIH, droits de l'homme, droit pénal international) se font écho et se consolident entre elles, assurant ainsi une complémentarité essentielle ».[112] Une Déclaration du G8 en 2013 fait remarquer que « le droit humanitaire international présente une interdiction de longue date [...] et lorsque faisant partie d'une attaque systématique ou répandue contre une population civile, peut représenter un crime contre l'humanité et un acte constitutif du génocide ».[113] Un récent rapport d'une commission d'enquête parlementaire de la Chambre des Lords a « étudié la question d'un renforcement du droit international [...] [mais] a conclu que les dispositions actuelles sont satisfai-

109 Bureau des Affaires Étrangères et du Commonwealth, "Foreign Secretary William Hague, Angelina Jolie and Zainab Hawa Bangura launch G8 Declaration on Preventing Sexual Violence in Conflict."

110 Gloria Gaggioli, "Sexual violence in armed conflicts: A violation of international humanitarian law and human rights law," *International Review of the Red Cross* 96(894) (2014), <doi:10.1017/S1816383115000211> (consulté le 11 janvier 2016), 537.

111 Ibid.

112 Ibid.

113 Bureau des Affaires Étrangères et du Commonwealth, "Declaration on Preventing Sexual Violence in Conflict Bureau des Affaires étrangères et du Commonwealth avril 2013), <https://www.gov.uk/government/uploads/system/uploads/attachment_data/file/185008/G8_PSVI_Declaration_-_FINAL.pdf> (consulté le 27 novembre 2015).

santes ».[114] Il semblerait donc que les dispositions légales soient, du moins en théorie, suffisamment solides.

Bien que la revue de littérature n'ait pas mis en évidence le besoin d'accroître la législation en la matière, elle a cependant mis l'accent sur sa mise en œuvre. Par exemple, Gaggioli appelle à « une meilleure mise en œuvre des règles existantes au sein d'un pays et des poursuites effectives des auteurs de crimes sexuels aux niveaux national et international ».[115] En 2013, le G8 soutient « le déploiement d'experts internationaux pour aider à construire les capacités judiciaires, enquêtrices et légales d'autres pays ».[116] Le CICR recommande que « Les autorités doivent s'assurer que des dispositifs adéquats soient en place afin que les victimes puissent rendre compte des violences de manière sécurisée et confidentielle »[117]. Ils appellent également à « une sensibilisation adéquate du personnel légal, des arrangements techniques spécifiques concernant la date et l'heure de l'audience, et une assistance légale adaptée pour tous les auteurs présumés ».[118]

Bien que cela représente un engagement considérable, certaines organisations aident les pays à améliorer leurs procédures légales. Par exemple, un rapport du G7 de 2015 a mis en relief le travail de « Justice Rapid Response » (JRR), un mécanisme intergouvernemental travaillant conjointement avec les Nations Unies. Ce rapport explique que JRR tient des listes d'experts en justice pénale (plus de 500 personnes) et des enquêteurs prêts à être missionnés, ces derniers entreprenant des investigations plus poussées.[119] Le site internet de JRR souligne que ces experts représentent 60 professions, « viennent de plus de 95 pays et parlent plus de 80 langues. Les membres du vivier de JRR proviennent à plus de 40% de l'hémisphère sud et plus de 50% sont des femmes ».[120]

---

114 Chambre des Lords, "Select Committee on Sexual Violence in Conflict: Report of Session 2015-16: Sexual Violence in Conflict: A War Crime," Chambre des Lords, HL Paper 123 12 avril 2016), <http://www.publications.parliament.uk/pa/ld201516/ldselect/ldsvc/123/123.pdf> (accessed April 15, 2016), 8.

115 Gaggioli, "Sexual violence in armed conflicts: violation of international humanitarian law and human rights law," 533.

116 Bureau des Affaires Étrangères et du Commonwealth, "Foreign Secretary William Hague, Angelina Jolie and Zainab Hawa Bangura launch G8 Declaration on Preventing Sexual Violence in Conflict."

117 CICR, "Sexual Violence in Armed Conflict: E-Briefing," Partie 3.

118 Ibid.

119 G7, "G7 Report on the Implementation of the G8 Declaration on Preventing Sexual Violence in Conflict," 7.

120 Justice Rapid Response, "Justice Rapid Response welcomes UN Women and Draper Richards Kaplan Foundation to its Executive Board," JRR novembre 2015), <http://www.justicerapidresponse.org/justice-rapid-response-welcomes-un-women-and-draper-richards-kaplan-foundation-to-its-executive-board/> (consulté le 7 janvier 2016).

En moins de six ans, JRR a mené près de 70 enquêtes, y compris en Syrie et en Irak[121]. Le Royaume-Uni a également monté sa propre équipe de plus de 70 experts qui couvrent un ensemble de domaines, comprenant la police scientifique et la médecine légale.[122] Elle a travaillé sur 17 projets dans 13 pays, y compris la frontière de la Syrie afin de « faire progresser les enquêtes et améliorer les poursuites à l'encontre des auteurs de violence sexuelle en conflit »,[123] entre autres. En outre, les Ministres des affaires étrangères du G8 ont convenu, en 2013, de lancer un Protocole international relatif aux enquêtes sur les violences sexuelles dans les situations de conflits. Conçu par des fonctionnaires britanniques avec l'aide d'experts, il est révélé au Sommet mondial de 2014 pour « aider à la consolidation des preuves visant à porter les auteurs en justice ».[124] Depuis, le Royaume-Uni a développé un plan de formation et traduit le Protocole en plusieurs langues, y compris l'arabe, et aidé plusieurs pays à en faire usage, comme la Bosnie, la Colombie et l'Ouganda.[125] La profession médicale a également reconnu son rôle dans la collecte de preuves, bien que cette approche ne soit pas totalement honnête, étant donné que la fonction première de cette profession soit le traitement des patients et non le maintien de l'ordre. Cependant, depuis 2011, Physicians for Human Rights réunit les travailleurs du domaine de la santé et les professionnels du droit pour renforcer leurs efforts conjoints : « [Les praticiens cliniques] sont les premiers à tomber sur les éléments qui constituent des preuves ; ils doivent donc les identifier et les préserver dans l'optique de pouvoir les soumettre lors d'un procès au long cours ».[126] Il semblerait ainsi que la communauté internationale ait reconnu la nécessité d'aider les nations à améliorer leurs pratiques juridiques, et franchi des étapes pour instaurer un changement. Néanmoins, pour garantir un réel effet en tant que mesure préventive, cela requerra un engagement national et

121 Ibid. & G7, "G7 Report on the Implementation of the G8 Declaration on Preventing Sexual Violence in Conflict," 7.

122 Bureau des Affaires Étrangères et du Commonwealth, "Foreign Secretary William Hague, Angelina Jolie and Zainab Hawa Bangura launch G8 Declaration on Preventing Sexual Violence in Conflict."

123 G7, "G7 Report on the Implementation of the G8 Declaration on Preventing Sexual Violence in Conflict," 7.

124 Bureau des Affaires Étrangères et du Commonwealth, "Chair's Summary: Global Summit to End Sexual Violence in Conflict," Foreign & Commonwealth Office juin 2014), <https://www.gov.uk/government/publications/chairs-summary-global-summit-to-end-sexual-violence-in-conflict/chairs-summary-global-summit-to-end-sexual-violence-in-conflict> (consulté le 27 novembre 2015).

125 G7, "G7 Report on the Implementation of the G8 Declaration on Preventing Sexual Violence in Conflict," 5-6.

126 Alcorn, "Responding to sexual violence in armed conflict," 2037.

international, une formation et un mentorat de long terme ainsi que des ressources afin d'intégrer de bonnes pratiques et d'assurer une meilleure application de la législation adéquate. Il faudrait probablement aborder ce problème de manière plus approfondie, mais une fois que les états sont convaincus d'avoir adopté la législation appropriée, il est du devoir de la communauté internationale de les assister et de s'assurer de son application.

Le dernier aspect à l'étude en matière de législation est son efficacité en tant que moyen de dissuasion. Une des critiques majeures de la PSVI formulée par Kirby se fonde sur la fin de l'impunité : « l'hypothèse principale de l'impunité, selon laquelle l'augmentation des poursuites éviterait de futures atrocités, se heurte à une considérable opposition fondée sur son efficacité, son coût et la clarté de son but ».[127] Kirby rappelle que les coûts moyens d'emprisonnement d'une personne aux Tribunaux pénaux internationaux pour l'ex-Yougoslavie et le Rwanda s'élèvent respectivement à 35 millions de dollars et 39 millions de livres.[128] Il met également en évidence que « les vainqueurs et les vaincus ne sont pas égaux devant la loi ».[129] Human Rights Watch note que les critiques du Tribunal Pénal International pour le Rwanda (TPIR) ciblent le coût, la lenteur des procédures, le peu d'affaires traitées, la quantité de temps considérable, permettant ainsi aux condamnés de s'adresser aux médias, le manque de compensation pour les survivants, et l'abandon des charges à l'encontre des « vainqueurs » du Front patriotique rwandais.[130] Il semblerait que la perspective de peines de long terme puisse être annulée par l'opportunité à court terme de gagner une guerre.

Cependant, le TPIR a bien écroué l'ancien Premier ministre, chef d'État-Major des armées et le chef de cabinet du ministère de la Défense,[131] ainsi que la première femme auteur de génocide, crimes de guerre et crimes contre l'humanité, Pauline Nyiramasuhuko.[132] Parmi d'autres affaires faisant date, on compte celle de Duško Tadić, qui fut le premier à être condamné pour de violents crimes de guerre sexuels contre des hommes en 1997.[133] En 2014, le Général Kakwavu et le « Colonel 106 » ont été déclarés coupables de crimes de violence sexuelle en République Démocratique du Congo, des condamnations

127 Kirby, "Ending sexual violence in conflict: Preventing Sexual Violence Initiative and its critics," 464.

128 Ibid., 465.

129 Ibid.

130 Human Rights Watch, "Rwanda: International Tribunal Closing Its Doors."

131 Ibid.

132 Mollmann, "Rape in war: No more excuses."

133 Watson, "Bad apples or bad apple trees? Examination of contexts in which sexual violence against men takes place," 3.

décrites par les Nations Unies comme « marquant une étape importante pour faire répondre les hauts gradés de leurs actes ».[134] En mars 2016, la Cour Pénale Internationale obtient sa première condamnation pour violences sexuelles en situation de conflit (y compris contre des hommes) avec Jean-Pierre Bemba. C'est également la première fois que la CPI poursuit un individu pour ses « responsabilités de commandement », Bemba occupant les fonctions de Président et chef d'État-Major du mouvement de libération du Congo.[135] Le CICR remarque l'importance symbolique des poursuites engagées contre ces individus, pour le message qu'elles font passer à d'autres, et la reconnaissance qu'elles apportent aux survivants.[136] Les résultats de la revue de littérature précédemment évoqués indiquent que la violence sexuelle utilisée comme arme de guerre peut résulter d'un sentiment d'impunité. Par conséquent, le succès des poursuites contre des hommes politiques, des officiers de police et militaires de grade intermédiaire et supérieur, des membres de groupes étatiques et non-étatiques est une condition nécessaire pour empêcher que la violence sexuelle ne soit employée comme arme de guerre lors de futurs conflits. Il semblerait toutefois que bien davantage ne doive être accompli dans ce domaine pour en faire une mesure préventive.

***Résumé des approches préventives actuelles***

L'évaluation des approches préventives actuelles montre que des mesures efficaces sont en place, bien que des améliorations soient requises. Le haut degré de compréhension du sujet représente le point positif, qui a permis l'élaboration et la mise en place de stratégies de prévention et de plans de formation. Il y a également un soutien considérable de membres-clés de la communauté international, qui a alloué des ressources au problème et impulsé des actions. Des milliers d'effectifs des forces civiles et militaires reçoivent un entraînement et des sanctions sont prises à l'encontre des soldats de la paix lorsqu' ils désobéissent aux ordres. Les dispositions légales sont substantielles, des preuves sont collectées et des poursuites sont engagées. Concernant les améliorations, davantage de recherches sont nécessaires pour approfondir la compréhension et concevoir des approches préventives supplémentaires (par exemple, empêcher les femmes d'avoir recours à la violence sexuelle). Davantage de ressources et un engagement durable de la communauté internationale sont nécessaires. Le soutien et le financement internationaux doivent

134 Secrétaire Général des Nations Unies, "Conflict-related sexual violence: Report of Secretary General," 8/33.

135 Chambre des Lords, "Select Committee on Sexual Violence in Conflict: Report of Session 2015-16: Sexual Violence in Conflict: A War Crime," 22

136 CICR, "Sexual Violence in Armed Conflict: E-Briefing," Partie 3.

venir d'organisations non-occidentales, comme l'UA, la Ligue des États arabes ou le Conseil de coopération du Golfe, et ce, de manière visible. Au vu des affaires dans lesquelles soldats de la paix ou forces de l'ordre commettent des violences sexuelles, une formation plus étendue et des stages de perfectionnement doivent être dispensés (et des poursuites engagées). L'impact de ces formations doit être mesuré et elles doivent être réajustées si nécessaire. La formation et les exercices doivent être basés sur des scénarios complexes pour évaluer la compréhension et la réponse des étudiants. Une assistance de long terme approfondie doit être donnée aux pays montrant un faible système judiciaire et de piètres procédures pour engager des poursuites efficaces. Davantage de personnes, y compris les soldats de la paix des Nations Unies ou de l'UA et les vainqueurs, doivent être portés devant la justice plus rapidement, dans le but de réduire le sentiment d'impunité (et son coût). Il apparaît donc qu'il existe fondation solide sur laquelle se baser, mais les approches préventives actuelles requièrent un approfondissement si l'on veut les rendre capables de lutter plus systématiquement et de manière exhaustive contre la violence sexuelle en conflit.

## Etude de cas : Daech[137]

### *Le mode opératoire de Daech*

Ce travail va maintenant s'intéresser au cas de Daech et à son usage actuel de la violence sexuelle en Irak et en Syrie. Il considérera l'approche de Daech à la lumière des résultats de la revue de littérature et évaluera l'efficacité des méthodes de prévention existantes en tant que moyen d'empêcher l'organisation d'avoir recours à la violence sexuelle à l'avenir. Le SGONU décrit les « actes abominables de violence sexuelle liée au conflit »[138] commis par Daech depuis 2014 et confirmés par un rapport du G7.[139] Le rapport annuel du SGONU faisant la liste des groupes armés commettant des violences sexuelles en conflit, décrit le mode opératoire de Daech en Irak : « La violence sexuelle a été utilisée par l'EIIL comme instrument de sa stratégie consistant à répandre la terreur, persécuter les minorités ethniques et religieuses et éradiquer les communautés

137 Voir note n°3 pour la justification de l'orthographe.

138 Secrétaire Général des Nations Unies, "Conflict-related sexual violence: Report of Secretary General," 24/33.

139 G7, "G7 Report on the Implementation of the G8 Declaration on Preventing Sexual Violence in Conflict," 1.

s'opposant à son idéologie ».[140] Dans un rapport ultérieur, l'ONU affirme que Daech emploie la violence sexuelle en tant que « tactique de guerre »,[141] ce qui est également évoqué par Wood et sa vision de Daech comme un groupe qui « a résolument opté pour l'utilisation de la violence sexuelle pour poursuivre des objectifs organisationnels, ce qui en fait une stratégie ».[142] L'usage de violence sexuelle par Daech a également été rapporté dans des camps de détention et de réfugiés, et lors de contrôles aux frontières.[143] Tout comme les résultats de la revue de littérature, de telles caractéristiques confirment le postulat que la violence sexuelle peut être utilisée pour exercer un pouvoir, neutraliser la résistance communautaire, poursuivre des buts militaro-politiques et obtenir des informations. Il apparaît qu'elle ait également eu lieu dans des espaces dits vulnérables.

Cependant, certains éléments dans l'usage de la violence sexuelle par Daech semblent différer ou présenter une forme plus accentuée que ceux rapportés par la revue de littérature. Par exemple, l'on peut affirmer que Daech y ait recours pour détruire les droits des femmes et leur valeur au sein de la société. Le Représentant Spécial du SGONU pour la violence sexuelle en conflit note ainsi que « la célèbre offensive du Mont Sinjar d'août 2014 a été considérée comme une conquête tout autant sexuelle que territoriale ».[144] Dans des villes comme Raqqa, des marchés ont été créés pour vendre des femmes et des filles, des « régulations » de Daech spécifiant le taux du marché applicable selon leur âge.[145] L'approche de Daech comprend également la prise d'otage de femmes et de filles, décrite comme « une nouvelle et inquiétante dimension »[146] par le G7. Les membres notent qu'elle ne se réduit pas à Daech et prennent l'exemple des 270 écolières prises en otage à Chibok, au Nigeria, en avril 2014.[147] L'ONU

---

140 Secrétaire Général des Nations Unies, "Conflict-related sexual violence: Report of Secretary General," 9/33.

141 Nations Unies, "Report on Protection of Civilians in Armed Conflict in Iraq: 1 mai – 31 octobre 2015," 32.

142 Wood, "Conflict-related sexual violence and the policy implications of recent research," 472.

143 Secrétaire Général des Nations unies, "Conflict-related sexual violence: Report of Secretary General," 18/33.

144 Zainab Bangura, "Faith in Islam & Faith in Women: Why Gender Justice is Key to an Islam Without Extremes," International Crisis Group octobre 2015),<https://medium.com/the-future-of-conflict/faith-in-islam-faith-in-women-why-gender-justice-is-key-to-an-islam-without-extremes-8920277ef674#.dkjeoo8jg> (consulté le 6 janvier 2016).

145 Secrétaire Général des Nations Unies, "Conflict-related sexual violence: Report of Secretary General," 10/33.

146 G7, "G7 Report on the Implementation of the G8 Declaration on Preventing Sexual Violence in Conflict," 1.

147 Ibid.

identifie également le rapport : « les mêmes idéologies et objectifs qui encouragent Boko Haram à enlever des femmes et des filles au Nigeria incitent également l'EIIL à les réduire en esclavage en République arabe syrienne et en Irak ».[148] Un rapport d'Amnesty International de décembre 2014 constate que des milliers de femmes et de filles sont retenues prisonnières de Daech[149] et un rapport de l'ONU de janvier 2016 mentionne que le phénomène s'étend à d'autres minorités, avec environ 3500 yézidis réduits en esclavage.[150] Par ailleurs, les violences sexuelles faites aux femmes font « partie de l'économie politique utilisée pour générer des revenus par le trafic, le commerce et le rançonnage de femmes et de filles. Les femmes sont devenues partie intégrante de la devise que l'EIIL utilise pour renforcer son pouvoir et sont monétisées comme un « butin de guerre » ».[151] Le SGONU fait également allusion à une forme de construction nationale à travers la création de « bureaux matrimoniaux » vendant des femmes aux membres de Daech pour produire la prochaine génération.[152] Ainsi, cela montre que Daech utilise la violence sexuelle pour atteindre ses objectifs stratégiques politiques et militaires.

La plupart des rapports traitant des méthodes de Daech se concentrent sur les violences sexuelles faites aux femmes et aux filles. Cependant, un rapport de l'ONU de 2016 reconnaît qu'entre 800 et 900 garçons ont été enlevés à Mossoul en juin 2015 et ceux « qui refusent d'obéir aux ordres de l'EIIL ont été fouettés, torturés ou violés ».[153] Le même document affirme en outre que « UNAMI et le HCDH ont vérifié un certain nombre de rapports sur des meurtres perpétrés par l'EIIL à l'encontre de personnes homosexuelles (en les jetant du haut d'un immeuble) ».[154] Le SGONU fait également état de violences sexuelles contre « des personnes lesbiennes, gay, bisexuelles, transgenre et intersexuées

---

148 Secrétaire Général des Nations Unies, "Conflict-related sexual violence: Report of Secretary General," 25/33.

149 Amnesty International, "Escape from Hell: Torture and Sexual Slavery in Islamic State Captivity in Iraq," Amnesty International, MDE 14/021/2014 décembre 2014), <http://www.amnesty.org.uk/sites/default/files/escape_from_hell_-_torture_and_sexual_slavery_in_islamic_state_captivity_in_iraq_-_english_2.pdf(consulté le 7 janvier 2016), 5-6.

150 Nations Unies, "Report on Protection of Civilians in Armed Conflict in Iraq: 1 mai – 31 octobre 2015," 18.

151 Bangura, "Faith in Islam & Faith in Women: Why Gender Justice is Key to Islam without Extremes".

152 Secrétaire Général des Nations Unies, "Conflict-related sexual violence: Report of Secretary General," 25/33.

153 Nations Unies, "Report on Protection of Civilians in Armed Conflict in Iraq: 1 mai – 31 octobre 2015," 14.

154 Ibid., 17.

[…] comme une forme de « nettoyage moral » »[155] et comme « une forme de contrôle social » exercées par Daech à la fois en Irak et en Syrie.[156]

Enfin, le SGONU décrit une autre caractéristique-clé du type de violence sexuelle utilisée par Daech : « l'EIIL affiche de manière flagrante ses abus [sexuels] ».[157] Amnesty International remarque : « Plus que tout autre groupe, il a fait de grands efforts pour faire la publicité des horribles détails des atrocités qu'il commet […] les mettant en perspective dans des vidéos et des communiqués largement relayés sur les réseaux sociaux, souvent en plusieurs langues ».[158] Amnesty International estime que cette technique a été déployée afin de « propager la peur chez ses ennemis et quiconque se trouvant sur son chemin ».[159] Ces méthodes présentent probablement un caractère d'autant plus intimidant que Daech défie des tabous religieux et culturels traditionnels. Le SGONU suggère que « les réseaux sociaux ont converti la brutalité en une forme de propagande pour inciter, radicaliser et attirer des recrues ».[160] Le même rapport note également l'usage de violence sexuelle à travers « les mariages forcés à des combattants étrangers ».[161] Une autre raison expliquant la politique de violence sexuelle de Daech serait d'encourager les individus ne provenant ni d'Irak, ni de Syrie, de rejoindre le groupe. Ainsi, en exploitant les réseaux sociaux afin de toucher un public mondial, Daech a délibérément communiqué sur sa perpétration de violences sexuelles contre les femmes, les hommes, les enfants, les homosexuels et autres, servant le triple but de terrifier, attirer et faire la une des médias pour promouvoir son message principal.

Par conséquent, alors que les violences sexuelles perpétrées par Daech sont cohérentes avec les conclusions de la revue de littérature, sa stratégie implique également : l'avilissement des femmes (en tant qu'attaque contre les valeurs occidentales), la recherche de l'éradication des non-hétérosexuels, la violence sexuelle pour lever des fonds et le recrutement externe, et une campagne de communication ciblant la violence sexuelle. Le mode opératoire de Daech n'est pas unique en son genre, mais l'étude de cas révèle toutefois des aspects particuliers dans son approche.

---

155 Secrétaire Général des Nations Unies, "Conflict-related sexual violence: Report of Secretary General," 10/33.

156 Ibid., 2/33.

157 Bangura, "Faith in Islam & Faith in Women: Why Gender Justice is Key to Islam without Extremes".

158 Amnesty International, "Escape from Hell: Torture and Sexual Slavery in Islamic State Captivity in Iraq," 11.

159 Ibid.

160 Secrétaire Général des Nations Unies, "Conflict-related sexual violence: Report of Secretary General," 25/33.

161 Ibid.

### *Mesures préventives pour lutter contre les violences sexuelles commises par Daech*

Ce travail va maintenant évaluer l'efficacité des méthodes de prévention existantes mentionnées précédemment (compréhension; soutien de haut niveau; formation; et législation), en tant que moyen d'empêcher Daech d'avoir recours à la violence sexuelle à l'avenir. Premièrement, une compréhension des tenants et des aboutissants du recours à la violence sexuelle par Daech semble être établie par des rapports exhaustifs de l'ONU, du G7 et d'Amnesty International, par exemple, en dépit des difficultés rapportés par l'ONU pour obtenir des statistiques précises.[162] Ces difficultés sont, semble-t-il, contrebalancées par les intentions claires de Daech de faire la publicité de son usage de violence sexuelle plutôt que de le cacher ou le nier, comme le font certains autres groupes. Deuxièmement, il existe un soutien de haut niveau s'attaquant à l'usage répandu de violence sexuelle par Daech. Par exemple, la National Security Strategy de l'an dernier stipule que la PVSI serait particulièrement étendue à la Syrie et l'Irak,[163] et un rapport du G7 de 2015 sur la mise en œuvre d'une Déclaration du G8 de 2013 sur la PSVI contient des éléments d'assistance à l'Irak et la Syrie. Par exemple, le Royaume-Uni a dispensé des formations de prévention aux troupes peshmerga, a également entraîné les défenseurs des droits de l'homme iraquiens et syriens à collecter des preuves dans le cadre du Protocole international relatif aux enquêtes sur les violences sexuelles dans les situations de conflits, et les États-Unis ont financé la documentation médico-légale pour des médecins syriens. Les canadiens ont financé enquêtes et aide aux survivants. La France a financé « Gynécologues Sans Frontières » pour aider les réfugiés syriens en Jordanie. L'Allemagne a financé le Centre pour les victimes de tortures de Berlin, pour les assister dans six provinces d'Irak, et également une station de radio irakienne qui aborde le problème de la violence sexuelle en conflit.[164] De même, le Royaume-Uni a financé « la formation de militants à l'usage de la radio pour donner du pouvoir aux femmes et impliquer les hommes dans le renversement des normes sociales quant au compte rendu de violences sexuelles ».[165] Le SGONU affirme : « Je condamne l'usage de violence sexuelle par l'EIIL» et recommande « Des programmes favorisant la

162 Ibid., 18/33.

163 Gouvernement britannique, *National Security Strategy and Strategic Defence and Security Review 2015: Secure and Prosperous United Kingdom*, 63.

164 G7, "G7 Report on the Implementation of the G8 Declaration on Preventing Sexual Violence in Conflict," 3-4, 6-7.

165 Bureau des Affaires Étrangères et du Commonwealth, "Angelina Jolie Pitt joins Baroness Anelay to chart next steps on tackling sexual violence".

réintégration sociale des femmes et filles libérées de la captivité ».[166] Il semblerait ainsi que le soutien international de haut niveau existe, au vu des actions entreprises, comme l'entraînement des forces peshmerga, des défenseurs des droits de l'homme, des médecins et des cybermilitants.

Cela conduit à examiner la quatrième méthode préventive présentée par la revue de littérature, à savoir la législation, et plus précisément ses aspects de dissuasion et de mise en œuvre. La revue de littérature a précédemment confirmé que « la violence sexuelle est prohibée de manière absolue et adéquate par le droit international ».[167] Cependant, cela n'a apparemment pas eu l'effet escompté sur l'usage qu'en fait Daech dans sa stratégie, ce qui appuie les critiques précédemment mentionnées de Kirby sur la PVSI. Le sentiment d'impunité de Daech ne semble connaître aucune limite en dépit de sa réputation sur la scène internationale et des condamnations venant des plus hauts niveaux. Amnesty International a déclaré que Daech est coupable de crimes de guerre et de crimes contre l'humanité, en partie pour avoir commis des violences sexuelles en Irak[168]. L'ONG a affirmé que le Droit International Humanitaire s'applique à Daech et que ses leaders civils et militaires « peuvent être pénalement responsables de crimes de guerre » et également des actes de leurs subordonnés forcés à les commettre ou ne les ayant pas empêchés.[169] Un rapport de l'ONU publié cette année convient que Daech a commis des crimes de guerre, des crimes contre l'humanité et « possiblement un génocide ».[170] Le Haut-Commissaire des Nations Unies aux droits de l'homme, Zeid Ra'ad Al Hussein, a déclaré que « La communauté internationale doit continuer à suivre de près la situation en Irak en vue d'assurer que les auteurs d'abus choquants et de violations graves des droits de l'homme et du droit international humanitaire soient tenus pour responsables ».[171] Dans ce même rapport, l'ONU enjoint le gouvernement irakien de modifier sa propre législation pour que les tribunaux irakiens entrent dans la juridiction internationale, et de renvoyer les affaires de violence sexuelle devant la Cour Pénale Internationale[172] (bien que cela semble improbable étant donné que le même rapport accuse les forces

---

166 Secrétaire Général des Nations Unies, "Conflict-related sexual violence: Report of Secretary General," 19/33 & 10/33.

167 Gaggioli, "Sexual violence in armed conflicts: violation of international humanitarian law and human rights law," 505.

168 Amnesty International, "Escape from Hell: Torture and Sexual Slavery in Islamic State Captivity in Iraq," 4

169 Ibid., 15.

170 Nations Unies, "Report on Protection of Civilians in Armed Conflict in Iraq: 1 mai – 31 octobre 2015," i.

171 Ibid., début du rapport (pas de numéro de page).

172 Ibid., ii.

armées irakiennes de violation du droit international humanitaire et des droits de l'homme).[173] Daech ne semble pas non plus découragé par les efforts entrepris par les membres du G7 pour collecter et étayer des preuves, comme cité précédemment, ou par le travail de la Commission d'enquête internationale en Syrie et de la Commission d'établissement de faits en Irak, soutenue par la Justice Rapid Response.[174] Ainsi, en dépit des efforts de collecte de preuves et d'accusations crédibles selon lesquelles les violences sexuelles commises par Daech équivalent à des crimes de guerre, des crimes contre l'humanité et possiblement des actes de génocide, l'organisation ne semble pas être découragée.

### *Conclusions sur Daech*

Pour conclure cette étude de cas, Daech se révèle être à la fois caractéristique et spécifique. Une grande partie des raisons de son usage de violence sexuelle comme arme de guerre fait écho aux résultats de la revue de littérature : un sentiment d'impunité manifeste, un objectif d'exercice du pouvoir et de neutralisation de la résistance communautaire, faisant partie d'une stratégie militaire planifiée de conquête territoriale. La plupart des actes de violence sexuelle semblent être commis à l'encontre de femmes et de filles, plus particulièrement si elles appartiennent à des minorités ethniques et religieuses, mais de tels actes ont néanmoins également été commis contre des hommes et des garçons, dans le but d'obtenir des informations ou de réprimer l'opposition. Cette violence se passe dans des lieux connus pour leur vulnérabilité, tels que les camps de réfugiés ou de détention, et les contrôles aux frontières. D'autres éléments renvoyant aux résultats de la revue de littérature comprennent également la honte ressentie par les survivants, qui a exacerbé les difficultés à obtenir de l'aide et à réunir des données tangibles. Amnesty International a mis en évidence le nombre de familles yézidi ayant nié que leurs proches avaient été victimes de violences sexuelles, tout en insistant sur la systématisation de ces actes contre les membres de leur communauté.[175] Amnesty International a également décrit les difficultés éprouvées par les survivants à obtenir de l'aide médicale de psychologique, dues à un manque de sensibilisation, aux distances géographiques, aux coûts et à la logistique nécessaires à l'accès aux services de soutien.[176] De nouveau, la revue de littérature avait identifié ces

173 Ibid.

174 G7, "G7 Report on the Implementation of the G8 Declaration on Preventing Sexual Violence in Conflict," 7.

175 Amnesty International, "Escape from Hell: Torture and Sexual Slavery in Islamic State Captivity in Iraq," 13-14.

176 Ibid., 13.

problèmes comme faisant partie des nombreux challenges de la gestion des répercussions.

La revue de littérature a mis en exergue que chaque conflit est différent, ce qui explique que les approches préventives exigent une compréhension approfondie du contexte et des réponses sur-mesure. La politique de Daech consistant à faire la publicité de son recours à la violence sexuelle via les canaux de communication les plus modernes sert un triple objectif : terroriser et soumettre la population d'Irak et de Syrie à l'organisation, attirer de nouveaux membres, et assurer la diffusion mondiale de son intention plus générale d'établir un califat islamique. Au cœur de sa campagne militaire, Daech semble mener une opération d'influence comprenant la violence sexuelle comme vecteur principal de son message. D'autres caractéristiques différant des résultats de la revue de littérature comprennent une politique financière et idéologique consistant à user de violence sexuelle pour rabaisser le statut des femmes et faire d'elles des consommables pouvant alimenter des fonds pour l'effort de guerre. L'organisation utilise également la violence sexuelle pour tenter d'éliminer les non-hétérosexuels, comme évoqué dans une moindre mesure dans la littérature.

En ce qui concerne les méthodes de prévention actuelles préalablement identifiées, l'étude du cas de Daech renvoie à la plupart des résultats de la revue de littérature. Il semble exister une bonne compréhension de la part de l'ONU, du G7 et d'Amnesty International, des tenants et des aboutissants de l'usage de la violence sexuelle par Daech, alors que des universitaires tels que Wood effectue déjà des recherches sur leurs méthodes. Le soutien international émane également des plus hauts niveaux, comme du SGONU, sa Représentante Spéciale sur la violence sexuelle liée au conflit et le Haut-Commissaire des Nations Unies aux droits de l'homme, ainsi que le G7. Tout comme pour la revue de littérature, un tel soutien international reflète un biais occidental, et l'engagement d'autres entités comme la Ligue des états arabes et le Conseil de coopération du Golfe, s'avèrerait utile. Ce soutien coïncide néanmoins avec des ressources entretenant un certain nombre de mesures, comme la formation des troupes peshmergas, des défenseurs des droits de l'homme, des médecins et des cybermilitants. La quatrième plage de stratégies de prévention existantes, la dissuasion par la législation, semble pourtant tristement inadaptée, malgré les tentatives de l'ONU et d'Amnesty International de réunir preuves et accusations tangibles concernant les violences sexuelles commises par Daech, et leur équivalence avec des crimes de guerre, crimes contre l'humanité et peut-être des actes de génocide. Daech reste stoïque.

Peu d'autres mesures de prévention ont été mises en place pour lutter contre l'usage de violence sexuelle comme arme de guerre par Daech. Souvent encouragés par les militants communautaires et parfois les membres des familles des victimes, les journalistes ont déployé d'importants efforts pour rapporter ses actions. Conséquence involontaire, cela peut avoir entraîné une pression malvenue sur les survivants pour les pousser à parler à la presse. Par conséquent, Amnesty International a appelé à un journalisme plus responsable et à une plus grande sensibilité de la part des leaders locaux et des militants.[177] Il est pourtant important que les médias internationaux demeurent engagés afin de ne pas dissimuler les actes de violence sexuelle de Daech aux leaders mondiaux, qui devront impulser les stratégies de prévention futures. Un autre aspect est le rôle joué par le guide spirituel yézidi, Baba Sheikh, qui s'est exprimé publiquement en février 2015 pour exhorter sa communauté à soutenir les femmes yézidi s'étant échappées de Daech.[178] Bien que premièrement destinée à aider les survivants, ce message a également servi à remettre en question la stratégie de Daech consistant à avilir les femmes. Cependant, de tels messages doivent être réitérés régulièrement par un panel de leaders religieux et communautaires pour parvenir à contrebalancer les efforts de communication dévoués de Daech. Bien qu'il soit encore trop tôt pour déterminer l'impact que pourraient avoir ces mesures préventives supplémentaires, il apparaît que d'autres méthodes doivent être mises en place pour détourner Daech de sa stratégie d'usage de violence sexuelle. Ce besoin se fait d'autant plus sentir que les méthodes existantes à l'œuvre contre Daech et décrites dans la revue de littérature n'ont que peu d'impact, et n'ont eu aucun effet apparent à ce jour.

## Mesures préventives supplémentaires

La littérature universitaire et spécialisée n'offre que peu de mesures pratiques de prévention allant au-delà de celles précédemment mentionnées dans cet ouvrage, et comporte les mêmes limites des approches existantes étudiées dans le cas de Daech. Cette dernière partie va donc brièvement considérer de possibles outils préventifs complémentaires. Bien que non exhaustive, cette liste se concentre sur l'apprentissage de groupes ayant cessé d'user de violence sexuelle, le rôle des acteurs de la société civile et le *soft power*, l'application aux groupes armés de la recherche dans d'autres domaines, et l'exploitation du potentiel des médias sociaux.

177 Ibid., 17.

178 Bangura, "Faith in Islam & Faith in Women: Why Gender Justice is Key to Islam without Extremes".

Premièrement, le CICR défend l'importance d'apprendre des groupes qui n'ont pas fait usage de violence sexuelle en situation de conflit.[179] En étudiant des cas individuels, Wood remarque que « le commandement d'un groupe armé peut interdire la violence sexuelle pour des raisons stratégiques, directives ou pratiques ».[180] Wood en identifie la raison principale : éviter de perdre le contrôle sur les subordonnés, établir une supériorité morale, obtenir des fonds et des ressources, et gagner la paix ainsi que la guerre pour assumer les futures fonctions du pouvoir.[181] En soulignant les avantages militaires, stratégiques et opérationnels réalisés par d'autres groupes armés, il est possible que de tels arguments puissent les persuader d'éviter, ou d'arrêter d'user de violence sexuelle. Une combinaison sur-mesure de récompenses et de sanctions, qui reflète une compréhension profonde de la hiérarchie, des acteurs, de la culture et des méthodes de violence de ces groupes, peut aider à prévenir leur usage de violence sexuelle, surtout si ceux ayant renoncé à y avoir recours dans leurs propres luttes armées peuvent en exprimer clairement les avantages.

En plus d'avoir recours à des chefs militaires crédibles, le rôle des acteurs de la société civile pourrait être mieux utilisé afin d'obtenir des résultats positifs. En se concentrant sur des modèles masculins positifs (bien que tout aussi applicable aux modèles féminins), MenEngage Alliance et le Fonds des Nations Unies pour la population ont mis en évidence que les fournisseurs de services pourraient « jouer un rôle important dans le [...] remaniement des normes sociales » pas seulement via leurs fonctions professionnelles, mais en raison de leurs statuts au sein de la société.[182] Hague, dans son résumé du Sommet mondial de 2014, reconnaît le rôle des groupes religieux : « A travers leurs réseaux, ils ont souvent accès aux communautés locales, qu'ils peuvent influencer comme aucun autre acteur. A ce titre, ils sont idéalement placés pour changer les croyances et les mentalités ».[183] Davantage de ressources pourraient être allouées aux organisations de femmes et d'hommes pour soutenir leurs efforts au sein de leurs propres sociétés. L'utilisation du soft power par des organisations telles que le British Council, l'ONU et les ONG, ainsi que par les militants individuels, est établie depuis longtemps. Cependant, la littérature ne cite que très peu d'exemples concernant des mesures pratiques pour prévenir la vio-

179 CICR, "Sexual Violence in Armed Conflict: E-Briefing," Partie 4.

180 Wood, "Rape is not inevitable during war," in Kuehnast et al., eds., *Women and War: Power & Protection in Twenty-First Century*, 54.

181 Ibid., 54-55.

182 MenEngage Alliance et FNUAP, "Sexual Violence in Conflict and Post-Conflict: Engaging Men and Boys," 7.

183 Bureau des Affaires Étrangères et du Commonwealth, "Chair's Summary: Global Summit to End Sexual Violence in Conflict."

lence sexuelle en conflit. Wood suggère que des leçons doivent être tirées d'autres campagnes, comme celles luttant contre le trafic de diamants de conflits, les enfants soldats et les mines terrestres, pour ensuite être appliquées à la prévention de violences sexuelles en conflit.[184] Un récent rapport de la Chambre des Lords sur ce sujet conclut : « Il existe des preuves tangibles de la capacité des programmes visant à modifier les comportements à aider à la prévention de la violence sexuelle en conflit ».[185]

Se tournant vers d'autres spécialités, Steffens et al. ont conduit des recherches pour comprendre la façon dont les adeptes s'identifient à certains leaders et l'importance des identités sociales partagées dans l'émergence d'un comportement de groupe,[186] alors que d'autres universitaires ont examiné les facteurs de cohésion du groupe militaire.[187] Par ailleurs, d'autres recherches ont étudié les raisons pour lesquelles des groupes commettent des meurtres de masse, comme pendant l'Holocauste. Par exemple, Haslam et Reicher proposent que « les groupes transforment les individus les rejoignant en modifiant le tempérament de leurs membres ».[188] En outre, Wood envisage que les résultats des recherches sur le viol sur les campus universitaires, ou dans les gangs de jeunes, les clubs de sport et les prisons puissent être appliqués à la violence sexuelle en conflit.[189] Elle considère également que « Les dynamiques de groupe à petite échelle qui conduisent à des normes unitaires qui promeuvent ou restreignent l'occurrence d'actes de violence sexuelle représentent une piste de recherches prometteuse ».[190] Ainsi, des recherches plus approfondies sur l'impact des leaders et des groupes sur le comportement pourraient donner lieu au développement futur de mesures complémentaires de prévention, en

184 Wood, "Conflict-related sexual violence and the policy implications of recent research," 476.

185 Chambre des Lords, "Select Committee on Sexual Violence in Conflict: Report of Session 2015-16: Sexual Violence in Conflict: A War Crime," 8.

186 Niklas K. Steffens, S. Alexander Haslam, et Stephen D. Reicher, "Up close and personal: Evidence that shared social identity is a basis for the 'special' relationship that binds followers to leaders," *The Leadership Quarterly* 25 (2015).

187 Guy, L. Siebold, "The Essence of Military Group Cohesion," *Armed Forces & Society* 33(2) (2007): 286-295 et Anthony King, "The Existence of Group Cohesion in the Armed Forces: A Response to Guy Siebold," *Armed Forces & Society* 33(4) (2007): 638-645.

188 S.A. Haslam, et S. Reicher, "Beyond the banality of evil: three dynamics of an interactionist social psychology of terrorism," *Personality and Social Psychology Bulletin*, 33(5) (2007): 620.

189 Wood, "Conflict-related sexual violence and the policy implications of recent research," 478.

190 Wood, "Sexual violence during war: toward an understanding of variation," in: *Order, Conflict and Violence*, eds. Stathis N. Kalyvas, Ian Shapiro et Tarek Masoud (New York and Cambridge: Cambridge University Press, 2008), 347.

ciblant particulièrement les leaders, qui exercent le plus leur influence sur leurs membres, en modifiant l'identité sociale d'un groupe et en exploitant la cohésion militaire comme des manières de changer les normes comportementales.

Enfin, il faut également prendre en considération le potentiel des médias sociaux. D'ici 2020, le taux de possession d'un smartphone dans le monde est prévu d'atteindre 70%, dont la plupart des nouveaux propriétaires viendraient des pays en développement.[191] L'analyse de sources publiques, comme les sites de réseaux sociaux, est déjà utilisée pour détecter des crises et pour acquérir une connaissance rapide de la situation. Par exemple, les journalistes citoyens tels que l'équipe « Bell¿ngcat », ont réuni des sites de média sociaux pour comprendre la situation de la zone de conflit ukrainienne.[192] Dans les quatre ou cinq prochaines années, l'introduction de smartphones dans les zones du monde les plus isolées et les plus sujettes aux conflits peut avoir un pouvoir transformatif dans la prévention de ce crime traditionnellement caché. Le sentiment d'impunité, décrit plus haut dans la revue de littérature comme l'une des raisons principales de l'usage de violence sexuelle en conflit, pourrait s'éroder si des technologies perturbatrices telles que les médias sociaux étaient exploitées pour apporter une connaissance de la situation et identifier des signes avant-coureurs. Là où il est impossible de prévenir la violence sexuelle, les médias sociaux pourraient contribuer à la collecte de données générales afin de produire une réponse militaire ou des forces de l'ordre, d'aider à cibler l'assistance médicale et potentiellement, de soutenir l'opération de collecte de preuves.

Ceci conclut le passage en revue de mesures complémentaires de prévention possibles, qui a couvert : l'application du retour d'expérience des groupes ayant choisi de ne pas avoir recours à la violence sexuelle; le rôle des acteurs de la société civile et du *soft power*; l'influence des leaders et des groupes; et les médias sociaux. Il s'est attaché à mettre en avant le cadre dont les universitaires et spécialistes de la prévention de la violence sexuelle en conflit disposent pour collaborer avec leurs confrères d'autres domaines et considérer des approches de prévention alternatives. Il semble improbable qu'une seule et même approche puisse empêcher l'usage de violence sexuelle en temps de guerre, mais une association sur-mesure de moyens de prévention prenant en

191 The Mobile Economy 2015), <http://gsmamobileeconomy.com/global/> (consulté le 12 mai 2016), 2.

192 Bell¿ngcat, "Confirming the Location of the Same Msta-S in Russia and Ukraine," Bell¿ngcat mai 2015), <https://www.bellingcat.com/resources/case-studies/2015/05/29/confirming-the-location-of-the-same-msta-s-in-russia-and-ukraine/> (consulté le 12 mai 2016).

compte le contexte et les spécificités d'un conflit armé donné pourrait être adoptée.

## Conclusion

En conclusion, ce travail a tenté de déterminer s'il est possible d'empêcher l'usage de violence sexuelle comme arme de guerre contre les femmes, les hommes et les enfants ou seulement d'en prévenir les répercussions. La revue de littérature a analysé cinq aspects du problème: les raisons pour lesquelles la violence sexuelle est utilisée en conflit; le manière dont les hommes et les garçons peuvent en être victimes, et les femmes les auteurs; la multitude de challenges que présente la gestion de ses répercussions ; les risques qu'entraînent la titrisation du problème et la négation de la progression du rôle des femmes dans la paix et la sécurité; et les preuves justifiant que la violence sexuelle en conflit n'est pas inévitable. Quatre approches préventives existantes ont été analysées, concernant la compréhension, le soutien de haut niveau, la formation, et la législation. Cette étude arrive à la conclusion qu'elles représentent des bases solides sur lesquelles l'on peut construire, mais que des améliorations, exigeant un financement de long terme et un effort soutenu, sont nécessaires. Le cas particulier de Daech a été étudié vis-à-vis des résultats de la revue de littérature, et cette étude suggère que l'usage de violence sexuelle par Daech va de pair avec les éléments mis en évidence dans la littérature, bien que des spécificités aient été identifiées, telles que leur stratégie consistant à faire la publicité, sur les médias sociaux, de leur recours à la violence sexuelle. L'étude du cas de Daech a révélé les défauts que présentent les approches préventives actuelles (en particulier le manque de dissuasion de la législation) et le besoin urgent d'autres méthodes. Aussi a-t-on pris en considération des approches préventives alternatives, qui amènent à conclure qu'une approche plus large et innovante, en collaboration avec des experts d'autres domaines, puisse donner des résultats. En définitive, les challenges que présentent la prévention de la violence sexuelle comme arme de guerre, la gestion de ses répercussions et de l'impact générationnel, requièrent l'entière exploitation de toute mesure adéquate.

Cet ouvrage s'est attaché à témoigner qu'il est possible d'empêcher que la violence sexuelle ne soit utilisée comme arme de guerre, mais il a cependant mis en évidence que la prévention exhaustive et systématique de la violence sexuelle présente des challenges considérables. Les résultats de la revue de littérature et l'exemple de Daech ont démontré le besoin d'amélioration des stratégies de prévention actuelles et d'introduction de nouvelles mesures. Ces résultats défendent la nécessité d'une approche coordonnée et rationnalisée entre praticiens, membres des forces de l'ordre et experts juridiques, qui serait pilotée localement et bénéficierait d'un soutien externe à maintenir sur le long terme. Chaque conflit requiert en particulier une compréhension approfondie de son contexte, ses acteurs et ses méthodes afin d'assurer une réponse adaptée, disposant de suffisamment de ressources et pouvant s'inscrire sur plusieurs niveaux, prenant ainsi en compte les différents besoins des femmes, des hommes et des enfants.

De plus, les résultats de la revue de littérature ont montré que la gestion des répercussions est une entreprise considérable, qui implique que des soins physiques et psychologiques soient dispensés aux individus. Les répercussions dans les sociétés doivent également être abordées afin de réduire la transmission d'IST, décourager les châtiments et reconstruire la cohésion de la communauté. D'une manière ou d'une autre, le cycle de la violence sexuelle doit être rompu. Les hommes et les femmes, auteurs, victimes et témoins, doivent être réintégrés, et les enfants nés de violences sexuelles, acceptés dans la société. Les survivants ont besoin de reconnaissance. Les auteurs de violences sexuelles doivent être jugés, de manière juste et rapide. Les coûts des soins médicaux de long terme, des procédures pénales, de l'éducation et de la reconstruction sont incalculables et probablement au-dessus des moyens de la plupart des pays déchirés par la guerre. Cependant, une gestion efficace des répercussions contribuerait à prévenir de futures vagues de violences sexuelles en aidant à sortir du cycle de la violence.

Si les challenges de la prévention semblent insurmontables, les preuves du caractère non inévitable de la violence sexuelle doivent être rappelées. Elles représentent un choix et non un incident, comme le soulignent les recherches et expériences du CICR :

> Il n'est plus défendable d'affirmer que la violence sexuelle représente simplement le côté sombre de nos pires pulsions humaines et un dommage collatéral de la guerre ; il est aujourd'hui largement admis que la violence sexuelle n'est pas une conséquence inévitable des conflits armés. Cela fait de la prévention un effort crucial, légitime et urgemment nécessaire.[193]

Gloria Steinem note que « la caractéristique la plus significative des êtres humains, celle qui permet à notre espèce de survivre, est notre capacité d'adapta-

193 CICR, "Sexual Violence in Armed Conflict: E-Briefing," Partie 4.

tion ».[194] Il est également remarquable que nos prédécesseurs aient réalisé ce qui était auparavant « impossible » dans la guerre : par exemple, proscrire l'exploitation d'enfants-soldats, l'utilisation d'armes à sous-munitions et de mines anti-personnel. Même si ces armes de guerre existent toujours, l'on peut espérer que leur utilisation en tant que stratégie de guerre, ainsi que la violence sexuelle, disparaîtront avec le temps. Kerry reconnaît que « l'impensable a été prohibé auparavant [...]. La violence sexuelle est un crime abominable contre l'humanité, et non simplement un produit excusable et inévitable de la guerre ».[195] En conclusion, empêcher la violence sexuelle d'être utilisée comme arme de guerre demeure extrêmement exigeant, et l'amplitude de cette entreprise ne doit pas être sous-estimée. Cependant, l'absence de violence sexuelle dans de nombreux conflits suggère qu'il est possible de l'empêcher de manière systématique ; cela requiert des efforts acharnés, peut-être sur des générations, mais il semble qu'une évolution positive soit en marche, avec une meilleure compréhension, le soutien et l'action internationaux de haut niveau, la formation et la législation :

> Nous sommes déterminés à mettre fin au recours au viol et à la violence sexuelle en conflit dans le monde. [...] La prévention de la violence sexuelle est d'une importance cruciale pour la paix, la sécurité et le développement durable [...] Il est du devoir moral de chaque individu de les dénoncer [...] et d'exiger un changement de perception et de réaction à ces crimes.[196]

## Bibliographie

Arieff, Alexis. "Sexual Violence in African Conflicts." *Congressional Research Service.* (November 2009). <http://web.a.ebscohost.com/ehost/pdfviewer/pdfviewer?sid=e00a61c4-d061-425e-9d6f-dac6e949281e%40sessionmgr4004&vid=15&hid=4212> (accessed May 17, 2016).

Al Achi, Dalia. "*Human Rights Day: Abuses rife in Central African Republic.*" UNHCR. (December 2015). <http://www.unhcr.org/5669a3a66.html> (accessed January 6, 2016).

194 Lauren Wolfe, "Gloria Steinem on Rape in War, Its Causes, and How to Stop It," *The Atlantic* 8 février 2012), <http://www.theatlantic.com/international/archive/2012/02/gloria-steinem-on-rape-in-war-its-causes-and-how-to-stop-it/252470/> (consulté le 18 janvier 2016).

195 Kerry, "Remarks at Global Summit to End Sexual Violence in Conflict".

196 Bureau des Affaires Étrangères et du Commonwealth, "Statement of Action – Global Summit to End Sexual Violence in Conflict".

Alcorn, Ted. "Responding to sexual violence in armed conflict." *The Lancet* Volume 383, No. 9934 2014): 2034-2037. <http://www.thelancet.com/journals/lancet/article/PIIS 0140-6736(14)60970-3/fulltext> (accessed January 18, 2016).

Amnesty International. "Escape from Hell: Torture and Sexual Slavery in Islamic State Captivity in Iraq." Amnesty International. MDE 14/021/2014. (December 2014). <http://www.amnesty.org.uk/sites/default/files/escape_from_hell_-_torture_and_sexual_slavery_in_islamic_state_captivity_in_iraq_-_english_2.pdf> (accessed January 7, 2016).

Baaz, Maria Eriksson, and Maria Stern. *Sexual Violence as a Weapon of War? Perceptions, Prescriptions, Problems in the Congo and Beyond.* London: Zed Books Ltd, 2013. eBook Collection. <http://web.a.ebscohost.com/ehost/ebookviewer/ebook/bmxlYmtfXzU3NzU1OF9fQU41?sid=e00a61c4-d061-425e-9d6f-dac6e949281e@sessionmgr4004&vid=73&format=EK&rid=2> (accessed May 18, 2016).

Baker, Aryn. "War and Rape." *Time* 187, no. 14 (2016): 36-41. <http://web.a.ebscohost.com/ehost/pdfviewer/pdfviewer?sid=0e34b8af-4d52-4955-9dfa-eb6e4e3bae87%40sessionmgr4004&vid=20&hid=4107> (accessed May 23, 2016).

Bangura, Zainab. "Faith in Islam & Faith in Women: Why Gender Justice is Key to an Islam Without Extremes." International Crisis Group. (October 2015). <https://medium.com/the-future-of-conflict/faith-in-islam-faith-in-women-why-gender-justice-is-key-to-an-islam-without-extremes-8920277ef674#.dkje008jg> (accessed January 6, 2016).

Bell¿ngcat. "Confirming the Location of the Same Msta-S in Russia and Ukraine." Bell¿ngcat. (May 2015). <https://www.bellingcat.com/resources/case-studies/2015/05/29/confirming-the-location-of-the-same-msta-s-in-russia-and-ukraine/> (accessed May 12, 2016).

Bernard, Vincent, and Durham, Helen. "Sexual violence in armed conflict: From breaking the silence to breaking the cycle." *International Review of the Red Cross* 96(894) (2014): 427-434. <doi:10.1017/S1816383115000442> (accessed January 11, 2016).

Bernard, Vincent, and Elvina Pothelet. "Through the eyes of a detention doctor: Interview with Raed Aburabi." *International Review of the Red Cross* 96(894) (2014): 479-484. <doi:10.1017/S1816383115000284> (accessed January 11, 2016).

Bouvier, Paul. "Sexual violence, health and humanitarian ethics: Towards a holistic, person-centred approach." *International Review of the Red Cross* 96(894) (2014): 565-584. <doi:10.1017/S1816383115000430> (accessed January 11, 2016).

Buckingham, Becks. "Rape and Sexual Violence: a Weapon of War?" Defence Research Paper, JSCSC, 2012.

Cannon, Patrick. "A Feminist Response to Rape as a Weapon of War in Eastern Congo." *Peace Review* 24, no. 4 (2012): 478-483. <http://web.a.ebscohost.com/ehost/pdfviewer/pdfviewer?sid=0e34b8af-4d52-4955-9dfa-eb6e4e3bae87%40sessionmgr4004&vid=30&hid=4107> (accessed May 23, 2016).

Carpenter, R. Charli. "Recognizing Gender-Based Violence Against Civilian Men and Boys in Conflict Situations." *Security Dialogue* 37(1) (2006): 83-103. <http://sdi.sagepub.com/content/37/1/83.full.pdf+html> (accessed May 19, 2016).

Carvajal, Doreen. "A Female Approach to Peacekeeping." New York Times. (March 5, 2010). <http://www.nytimes.com/2010/03/06/world/africa/06iht-ffpeace.html?_r=0> (accessed January 7, 2016).

Cohen, Dara Kay. "Female Combatants and the Perpetration of Violence: Wartime Rape in the Sierra Leone Civil War." *World Politics* 65, no. 3 (2013): 383-415. <doi: 10.1017/S0043887113000105> (accessed May 18, 2016).

Dammers, Tom. *"Paper commissioned for the EFA Global Monitoring Report 2011, The hidden crisis: Armed conflict and education".* United Nations Educational, Scientific and Cultural Organization. 2011/ED/EFA/MRT/PI/15. (2010). <http://unesdoc.unesco.org/images/0019/001907/190705e.pdf> (accessed May 23, 2016).

Davies, Mathew. "Women and Development, Not Gender and Politics: Explaining ASEAN's Failure to engage with the Women, Peace and Security agenda." *Contemporary Southeast Asia: A Journal of International & Strategic Affairs* 38, no. 1 (2016): 106-127. <http://web.a.ebscohost.com/ehost/pdfviewer/pdfviewer?vid=36&sid=0e34b8af-4d52-4955-9dfa-eb6e4e3bae87%40sessionmgr4004&hid=4107> (accessed May 23, 2016).

de Jonge Oudraat, Chantal. "UNSCR 1325 – Conundrums and Opportunities." *International Interactions* 39, no. 4 (2013): 612-619. <http://web.a.ebscohost.com/ehost/pdfviewer/pdfviewer?sid=0e34b8af-4d52-4955-9dfa-eb6e4e3bae87%40sessionmgr4004&vid=48&hid=4107> (accessed May 23, 2016).

Dolan, Chris. "Letting go of the gender binary: Charting new pathways for humanitarian interventions on gender-based violence." *International Review of the Red Cross* 96(894) (2014): 485-501. <doi:10.1017/S1816383115000120> (accessed January 10, 2016).

Dolan, Chris. "Into the Mainstream: Addressing Sexual Violence against Men and Boys in Conflict." Briefing Paper prepared for the Overseas Development Institute. (2014) <https://www.warchild.org.uk/sites/default/files/Into-the-Mainstream.pdf> (accessed May 23, 2016).

Duroch, Françoise, and Catrin Schulte-Hillen. "Care for victims of sexual violence, an organization pushed to its limits: The case of Médecins Sans Frontières." *International Review of the Red Cross*, 96(894) (2014): 601-624. <doi:10.1017/S1816383115000107> (accessed January 11, 2016).

Edström Jerker, Alexa Hassink, Thea Shahrokh, and Erin Stern, eds. "Engendering Men: A Collaborative Review of Evidence of Men and Boys in Social Change and Gender Equality." EMERGE Evidence Review, Promundo-US, Sonke Gender Justice and the Institute of Development Studies. (September 2015). <http://opendocs.ids.ac.uk/opendocs/bitstream/handle/123456789/7059/EMERGE.pdf?sequence=1> (accessed January 22, 2016).

Ensler, Eve. "Bureau of Sex Slavery: for Yanar and my sisters in Iraq and Syria." *Nation* 301, no. 17 (2015): 4-6. <http://web.a.ebscohost.com/ehost/pdfviewer/pdfviewer?sid=e00a61c4-d061-425e-9d6f-dac6e949281e%40sessionmgr4004&vid=97&hid=4212> (accessed May 19, 2016).

Feeley, Rebecca, and Colin Thomas-Jensen. "Getting Serious about Ending Conflict and Sexual Violence in Congo." ENOUGH Strategy Paper #15. (2008). <http://www.enoughproject.org/files/CongoSerious.pdf> (accessed May 23, 2016).

Foreign & Commonwealth Office. "Foreign Secretary launches new Government initiative to prevent sexual violence in conflict." Foreign & Commonwealth Office. (May 2012).<https://www.gov.uk/government/speeches/foreign-secretary-launches-new-government-initiative-to-prevent-sexual-violence-in-conflict> (accessed March 21, 2016).

Foreign & Commonwealth Office. "The Foreign Secretary William Hague, Angelina Jolie and Zainab Hawa Bangura launch G8 Declaration on Preventing Sexual Violence in Conflict." Foreign & Commonwealth Office. (April 2013). <https://www.gov.uk/government/news/g8-declaration-on-preventing-sexual-violence-in-conflict> (accessed November 27, 2015).

Foreign & Commonwealth Office. "Declaration on Preventing Sexual Violence in Conflict." Foreign & Commonwealth Office. (April 2013). <https://www.gov.uk/government/uploads/system/uploads/attachment_data/file/185008/G8_PSVI_Declaration_-_FINAL.pdf> (accessed November 27, 2015).

Foreign & Commonwealth Office. "Statement of Action - Global Summit to End Sexual Violence in Conflict." Foreign & Commonwealth Office. (June 2014). <https://www.gov.uk/government/publications/statement-of-action-global-summit-to-end-sexual-violence-in-conflict> (accessed November 26, 2015).

Foreign & Commonwealth Office. "Chair's Summary - Global Summit to End Sexual Violence in Conflict." Foreign & Commonwealth Office. (June 2014). <https://www.gov.uk/government/publications/chairs-summary-global-summit-to-end-sexual-violence-in-conflict/chairs-summary-global-summit-to-end-sexual-violence-in-conflict> (accessed November 27, 2015).

Foreign & Commonwealth Office. "Angelina Jolie Pitt joins Baroness Anelay to chart next steps on tackling sexual violence." Foreign & Commonwealth Office. (June 2015). <https://www.gov.uk/government/news/angelina-jolie-pitt-joins-baroness-anelay-to-chart-next-steps-on-tackling-sexual-violence> (accessed January 12, 2016).

G7. "G7 Report on the Implementation of the G8 Declaration on Preventing Sexual Violence in Conflict." G7. (November 2015). <https://www.g7germany.de/Content/EN/_Anlagen/G7/2015-11-24-g7-erklaerung_svc_en.pdf?__blob=publicationFile&v=3> (accessed January 7, 2016).

G7. "G7 Foreign Ministers Meeting: Joint Communique." G7. (April 2016). <http://www.mofa.go.jp/files/000147440.pdf> (accessed May 13, 2016).

Gaggioli, Gloria. "Sexual violence in armed conflicts: A violation of international humanitarian law and human rights law." *International Review of the Red Cross* 96(894) (2014): 503-538. <doi:10.1017/S1816383115000211> (accessed January 11, 2016).

Geneva Call. <http://www.genevacall.org/> (accessed January 21, 2016).

Gingerich, Tara, and Jennifer Leaning. "The Use of Rape as a Weapon of War in the Conflict in Darfur, Sudan." 2004. <http://reliefweb.int/sites/reliefweb.int/files/resources/B119C9EFB7DCAA2DC1256F5F004FBEA9-hu-sud-31oct.pdf> (accessed May 25, 2016).

Global Peace Operations Review. "Female Participation in UN Peace Operations." <http://peaceoperationsreview.org/featured-data/> (accessed January 12, 2016).

Haslam, S.A., and S. Reicher. "Beyond the banality of evil: three dynamics of an interactionist social psychology of terrorism." *Personality and Social Psychology Bulletin*, 33(5) (2007): 615-622.

Henry, Marsha. "Ten Reasons Not to Write Your Master's Dissertation on Sexual Violence in War." *The Disorder of Things*. (June 4, 2013). <http://thedisorderofthings.com/2013/06/04/ten-reasons-not-to-write-your-masters-dissertation-on-sexual-violence-in-war/> (accessed January 21 2016).

House of Lords. "Select Committee on Sexual Violence in Conflict: Report of Session 2015-16: Sexual Violence in Conflict: A War Crime." House of Lords. HL Paper 123. (April 12, 2016). <http://www.publications.parliament.uk/pa/ld201516/ldselect/ldsvc/123/123.pdf> (accessed April 15, 2016).

Human Rights Watch. "Rwanda: International Tribunal Closing Its Doors." HRW. (December 2015). <https://www.hrw.org/news/2015/12/23/rwanda-international-tribunal-closing-its-doors> (accessed January 6, 2016).

Human Security Report Project. *Human Security Report 2012: Sexual Violence, Education, and War: Beyond the Mainstream Narrative*. Vancouver: Human Security Press, 2012. <http://hsrgroup.org/human-security-reports/2012/text.aspx> (accessed May 23, 2016).

International Committee of the Red Cross. "Sexual Violence in Armed Conflict: E-Briefing." ICRC. (December 2015). <https://app.icrc.org/e-briefing/sexual-violence-armed-conflict/> (accessed January 7, 2016).

Jolie, Angelina. *In the Land of Blood and Honey*. (2011). DVD (accessed December 19, 2015).

Jones, Nicola, Janice Cooper, Elizabeth Presler-Marshall and David Walker. "The fallout of rape as a weapon of war: The life-long and intergenerational impacts of sexual violence in conflict." Overseas Development Institute. (2014). <http://www.odi.org/sites/odi.org.uk/files/odi-assets/publications-opinion-files/8990.pdf> (accessed May 23, 2016).

Justice Rapid Response. "Justice Rapid Response welcomes UN Women and Draper Richards Kaplan Foundation to its Executive Board." JRR. (November 2015). <http://www.justicerapidresponse.org/justice-rapid-response-welcomes-un-women-and-draper-richards-kaplan-foundation-to-its-executive-board/> (accessed January 7, 2016).

Kerry, John. "Remarks at The Global Summit to End Sexual Violence in Conflict." US Department of State. (June 2014). <http://www.state.gov/secretary/remarks/2014/06/227553.htm> (accessed November 27, 2015).

Kilcullen, David. *Out of the Mountains: the Coming of Age of the Urban Guerrilla*. London: C. Hurst & Co., 2013.

Kilmartin, Chris. "Men, Peace, and Security Symposium: Agents of Change." United States Institute of Peace. (October 29, 2013. Published November 13, 2013). <https://www.youtube.com/watch?v=rnXM8mvdzaw> (accessed January 22, 2016).

King, Anthony. "The Existence of Group Cohesion in the Armed Forces: A Response to Guy Siebold." *Armed Forces & Society* Vol 33, No. 4 (2007): 638-645.

Kirby, Paul. "How is rape a weapon of war? Feminist International Relations, modes of critical explanation and the study of wartime sexual violence." European Journal of International Relations 19(4) (2013): 773-796. <doi:10.1177/1354066111426621> (accessed May 18, 2016).

Kirby, Paul. "Ending sexual violence in conflict: the Preventing Sexual Violence Initiative and its critics." *International Affairs*, 91(3) (2015): 457-472. <doi:10.1111/1468-2346.12283> (accessed October 8, 2015).

Kuehnast, Kathleen, Chantal de Jonge Oudraat, and Helga Hernes, eds. *Women and War: Power and Protection in the Twenty-First Century*. Washington, DC: United States Institute of Peace Press, 2011.

Leatherman, Janie. "Sexual Violence and Armed Conflict: Complex Dynamics of Re-Victimization." *International Journal of Peace Studies* 12, no. 1 (2007): 53-71. <http://web.a.ebscohost.com/ehost/pdfviewer/pdfviewer?sid=e00a61c4-d061-425e-9d6f-dac6e949281e%40sessionmgr4004&vid=92&hid=4212> (accessed May 18, 2016).

Leiby, Michele L. "Wartime Sexual Violence in Guatemala and Peru." *International Studies Quarterly* 53, no. 2 (2009): 445-468. <http://web.a.ebscohost.com/ehost/pdfviewer/pdfviewer?sid=e00a61c4-d061-425e-9d6f-dac6e949281e%40sessionmgr4004&vid=109&hid=4212> (accessed May 19, 2016).

Lewis, Stephen. "Against the war on women: V-day in the Congo." *Peace & Conflict Monitor*. (April 2008). <http://web.a.ebscohost.com/ehost/detail/detail?vid=29&sid=e00a61c4-d061-425e-9d6f-dac6e949281e%40sessionmgr4004&hid=4212&bdata=JnNpdGU9ZWhvc3QtbGl2ZQ%3d%3d#AN=32019173&db=tsh> (accessed May 18, 2016).

Magner, K, JE Desrosiers, I Blunt, T Hawken, and E Brick. *The role of faith based organisations in preventing and responding to sexual, intimate partner and gender-based violence in conflict settings: A modified critical interpretive synthesis.* University of Otago for the Sexual Violence Research Initiative. (2015). <http://svri.org.dedi6.cpt3.host-h.net/sites/default/files/attachments/2016-04-13/FBOreview.pdf> (accessed May 22, 2016).

Matfess, Hilary. "Boko Haram's War on Women." *Newsweek Global* 166, no. 7 (February 19, 2016): 12-15. <http://web.a.ebscohost.com/ehost/pdfviewer/pdfviewer?vid=55&sid=0e34b8af-4d52-4955-9dfa-eb6e4e3bae87%40sessionmgr4004&hid=4107> (accessed May 23, 2016).

Mehari, Zeresenay Berhane. *Difret.* (2014). DVD (accessed December 20, 2015).

MenEngage Alliance and United Nations Population Fund. "Sexual Violence in Conflict and Post-Conflict: Engaging Men and Boys." (July 2012). <http://menengage.org/resources/sexual-violence-conflict-post-conflict-engaging-men-boys/> (accessed January 12, 2016).

Mollmann, Marianne. "Rape in war: No more excuses." Human Rights Watch. (July 2011). <https://www.hrw.org/news/2011/07/22/rape-war-no-more-excuses> (accessed January 6, 2016).

Morgan, A.J. "Sexual Violence and Gender Roles: From Peace to Conflict and Back Again." Gender Across Borders. (November 2011). <http://www.genderacrossborders.com/2011/11/28/sexual-violence-and-gender-roles-from-peace-to-conflict-and-back-again/> (accessed May 22, 2016).

NATO. "Remarks by NATO Deputy Secretary General Alexander Vershbow at the United Nations Security Council Open Debate on the High-Level Review of UNSCR 1325 – Women, Peace and Security." NATO. Last modified October 14, 2015. <http://www.nato.int/cps/en/natohq/opinions_123768.htm?selectedLocale=en> (accessed January 12, 2016).

Nelaeva, Galina. "The Impact of Transnational Advocacy Networks on the Prosecution of Wartime Rape and Sexual Violence: The Case of the ICTR." *International Social Science Review* 85, no. 1/2 (2010): 3-27. <http://web.a.ebscohost.com/ehost/pdfviewer/pdfviewer?vid=31&sid=0e34b8af-4d52-4955-9dfa-eb6e4e3bae87%40sessionmgr4004&hid=4107> (accessed May 23, 2016).

Nordås, Ragnhild, and Siri C.A. Rustad. "Sexual Exploitation and Abuse by Peacekeepers: Understanding Variation." *International Interactions* 39, no. 4 (2013): 511-534. <http://web.b.ebscohost.com/ehost/pdfviewer/pdfviewer?vid=87&sid=d9b58e6f-f0a9-428e-86e5-c8fba15262df%40sessionmgr106&hid=105> (accessed May 23, 2016).

Office of the Special Representative of the Secretary-General for Sexual Violence in Conflict. Homepage. <http://www.un.org/sexualviolenceinconflict/> (accessed May 13, 2016).

Oxford Learner's Dictionary. "Prevent." Oxford Learner's Dictionary. <http://www.oxfordlearnersdictionaries.com/definition/english/prevent?q=prevent> (accessed May 15, 2016).

Parliament. "House of Commons Debates 29 June 2015: Tunisia, and European Council." Parliament. (June 2015). <http://www.publications.parliament.uk/pa/cm201516/cmhansrd/cm150629/debtext/150629-0001.htm#1506295000001> (accessed April 7, 2016).

Peterman, Amber, Dara Kay Cohen, Tia Palermo, and Amelia Hoover. "Rape reporting during war: Why the numbers don't mean what you think they do." *Foreign Affairs.* (August 1, 2011). <https://www.foreignaffairs.com/articles/2011-08-01/rape-reporting-during-war?page=show> (accessed May 23, 2016).

Rees, Madeleine and Christine Chinkin. "Why we support the PSVI." Women's International League for Peace and Freedom. (June 2015). <http://wilpf.org/why-we-support-the-psvi/> (accessed May 20, 2016).

Reicher, Stephen. "The Context of Social Identity: Domination, Resistance, and Change." *Political Psychology.* 259(6) (2004): 921-945. <doi:10.1111/j.1467-9221.2004.00403.x.> (accessed January 19, 2016).

Rowley, Elizabeth, Garcia Moreno, and Elizabeth Dartnall. *Executive Summary: A Research Agenda for Sexual Violence In Humanitarian, Conflict and Post-Conflict Settings.* World Health Organization, UN Action, Sexual Violence Research Initiative and Medical Research Council South Africa. (2011). <https://www.researchgate.net/publication/233428122_Executive_Summary_A_Research_Agenda_for_Sexual_Violence_In_Humanitarian_Conflict_and_Post-Conflict_Settings> (accessed May 23, 2016).

Russell, Wynne. "Sexual violence against men and boys." *Forced Migration Review*, no. 27 (2007). <http://web.a.ebscohost.com/ehost/pdfviewer/pdfviewer?sid=e00a61c4-d061-425e-9d6f-dac6e949281e%40sessionmgr4004&vid=27&hid=4212> (accessed May 18, 2016).

Schuurman, Marriët. "NATO and the Women, Peace and Security Agenda: Time to Bring It Home." *Connections: The Quarterly Journal*, Vol XIV, No. 3 October 2015). <http://www.nato.int/cps/en/natohq/opinions_124032.htm?selectedLocale=en> (accessed January 12, 2016).

Shepherd, Laura J. and Jacqui True. "The Women, Peace and Security agenda and Australian leadership in the world: from rhetoric to commitment?' *Australian Journal of International Affairs*, Vol. 68, No. 3 (2014): 257-284. <http://dx.doi.org/10.1080/10357718.2014.903895> (accessed May 18, 2016).

Siebold, Guy, L. "The Essence of Military Group Cohesion." *Armed Forces & Society* Vol. 33, No. 2 (2007): 286-295.

Sivakumaran, Sandesh. "Lost in translation: UN responses to sexual violence against men and boys in situations of armed conflict." *International Review of the Red Cross*, 92(877) (2010): 259-277. <doi:10.1017/S1816383110000020> (accessed May 18, 2016).

Solangon, Sarah, and Preeti Patel. "Sexual violence against men in countries affected by armed conflict." *Conflict, Security and Development* 12(4) (2012): 417-42. <doi:10.1080/14678802.2012.724794> (accessed November 27, 2015).

Stauffer, Hilary and Erica Hall. "No Shame in Justice: addressing stigma against survivors to end sexual violence in conflict zones." World Vision UK. (December 2015). <http://9bb63f6dda0f744fa444-9471a7fca5768cc513a2e3c4a260910b.r43.cf3.rackcdn.com/files/1614/4888/7012/WVUK_No_Shame_in_Justice_low_res.pdf> (accessed May 19, 2016).

Steffens, Niklas K., S. Alexander Haslam, and Stephen D. Reicher. "Up close and personal: evidence that shared social identity is a basis for the 'special' relationship that binds followers to leaders." *The Leadership Quarterly* 25 (2015): 296-313.

The Mobile Economy. (2015). <http://gsmamobileeconomy.com/global/> (accessed May 12, 2016).

UNICEF (UK). "Sexual Violence in Conflict." (2014) <http://www.unicef.org.uk/Documents/Public-Affairs-Briefings/UNICEF-UK-Briefing-Sexual-Violence-in-Conflict.pdf> (accessed May 23, 2016).

United Kingdom Government. *National Security Strategy and Strategic Defence and Security Review 2015: A Secure and Prosperous United Kingdom*. Cm 9161. November 2015.

United Kingdom. Development, Concepts and Doctrine Centre. *UK Defence Doctrine*. Joint Doctrine Publication 0-01. 5th ed. Shrivenham: DCDC, 2014.

United Nations. "Report on the Protection of Civilians in the Armed Conflict in Iraq: 1 May – 31 October 2015." (January 2016). <http://www.uniraq.org/images/humanrights/UNAMI-OHCHR_%20POC%20Report_FINAL_01%20May-31%20October%202015_FINAL_11Jan2016.pdf> (accessed January 21, 2016).

United Nations Secretary General. "Conflict-related sexual violence: Report of the Secretary General." United Nations. S/2015/203 (March 23, 2015). <http://www.stoprapenow.org/uploads/advocacyresources/1428937312.pdf> (accessed January 6, 2016).

Verma, Baroness Sandip. "The UK firmly believes that the 15th anniversary must represent the start of a new era on Women, Peace and Security." UK Government. (October 13, 2015). <https://www.gov.uk/government/speeches/the-uk-firmly-believes-that-the-15th-anniversary-must-represent-the-start-of-a-new-era-on-women-peace-and-security> (accessed November 26, 2015).

Warner, Christopher H, George N. Appenzeller, Angela Mobbs, Jessica R. Parker, Carolynn M. Warner, Thomas Grieger, and Charles W. Hoge. "Effectiveness of battlefield-ethics training during combat deployment: a programme assessment." The *Lancet*. Vol 378 (2011): 915-924.

Watson, Callum. "Preventing and Responding to Sexual and Domestic Violence against Men: A Guidance Note for Security Sector Institutions." Democratic Control of the

Armed Forces. 2014. <http://www.dcaf.ch/Publications/Preventing-and-Responding-to-Sexual-and-Domestic-Violence-against-Men-A-Guidance-Note-for-Security-Sector-Institutions> (accessed January 19, 2016).

Watson, Callum. "Bad apples or bad apple trees? An examination of the contexts in which sexual violence against men takes place." Paper presented at a workshop entitled, 'Sexual Violence Against Men during Conflicts: Bridging the Gap between Theory and Practice.' *The Graduate Institute of International and Development Studies*, Geneva February 26-27, 2015).

Wolfe, Lauren. "Gloria Steinem on Rape in War, Its Causes, and How to Stop It." *The Atlantic.* (February 8, 2012). <http://www.theatlantic.com/international/archive/2012/02/gloria-steinem-on-rape-in-war-its-causes-and-how-to-stop-it/252470/> (accessed January 18, 2016).

Women's International League for Peace and Freedom. "Women organising for change in Syria and Bosnia." WILPF. (2014). <http://wilpf.org/wp-content/uploads/2014/07/Women-Organising-for-Change-in-Bosnia-and-Syria.pdf> (accessed May 15, 2016).

Women's International League for Peace and Freedom. "WILPF reflects on the Global Summit to end Sexual Violence in Conflict." WILPF. (2014). <http://wilpf.org/wilpf-reflects-on-the-global-summit-to-end-sexual-violence-in-conflict/> (accessed May 20, 2016).

WomenPolice. "The Ongoing Fight to End Sexual Violence in Conflict." *WomenPolice.* (August 2015). <http://web.a.ebscohost.com/ehost/pdfviewer/pdfviewer?vid=9&sid=e00a61c4-d061-425e-9d6f-dac6e949281e%40sessionmgr4004&hid=4212> (accessed May 17, 2016).

Wood, Elizabeth Jean. "Sexual violence during war: toward an understanding of variation." in *Order, Conflict and Violence*, edited by Stathis N. Kalyvas, Ian Shapiro and Tarek Masoud. New York and Cambridge: Cambridge University Press, 2008.

Wood, Elizabeth Jean. "Armed Groups and Sexual Violence: When is Wartime Rape Rare?" *Politics and Society*, 37(1) (2009): 131-161.

Wood, Elizabeth Jean. "Conflict-related sexual violence and the policy implications of recent research." *International Review of the Red Cross* 96(894) (2014): 457-478. <doi:10.1017/S1816383115000077> (accessed January 7, 2016).

Zawati, Hilmi M., "Re-thinking rape law." *Journal of International Law and International Relations*, Vol. 102014): 31-43. <http://web.b.ebscohost.com/ehost/pdfviewer/pdfviewer?vid=58&sid=d9b58e6f-f0a9-428e-86e5-c8fba15262df%40sessionmgr106&hid=105> (accessed May 23, 2016).

Zawati, Hilmi M., "The Challenge of Prosecuting Conflict-Related Gender-Based Crimes under Libyan Transitional Justice." *Journal of International Law & International Relations* Vol. 102014): 44-91. <http://web.b.ebscohost.com/ehost/pdfviewer/pdfviewer?sid=d9b58e6f-f0a9-428e-86e5-c8fba15262df%40sessionmgr106&vid=62&hid=105> (accessed May 23, 2016).

Zimbardo, Philip. *The Lucifer Effect: How Good People Turn Evil.* London: Rider, 2007.

www.ingramcontent.com/pod-product-compliance
Lightning Source LLC
Chambersburg PA
CBHW071344230926
51846CB00002B/442
*9789004396838*